THE DIVINE LITURGY
A COMMENTARY IN THE LIGHT OF THE FATHERS

Hieromonk Gregorios

THE DIVINE LITURGY

A COMMENTARY IN THE LIGHT OF THE FATHERS

It is needful to understand the miracle of the Mysteries:
what it is, why it was given, and what is its profit.

St John Chrysostom

CELL OF ST JOHN THE THEOLOGIAN
KOUTLOUMOUSIOU MONASTERY

MOUNT ATHOS * 2009
Hieromonk Gregorios
THE DIVINE LITURGY
A Commentary in the Light of the Fathers

First published in 2009
by the Cell of St John the Theologian
Koutloumousiou Monastery
P.O. Box 13
630 86 Karyes
Mount Athos
Greece

© Hieromonk Gregorios

Translated by Elizabeth Theokritoff
from the fourth Greek edition entitled
Ἡ θεία Λειτουργία, Σχόλια (Mount Athos, 2006)

ISBN 978-960-89067-9-2

Distribution

Within Greece and Cyprus
Orthodox Logos Bookshop
Mesogeion 419, Aghia Paraskevi, 153 43 Athens, Greece
Tel. (0030) 210 639 9002, Fax (0030) 210 639 9016
e-mail: info@orthodoxoslogos.gr

Rest of the world
Denise Harvey, 340 05 Limni, Evia, Greece
Tel./Fax (0030) 22270 31154
e-mail: orders@deniseharveypublisher.gr

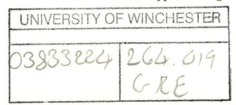

CONTENTS

NOTE ON THE ENGLISH TRANSLATION

This present edition of *The Divine Liturgy: A Commentary in the Light of the Fathers* has been published following the wish expressed by numerous people for an English translation of the Greek edition which has been in circulation for many years. The knowledge that the English text may be read internationally, and possibly will constitute a reference point for other such studies, has made us acutely aware of our responsibility in ensuring the accurate translation of the original, and every attempt has been made to provide a faithful and efficacious rendering of the Greek text. For this reason we express our thanks to the translator Elizabeth Theokritoff as well as to Dionysia Harvey for her valuable contribution to its philological content and final presentation. We pray that God will reward the great pains they have taken.

All Biblical references are acccording to the Greek Septuagint, which is used by the Orthodox Church. The main differences between the Hebrew, as reproduced in the Authorised Version (King James Bible), and the Septuagint are in the Deuterocanonical Books and the Psalms. The difference in the numbering of the Psalms are as follows:

Hebrew (Authorised Version)	Greek (Septuagint)
1–8	1–8
9 and 10	9
11–113	Subtract one from the number of each Psalm in the Hebrew
114 and 115	113
116: 1–9	114
116: 10–16	115
117–146	Subtract one from the number of each Psalm in the Hebrew

In this English edition a number of explanatory details have been added to the original Greek text as an aid for those unfamiliar with the Orthodox Christian tradition, as well as a Glossary of liturgical terms. An asterisk (*) is used to denote a word defined in the Glossary when it occurs for the first time. Biblical quotations and the words of the Divine Liturgy are italicised in the text.

January, 2009   Hieromonk Gregorios

Addendum to the first edition of *The Divine Liturgy*

The text of the Divine Liturgy and its related Offices used in this commentary has been compiled and adapted by the Cell of Saint John the Theologian from the many translations into English that have circulated in the English-speaking world in past decades. It is hoped that in time a universal English text will be established which will adequately convey the meaning, power and beauty of the original Greek and be freely available to all.

ABBREVIATIONS

ANF	Alexander Roberts, D. D., & James Donaldson, LL.D., ed., *Ante-Nicene Fathers*, 10 vols (repr. Massachusetts: Peabody, 1994)
Asc. Hom.	*The Ascetical Homilies of St Isaac the Syrian*, translated and published by Holy Transfiguration Monastery (Boston, 1984)
Comm. Liturgy	St Nicholas Cabasilas, *Commentary on the Divine Liturgy*, PG 150.367–492
Chrestou	P. Chrestou, ed., *Grigoriou tou Palama syngrammata*, vols 1–5 (Thessaloniki: P. Chrestou, 1962–1992)
Church Building	St Symeon of Thessaloniki, *Commentary on the holy Church Building*, PG 155. 697–749
Consecration	St Symeon of Thessaloniki, *On the Church Building and its Consecration*, PG 155.305–61
Contemplation	St Germanus of Constantinople, *Church History and Mystical Contemplation*, PG 98.384–453
Halkin	F. Halkin, ed., *Douze récits byzantines sur Saint Jean Chrysostome* (Bruxelles: Societé des Bollandistes, 1977)
Leitourgiai	P. Trembelas, *Ai treis Leitourgiai [The three Liturgies]* (Athens: M. Patriarchiki Epistimoniki Epitropi, 1935)
Oikonomou	Sophocles of Oikonomoi, *Tou en agiois patros imon Grigoriou Archiepiscopou Thessalonikis tou Palama Omiliai 22* (Athens, 1861)
Philokalia	*The Philokalia*: The Complete Text, 4 vols, vol. 5 in preparation, tr. G. E. H. Palmer, Philip Sherrard and Kallistos Ware (London: Faber and Faber, 1979–)
PG	J. P. Migne, ed., *Patrologia Graeca*, vols 1–161, Paris

PL	J. P. Migne, ed., *Patrologia Latina*, vols 1–221, Paris
PO	R. Graffin, ed., *Patrologia Orientalis*, Paris
Protheoria	Theodore Bishop of Andida, *On the Symbols and Mysteries in the Divine Liturgy*, PG 140.417–68
SC	Sources Chrétiennes (Paris, 1946–)
Theotokos	Theophanes Bishop of Nicaea, *Logos eis tin Theo-tokon*, ed. M. Jugie (Rome: Facultas Theologica Pontificii Athenaei Seminarii Romani, 1935)

FOREWORD TO THE FIRST GREEK EDITION

The Divine Liturgy is Christ

When Christ first spoke about the Mystery of the Divine Eucharist,* He called Himself the 'Bread of life', which came down from heaven to be offered *for the life and salvation of the world:*[1] *I am the bread of life...which comes down from heaven... I am the living bread which came down from heaven; if anyone eats of this bread, he will live for ever. And the bread which I shall give for the life of the world is my flesh* (John 6: 48–51).

Christ is the 'Bread of life' which came down from heaven through the power of the Holy Spirit. It came down on the day of the Annunciation into the most blessed Virgin, and the Virgin became the 'good earth and blessed' which brought forth the Bread of life.[2]

Christ is the 'Bread of life' which comes down from heaven continually through the power of the Holy Spirit. It comes down at the moment of the eucharistic annunciation into the virgin Church, and the holy Church becomes the 'good earth and blessed' which brings forth the Bread of life. It is this reality of Christ's descent and His presence within the Church that we experience in the Divine Liturgy. For the Liturgy is Christ in our midst: *And lo, I am with you always, until the end of all time* (Matt. 28: 20).

Because the Divine Liturgy is Christ with us, any commentary on the Liturgy is in reality a homily about Christ. The holy Evangelists and the God-bearing Fathers spoke to us of Christ as they

---

[1] Service of Preparation of the Eucharistic Gifts, see p. 76 below.
[2] Service of Preparation for Holy Communion, Canon,* ode* 1.

experienced Him when He was with them, as they experienced Him as a living reality in the Divine Liturgy: *That which was from the beginning, which we have heard, which we have seen with our eyes, which we have looked upon and touched with our hands, concerning the Word of life — the life was made manifest, and we saw it, and testify to it, and proclaim to you eternal life* (1 John 1: 1–2).

Some may say that a contemporary commentary on the Divine Liturgy should reflect how a contemporary Christian sees, hears and touches Christ, but on account of the present author's spiritual blindness, deafness and insensibility he has turned to those who have seen the true Light, who have heard the Word and 'touched the immaculate head of the Master',[3] and who are eternally contemporary. And so this book is compiled from the eucharistic experiences of the saints and presents the Divine Liturgy as it was actually lived by them, and as it is still lived within the Church. For even today, in these difficult times, there are hearts that burn with His love (cf. Luke 24: 32) and experience His presence at the Altar and people who during the Divine Liturgy concelebrate with the angels and saints, and truly live in the blessed Kingdom of the Triune God.

It could be that someone reading about these experiences of the saints will be helped to come close to them, which is to come close to Christ. There in the Kingdom of God, I ask such readers to pray *with all the saints* (Eph. 3: 18) for the present author who has gathered from the honeycombs of these holy men the spiritual honey which sweetens and nourishes all humankind.[4]

January, 1982   Hieromonk Gregorios

---

[3] Royal Hours* for the feast of Theophany; *idiomelon* at the Ninth Hour.

[4] Cf. Prov. 24: 13–4: *My son, eat honey, for the honeycomb is good, that your throat may be sweetened. Thus you shall discern wisdom for your soul.*

FOREWORD TO THE FOURTH GREEK EDITION

Ever since its first publication this book has been most warmly received, and that has given us a heightened sense of responsibility with regard to its presentation, both theological and stylistic. Accordingly, in this edition we have tried to render the theological ideas in a more readily understandable manner and also made changes in the texts of the commentaries, as well as some essential corrections. So, twenty-four years after its initial publication, the book is now available in a new and substantially revised form.

We would like to take this opportunity to express a humble prayer: that this new edition, too, may contribute to our better understanding of the Divine Liturgy and to our deeper participation in it, and that we may all come to know at first hand 'the miracle of the Mysteries:* what it is, why it was given, and what is its profit.'[5] In other words, that we may understand that the Divine Liturgy is the mystery of God's love; that it was given because He first loved us; and that from it we obtain the beneficence of becoming participants in Christ and images of His love.

May the experience of His love challenge us in turn to love Him with all our heart.

Theophany, 2006   Hieromonk Gregorios

---

[5] St John Chrysostom, *On John*, 46.2, PG 59.260.

Come, let us partake of the new fruit of the vine of divine gladness on this auspicious day of awakening, and of the Kingdom of Christ, singing praises to Him as God unto the ages.

(Easter Canon)

INTRODUCTION

Holy are you and All-holy, you and your only-begotten Son and your Holy Spirit. Holy are you and All-holy, and magnificent is your glory, who did so love your world as to give your only-begotten Son, that everyone who believes in him might not perish, but have life everlasting.

(Divine Liturgy, Prayer of the Anaphora)

Come, O believers,
and in the upper room on high
raising our minds,
let us enjoy the Master's hospitality
and the Table of immortality.
But first let us hear the exalted
teaching of the Word
whom we magnify.

(Canon of Holy Thursday)

1. The Last Supper and the early Christian Liturgy

At a Jewish Passover supper, Jesus Christ celebrated for the first time the Mystery of the Divine Liturgy, the Passover Supper of the Church. It was the last Passover that Christ celebrated with His disciples in His earthly life.

The day before the feast of the Passover, the disciples asked the Lord, 'Where do you want us to prepare the Passover meal?' And Christ answered them: 'Go to so-and-so in the city and tell him: The Master says, "The time of my Passion is approaching. I am going to keep the Passover at your house, with my disciples."' The disciples did as the Lord told them, and prepared the place where they were to celebrate the Passover together (cf. Matt. 26: 17–9).

When the disciples asked Christ where they should prepare the Passover meal, they were of course talking about the Jewish Passover. And that was what they prepared. 'Whereas our Passover, the Christian Passover, has been prepared by Christ. And He has not only prepared it, but He Himself has become the Passover.' At the Last Supper, Christ celebrated both the Jewish and the Christian Passover, 'both the Passover that was the type and the Passover that was the reality. Christ was doing exactly what an artist does when on the same canvas he first draws an outline and puts in the shading, and then adds the actual colours. At the very same table, He both sketched out the Passover that was a type and added in the true Passover.'[1]

The first three Evangelists and the Apostle Paul give us a description of the first Divine Liturgy: *Jesus took bread, and when He had given thanks He broke it, and gave it to His disciples and said: 'Take, eat; this is my body which is given for you. Do this in remembrance of me.' And He took the cup, and when He had given*

---

[1] St John Chrysostom, *On the Betrayal of Judas*, 1.4, PG 49.378–9.

thanks He gave it to them, saying, 'Drink of it, all of you; for this is my blood of the new covenant, which is poured out for many for the forgiveness of sins. Do this, as often as you drink it, in remembrance of me. I tell you I shall not drink again of this fruit of the vine until that day when I drink it new with you in my Father's Kingdom' (Matt. 26: 26–9; Mark 14: 22–5; Luke 22: 15–20; 1 Cor. 11: 23–6).

This description of the first Divine Liturgy is at the same time a description of the eucharistic *synaxis** — assembly — of apostolic times, except that in the place of the leader of the *synaxis* there is no longer Christ but the holy Apostles, living icons of the Teacher. In the Divine Eucharist, the first Christians experienced the presence of Christ and awaited His return in glory. The awareness of Christ's presence and the expectation of His Second Coming gave the eucharistic assemblies of the early Christians an atmosphere of joy and gladness (cf. Acts 2: 46–7).

In apostolic times, an *agape* meal* was offered before the Divine Liturgy. Christians also experienced the Divine Eucharist as an *agape* meal, a feast of love, precisely because the Mystical Supper was the supper of Christ's boundless love for His disciples (cf. John 13: 1, 34). But as time went on, because of the occurrence of various improprieties, the Divine Liturgy was separated from the *agape* meal (1 Cor. 11: 17ff.).

When the Apostles began sending letters to the local Churches, the eucharistic *synaxis* would begin with the reading of a letter[2] (cf. Col. 4: 16, 1 Thes. 5: 27). There followed the kiss of love to which St Paul refers in his epistles (cf. 2 Cor. 13: 12, Rom. 16: 16). Then the celebrant would bless the faithful: *The grace of our Lord Jesus Christ and the love of God and the communion of the Holy Spirit be with you all. Amen** (2 Cor. 13: 13). After the blessing, the prayer of thanksgiving was said, and the words of the Lord: *Take, eat… Drink of this, all of you…* (cf. 1 Cor. 11: 23–5). This

---

[2] The assemblies of the faithful took place in the evening, in the upper room of a house (cf. Acts 20: 7ff.).

was followed by the prayer of the *epiklesis** or invocation of the Holy Spirit, which has its basis in Christ's words after the institution of the Mystery: *When the Comforter comes... He will bear witness to me... He will glorify me* (John 15: 26; 16: 14). Finally, the holy Body of Christ was divided up, and this was followed by Holy Communion.* In this manner was the Divine Eucharist celebrated in apostolic times.

2. The earliest liturgical prayers

The second and third centuries were the time of persecutions. We have some liturgical prayers from that period, such as those found in the *Didache* (Teaching of the Twelve Apostles) and the *Apostolic Tradition* of St Hippolytus. It seems that there was then still a comparative freedom in the formulation of prayers in the Liturgy. Thus the *Didache* says: 'Those who have the gift of prophecy should be allowed to give thanks as long as they like'; and St Justin Martyr writes that the celebrant 'offers up prayers and thanksgiving according to his ability'.[3]

The beginning of this period coincides with the definitive separation of the Eucharist from the *agape* meal. The Church was then moving from the age of the Apostles, prophets and charismatic teachers, who would travel around the local Churches, to the age of permanent pastors. The eucharistic *synaxis* took place in the morning rather than the evening, and it was celebrated at the tombs of the early Christian martyrs. During the last years of the first century, the Triumphal Hymn* was added to the Liturgy.[4]

In the *Didache*, which was written about 100 AD, we find the first prayers for the Liturgy: 'With regard to the Eucharist, give thanks in this way: First, for the Cup: "We thank You, our Father, for the holy vine of David Your servant, which You have made

---

[3] *Didache*, 10.7, *ANF* 7, p. 380; *First Apology*, 67, *PG* 6.429BC.
[4] Cf. St Clement of Rome, *First Epistle to the Corinthians*, 34.5-7, *PG* 1.277A.

known to us through Jesus Your child. To You be glory unto the ages." For the breaking [of the bread]: "We thank You, our Father, for the life and knowledge which You have made known to us through Jesus Your child. To You be glory unto the ages. As this bread which is broken was scattered on the mountains and was gathered up and became one, so may Your Church be gathered up[5] from the ends of the earth into Your Kingdom. For Yours is the glory and power through Jesus Christ unto the ages."'

The *Didache* then goes on to give some phrases which were probably a dialogue between the celebrant and the people:

> Celebrant: Let grace come [variant reading: Let Christ come] and let this world pass away.
>
> People: Hosanna to the God of David.
>
> Celebrant: If any is holy, let him come. If any is not, let him repent: *Maran atha* [that is, our Lord is coming].
>
> People: Amen.[6]

St Justin, in his *First Apology* (written about 150 AD), gives us two outlines of the Divine Liturgy. The eucharistic *synaxis* begins with readings from Scripture, after which the celebrant preaches to the faithful. This is followed by communal prayers, the kiss of love, the offering of the bread and wine* and the prayers offered up by the celebrant. The people pronounce the 'Amen', whereupon 'those present partake in the "eucharistic things" [that is, the consecrated Holy Gifts] over which thanks has been given. To those who are absent [the Gifts], are sent with the deacons.*' St Justin also refers to the invocation* of the Holy Spirit, which he calls 'the prayer of the word'.[7]

---

[5] The root of the verb 'to gather up' is also that of the noun *synaxis*, referring to the gathering of the Church. — Trans.

[6] *Didache*, 9.1–4 and 10.6, *ANF* 7, pp. 379–80.

[7] *First Apology*, 67, 66, *PG* 6.429C, 428C. There is also another instance where St Justin calls the Comforter 'word': *First Apology*, 33, *PG* 6.381B.

St Ignatius of Antioch (martyred about 113 AD) and St Irenaeus of Lyon (140–202) say less about the form of the prayers and more about the theology of the Mystery. St Irenaeus calls the Holy Anaphora* the 'invocation of God' or 'word of God'.[8]

In the *Apostolic Tradition* of St Hippolytus (written about 217), we have the following dialogue between the celebrant and the people:

Celebrant: The Lord [be] with you all.
    People: And with your spirit.
Celebrant: Your hearts on high.
    People: We have [them] with the Lord.
Celebrant: Let us give thanks to the Lord.
    People: [It is] right and fitting.

After this, the Anaphora begins:
'We give thanks to You, O God, through Your beloved child Jesus Christ, whom in the last times You sent to us as saviour and redeemer and messenger of Your counsel... Who, when He was giving Himself up to His voluntary Passion, took bread and gave thanks and said: "Take, eat; this is my body which is broken for you." And likewise also the cup, saying: "This is my blood which is poured out for you; as often as you do this, do it in remembrance of me."

'Calling to remembrance therefore His death and Resurrection, we offer You the bread and the cup, giving thanks to You... And we implore You to send down Your Holy Spirit upon the Sacrifice of the holy Church. Bringing [them] together, grant to all who partake in the Holy [Things] [that they may partake] unto fullness of the Holy Spirit for the assurance of faith in truth, that we may praise and glorify You through Your child Jesus Christ, through Whom be glory and honour to the Father and to the Son

---

[8] *Against Heresies*, 4.18.5, *SC* 100, p. 611, and 5.2.3, *SC* 153, p. 37.

and to the Holy Spirit in Your holy Church, both now and to the ages of ages. Amen.'[9]

The liturgical elements of the dialogue, the words of Christ, the *anamnesis*,* and the invocation (*epiklesis*) of the Holy Spirit are already clearly discernible in this Anaphora of the *Apostolic Tradition*.

3. The first written texts of the Divine Liturgy

The Divine Liturgy as we know it today took shape at the beginning of the fourth century. By that time, each local Church (such as at Jerusalem, Constantinople, Alexandria) had developed its own form of Liturgy. Thus we have the Liturgies of St Mark the Apostle, St James the Brother of the Lord, St Clement, St Basil the Great and St John Chrysostom.

Today, the following Liturgies are celebrated in the Orthodox Church:

1. *The Liturgy of St James.* The core of this Liturgy is of apostolic origin, but the form in which it is preserved is fourth century, with some later additions. The simplicity of its vocabulary, the Old Testament readings* and the petitions referring to persecutions of Christians confirm its antiquity.

This Liturgy took shape in Jerusalem, and from there spread to numerous local Churches. Many holy Fathers speak of this Liturgy: St Cyril of Jerusalem (who expounds it but without mentioning the name of St James), St Proclus of Constantinople, St Mark Evgenikos of Ephesus,[10] the Quinisext Ecumenical Council (in the

---

[9] *Apostolic Tradition*, 4, *SC* 11bis, pp. 46–52 and P. Trembelas, *Archai kai charaktir tis christianikis latreias* [*Principles and character of Christian worship*], (Athens: Sotir, 1962), pp. 175–6. The interpretation 'Bringing [them] together, grant to all who partake in the Holy [Things] [that they may partake] unto fullness of the Holy Spirit' follows Botte's translation, *SC* 11bis, p. 53.

[10] *Mystagogical Catechesis*, 5, *PG* 33.1109–1128; *Homily on the Tradition of the holy Liturgy*, *PG* 65.849B–852B; *On the holy Eucharist*, *PG* 160.1081B.

32nd Canon) and others. The Liturgy of St James is celebrated on the days when he is commemorated: on 23 October and the first Sunday after Christmas.

2. *The Liturgy of St Basil the Great*. This takes us to Caesarea in Cappadocia. St Basil must have written it while he was a priest (c. 365), because St Gregory the Theologian, referring to St Basil's activities during that period, says that his contributions to the Church included prayers for the Liturgy, and the order of service (*diataxis*) according to which they were to be read.[11] This Liturgy was brought to Constantinople by St Gregory the Theologian, and from there became known in Alexandria too. Today it is celebrated ten times a year, on the Sundays in Lent, on Thursday in Holy Week, on the eves of Easter, Christmas and Epiphany, and on the feast of St Basil (1 January).

3. *The Liturgy of St John Chrysostom*, to which we will now turn.

4. St John Chrysostom and the Divine Liturgy

i. The life of the saint

St John Chrysostom was born to devout Christian parents in Antioch, around 350 AD. His father, Secundus, was a general, and his mother, Anthusa, came from a noble family. A few months after the saint was born his father died, and his mother undertook the task of raising him.

At a very young age St John studied rhetoric and philosophy. The bishop of Antioch at the time was St Meletius, who thought highly of the youth and took him under his wing, for 'he loved the beauty of his heart, and with a prophetic eye foresaw how the young man would develop'.[12]

---

[11] See *Homily 43*, 34, *PG* 36.541C.

[12] Palladius of Hellenopolis, *Dialogue concerning St John Chrysostom*, 5, *PG* 47.18.

At the age of eighteen St John was baptised, and subsequently studied for three years at the theological school of Antioch. In 371 he was ordained reader,* and in accordance with the practice of the time would read the Holy Scriptures and explain them to the people.

In 372, the saint's mother died. Fulfilling his long-held desire, he retreated into the wilderness, where he remained six years in all. The first four years he spent in obedience to an ascetic, while for the next two years he lived alone in caves, following a very rigorous way of life. During those two years he did not lie down at all, but 'spent most of the time without sleep, learning the Holy Scriptures'.[13] The extreme cold and ascetic practices, however, played havoc with his health and he was forced to return to Antioch, where in 380 or 381 he was ordained deacon by St Meletius. Five years later, he was ordained priest by the new archbishop of Antioch, St Flavian.

St John served as a priest in Antioch until 397. A riveting preacher, he taught his flock ceaselessly and gave them encouragement at times of difficulty. His fame spread beyond Antioch and Syria, and everyone expected that he would succeed to the episcopal throne of Antioch after St Flavian. Following the death of Patriarch Nektarios of Constantinople however, God directed St John's steps to the imperial city, where he was elected its bishop on 15 December 397 and enthroned on 26 February 398.

New struggles awaited the saint in Constantinople. Paganism was still at war with the Christian faith. Heretics (Arians, Apollinarians, and others) were breaking apart the unity of the Church. Clergy with no sense of their mission were scandalising the people. It was in the midst of all these difficulties that St John carried on his work. With the inspired words of his 'golden tongue', he captivated the people. He comforted those who were suffering, he gave courage to the despairing, he preached repentance. In words and actions, he struck at evil wherever it was to be found. He pun-

---

[13] Palladius of Hellenopolis, *Dialogue concerning St John Chrysostom*, 5, PG 47.18.

ished unworthy members of the clergy and organised the spiritual work and philanthropic activity of the Church. He sent mis-
sionaries to the Goths, to Scythia and to Phoenicia. He instituted
services at night, so that working people could take part.

His wide-ranging activity, and in particular his punishment of
unworthy clergy, provoked enormous opposition. The saint's enemies, with the support of the Empress Eudoxia, took steps to remove him and send him into exile.[14] That exile lasted one day.
The saint had got as far as Bithynia but the reaction of the people
and an extraordinary event that alarmed Eudoxia made her ask
for him to return. St John came back to the imperial city, where
the people received him with honour and tears of joy.

His enemies, however, did not remain idle. With their constant machinations and slanders, they again aroused Eudoxia's
anger against him and persuaded the emperor to put the saint
under house arrest. On the night of Holy Saturday 404, terrible
outrages took place in the churches where those who had remained loyal to the saint were gathering: just as preparations
were taking place to baptise the catechumens* and celebrate
Easter, the catechumens, men and women alike, were attacked
by soldiers and driven out naked. As the saint relates, 'the blessed
waters [in the fonts] turned red from their wounds...and in the
uproar, the most holy Blood of Christ was spilled over the soldiers' clothes.'[15]

Finally, on 20 June 404, the saint bade farewell to his clergy
and unbeknown to the people gave himself up to his enemies and
was sent into exile in Caucason in Armenia. After unimaginable
physical and mental hardships lasting more than three years, on
14 September 407, while on his way to a new place of exile in Pity-
on, he fell asleep in the Lord having received the most pure Mysteries and uttered his beloved words: 'Glory to God for all things.'[16]

---

[14] The 'Robber' Synod of the Oak, which took place 403 AD.
[15] Palladius of Hellenopolis, *Dialogue concerning St John Chrysostom*, 2, *PG* 47.11.
[16] Theodore, Bishop of Trimythous, *Life of St John Chrysostom*, 25, *Halkin*, p. 31.

In 438, the holy relic of the saint's body was taken up and translated to Constantinople. 'It was brought first into the church of St Thomas the Apostle...then to the church of St Irene; there the holy relic was placed on the episcopal throne and everyone cried out, "Reclaim your throne, holy one!" After that, they put the reliquary in a royal carriage and brought it to the church of the Holy Apostles. There they placed the holy relic on the bishop's throne and, wondrous to relate, it pronounced to the people, "Peace be with you all!".'[17]

St John's life of martyrdom was ended. Once again, truth had triumphed. And the saint, fully alive after his repose, offered the peace of God to all: to those who were his enemies and to those who loved him.

ii. The Divine Liturgy

The end of St John Chrysostom's holy life of martyrdom brings us to the beginning of his Divine Liturgy, for in his time the Liturgy began with the entrance of the bishop into the church and the offering of peace to the people.[18] The people then replied to the bishop: 'And with your spirit.' There followed three readings from the Scriptures: one from the Prophets, one from the Epistles and one from the Gospel Book.[19] The bishop then preached the word of God, and afterwards prayers were said for the catechumens and the penitents. Once the catechumens and the penitents left, the doors of the church were shut. The prayers of the faithful were then said, followed by the Great Entrance* and the kiss

---

[17] St Nikodimus of the Holy Mountain, *Synaxaristis ton dodeka minon* [*Synaxarion for the twelve months*], vol. 3 (Thessaloniki: Orthodoxos Kypseli, 1982), p. 163 (27 January).

[18] St John Chrysostom writes: 'When the bishop enters the church, he does not go up to his throne until he has wished peace to all the faithful' (*Against the Jews*, 3.6, PG 48.870).

[19] St John Chrysostom, *On Pentecost 1*, 4, PG 50.458. Cf. *On the Prophetic Saying*, 3, PG 56.145–6.

of love. After this came the Holy Anaphora, the Triumphal Hymn, the words of Christ and the invocation of the All-holy Spirit. Finally the Lord's Prayer was said, followed by Holy Communion and the Dismissal.*

In addition to the prayers which he himself wrote, St John also used in his Liturgy certain more ancient liturgical prayers. His biographer, Bishop George of Alexandria, relates that while the saint was in Armenia he ordained seven bishops and a large number of presbyters and deacons for the needs of the Church there, and 'laid down the way they should sing and taught them the divine mystagogy'.*[20]

Study of the saint's work leads to the conclusion that 'the core of his Divine Liturgy consists of a series of prayers that have come down to us essentially in the form in which the saint pronounced them when he was Bishop of Constantinople.' Content and style alike testify that these prayers belong to the work of this holy Father.[21]

The Divine Liturgy of St John in the form we have it today includes later additions: a different beginning, the hymn 'Only-begotten Son' and the Cherubic Hymn.* The reading from the prophets has been removed, and since the eighth century the Service of the Proskomide,* the Service of Preparation, has been celebrated before the beginning of the Liturgy.

It is not necessary, however, to dwell on the history of the composition of the Liturgy. For the faithful, what matters is not when the prayers were written or by whom, but how in every age those with their *hearts burning within* (Luke 24: 32) with Christ's love, recognise Him *in the breaking of bread* (Luke 24: 35).

[20] George of Alexandria, *Life of St John Chrysostom*, 59, *Halkin*, p. 238.
[21] Georg Wagner (Bishop of Eudokias), *Der Ursprung der Chrysostomusliturgie*, (Münster: Aschendorff, 1973), p. 133.

iii. The celebrant

The primary evidence concerning St John Chrysostom as celebrant is provided by his own writings. When the saint speaks of the liturgical ministry of the priest, he is revealing to us his own experience of celebrating the Liturgy.

The real celebrant of the eucharistic Mystery is Christ: He who celebrated the Divine Eucharist 'at the Last Supper is the same One who now also performs these Mysteries. We priests are in the position of servants. The One who sanctifies and changes [the Holy Gifts] is Christ.'[22] The celebrant is the instrument of the Holy Spirit; he stands in the place of Christ.

St John Chrysostom, who knew from experience the loftiness of the priestly ministry, writes that the priest 'stands between God and humanity, transmitting honours to us from heaven and raising up thither our petitions'. The celebration of the Eucharist places the celebrant in heaven: 'The throne of the priesthood is situated in the heavens.' For this reason, angelic purity is required of the celebrant, so that he may minister in the task that God has not entrusted even to angels. For 'the priest invokes the Holy Spirit, performs this Sacrifice which is full of awe and dread, and constantly touches the Master of all'.[23]

The priest is on earth, yet the sphere of his activity is in heaven. He stands with the holy angels, glorifies God with the archangels, concelebrates with Christ.[24] St John testifies that during the Divine Liturgy, 'heavenly powers occupy the entire sanctuary, and cooperate with us in the celebration of the service'. And his contemporaries bear witness to this concerning the saint himself: 'During the course of the Divine Liturgy, the true nature of the one who sees the invisible world was revealed. For he did

---

[22] *On Matthew*, 82.5, PG 58.744.

[23] *Homily on Isaiah 5*, 1, PG 56.131, 130–1; *On the Priesthood*, 6.4, PG 48.681.

[24] Cf. St Gregory the Theologian, *Homily 2*, 73, PG 35.481AB.

not look like a human being clothed in mortal flesh, but more like an angel in human form.'[25]

That is how saints celebrate the Liturgy; that is how the divine Chrysostom used to celebrate 'the miracle of the Mysteries'.[26] Before the holy Altar he lived the mystery of God's love. He received divine love from heaven and offered it to his children on earth. In consequence, his life, his words and his sufferings provide the best means for interpreting the Divine Liturgy: for the Divine Liturgy, which is Christ, was his life, and his life was one continuous Divine Liturgy and thanksgiving to God.

5. What is the Divine Liturgy?

i. A recapitulation of the entire divine economy*

The totality of the wondrous events performed by God, in order to bring man after his disobedience back to His house and make him His own once more, is called divine *economy* or dispensation: 'The divine economy of our God and Saviour is the raising up of man from his fallen state and his return from the alienation produced by his disobedience to intimacy with God.'[27]

This reality of our salvation in Christ is what we experience at every Divine Liturgy, for which we give thanks to God: 'The awesome Mysteries which are performed at every assembly of the faithful and which offer salvation in abundance are called the Eucharist ['thanksgiving'] because they consist of the recollection of many benefactions, and reveal to us the culmination of divine providence.' The Divine Liturgy is the sacramental re-living of these things and the 'recapitulation of the entire divine economy'.[28]

---

[25] Anonymous, *Life of St John Chrysostom*, 14, *Halkin*, p. 399.
[26] St John Chrysostom, *On John*, 46.2, PG 59.260.
[27] St Basil the Great, *On the Holy Spirit*, 15.35, PG 32.128C.
[28] St John Chrysostom, *On Matthew*, 25.3, PG 57.331; St Theodore the Studite, *Antirrheticus*, 1, PG 99.340C.

That is why at the end of the Divine Liturgy of St Basil the celebrant says: 'The Mystery of Your dispensation, O Christ our God,
has been accomplished and perfected.'

The mystery of the divine economy was made manifest at the
same time as man's disobedience. The Master who loves mankind
'at once saw the fall and the magnitude of the wound, and has-
tened to treat the wound so that it would not grow and turn into
an incurable injury... Spurred on by His love, not for one moment did He cease to provide for man.'[29] Through wonderful
deeds and prophetic words, God prepared man to partake in the
fullness of life and love.

A number of events and prophecies in the Old Testament fore-
shadow the Mystery of the Divine Eucharist.

The first of these is the offering of bread and wine by Melchizedek (cf. Gen. 14: 18–20), who was 'a prefiguration and image
of Christ, the true High Priest [cf. Ps. 109: 4]', and his offering was
an imitation of the Lord's offering. Melchizedek, 'moved by a gift
of prophecy, envisioned the future offering which would be made
on behalf of the gentiles. Therefore, in imitation of Christ who
was to come, he glorified God, offering bread and wine.'[30] In the
Holy Spirit, Melchizedek lives the future in the present, and imitates that which has not yet taken place.

Another prefiguration of Christ's sacrifice and the Divine Eucharist is the sacrifice of Isaac by Abraham (cf. Gen. 22: 1–14), and
the sacrifice performed by the Prophet Elijah (cf. 3 Kingdoms [1
Kings] 18: 17–40). Isaiah's vision (cf. Isa. 6: 1–7), too, has liturgical
overtones: the Lord is seated on a throne, attended by Seraphim
who sing the Thrice-holy Hymn,* while a sacrifice of incense is be-

---

[29] St John Chrysostom, *On Genesis*, 17.2, PG 53.136.

[30] Melchizedek (whose name means 'king of peace') blessed the patriarch
Abraham after the latter returned from his victory over the king of Elam.
Abraham offered Melchizedek a tithe of the spoils, and Melchizedek offered
him bread and wine (cf. Heb. 7: 2); St John of Damascus, *On the Orthodox
Faith*, 4.86, PG 94.1149C; St John Chrysostom, *On Melchizedek*, 3, PG 56.261.

ing offered. According to the holy Fathers, a prophecy by the patriarch Jacob (cf. Gen. 49: 10–1) and another by the Prophet Malachi (cf. Mal. 1: 11) also refer to the Eucharist.[31]

The supreme event prefiguring the Divine Eucharist, however, was the feast of the Jewish Passover. This feast was a continuous commemoration of the salvation of the Hebrews from the Egyptians and thanksgiving to God for His benefactions. The events that took place when the Hebrews escaped from Egypt were 'fearful mysteries of profound significance. And if the prefigurations were so fearful, how much more the reality... [For] the reality is that we eat Christ as our Passover!'[32]

All these events prepared the way for the coming of Christ. Having hitherto been foreshadowed in ways that were obscure, the Truth was made manifest in the fullness of time. At the same instant, the true extent of the mystery of the divine economy was also made manifest, because Christ is the recapitulation of this mystery.

In the Divine Liturgy, all the events of Christ's life are ritually enacted: 'All the actions performed in the divine service are a type of Christ's saving Passion, His burial and His Resurrection...and of the whole of His redeeming life on earth and the divine economy.' In the Liturgy, the celebrant stands 'before the divine Altar' and 'praises the sacred and divine works of Jesus Christ... Then he performs the divine Mysteries and brings before our eyes all those things that he has previously extolled.' The life of Christ is revealed before our eyes, because 'the entire mystagogy is like an integrated image of a body — that of the earthly life of the Saviour.'[33]

---

[31] Cf. St Justin, *First Apology*, 32, *PG* 6.377–380; cf. St John Chrysostom, *Against the Jews*, 5.12, *PG* 48.902–3.

[32] St John Chrysostom, *On Ephesians*, 23.2, *PG* 62.165–6.

[33] Theodore of Andida, *On the Symbols of the Divine Liturgy*, 1, *PG* 140.417A; St Dionysius the Areopagite, *On the Church Hierarchy*, 3.3.12, *PG* 3.441C–444A; St Nicholas Cabasilas, *Comm. Liturgy*, 1, *PG* 150.372B.

St John Chrysostom writes that 'things invisible are seen with the eye of faith'.[34] Let us listen, then, to this saint who in the Divine Liturgy perceived things unseen.

The church where the Liturgy is celebrated is Bethlehem: 'Let us hasten to Bethlehem [that is, to the church], which is the house of the spiritual Bread.' In a little while, we shall take part in the Mystical Supper in the upper room in Sion, together with the disciples. For in the Liturgy 'that very same Supper at which Christ was present is accomplished. The eucharistic Supper does not differ from that Supper in any way.' 'This holy church is the upper room where Christ and the disciples were assembled; it was from here that they went out to the Mount of Olives.'[35]

Later on, the Altar becomes the place of the skull, the terrible Golgotha: the Mystery of the Divine Eucharist 'is a type of that sacrifice [on Golgotha]... The sacrifice that was offered then, we offer now too.' After Golgotha, we experience the Resurrection: 'The Mystery we celebrate at Easter contains nothing additional to what we celebrate now. It is one and the same, the same grace of the Holy Spirit. It is always Easter.'[36]

The Divine Eucharist is the unceasing Passover of the Church. It is the beginning of the new age which irrupts into the old and renews it. It is the charismatic presence of the Kingdom which is to come: *You left nothing undone until you had brought us back to heaven and granted us Your Kingdom that is to come.* Christ has given us even now the Kingdom which is to come and 'He has made heaven accessible'.[37] And more awesome yet: He has accounted us worthy to receive within us the Master of heaven.

The Divine Liturgy is the mystery of Christ. In it, things near and things far, the beginning and the end, co-exist side by side:

---

[34] *On the words 'In the last days'*, 2, *PG* 56.272.
[35] St John Chrysostom, *On Matthew*, 7.5, 50.3 and 82.5, *PG* 57.78, *PG* 58.507, 744.
[36] Ibid. *On Hebrews*, 17.3, *PG* 63.131; *On 1 Timothy*, 5.3, *PG* 62.529–30.
[37] Anaphora prayer; St John Chrysostom, *On John*, 46.3, *PG* 59.261.

'The Passover of the Lord appears, the ages are brought together [that is, differences of time are removed], heaven and the earthly world are made one.'[38] As Christ is *Alpha and Omega, the first and last, the beginning and the end* (Rev. 22: 13), so the Divine Liturgy is the *synaxis* of space and time in Christ and their transfiguration into liturgical space* and time.*

ii. A theophany of the Trinity

The divine economy is the manifestation of the triune God's love for man: the author of our salvation is the Word of God, the Father is well pleased with the work of the Son in which the All-holy Spirit cooperates. 'The divine-human theophany, made flesh through the Ever-Virgin Mary, is realised by the will of the Father, by the Incarnation of the Son and by the cooperation of the Holy Spirit.'[39]

The mystery of the divine economy is a theophany of the Trinity, and hence the Divine Liturgy — in which we re-live this mystery by grace — is also a theophany of the Trinity. The celebrant 'reveals the Holy Trinity to us' through the Liturgy.[40]

From beginning to end, the Liturgy helps us to experience the mystery of the trinitarian presence. The priest begins with a doxology of the Holy Trinity: *Blessed is the Kingdom of the Father, and of the Son, and of the Holy Spirit.*[41] This is followed by trinitarian exclamations, the three antiphons* and the Trisagion Hymn* which we sing to the life-giving Trinity. As the time for the Holy Anaphora draws near, the celebrant bestows on us *the grace of our Lord Jesus Christ, and the love of God the Father, and the communion of the Holy Spirit.*

---

[38] *Epistle to Diognetus*, 12.9, *ANF* 1, p. 30.
[39] St Caesareus of Nazianzus, *Dialogue 3*, 167, *PG* 38.1129.
[40] St Gregory the Theologian, *Homily 43*, 72, *PG* 36.593C.
[41] Cf. St Germanus, *Contemplation*, *PG* 98.401B.

After this, we thank God for all that His love has done for us: *You brought us out of non-existence into being, and when we had fallen you raised us up again, and left nothing undone until you had brought us up to heaven and granted us your Kingdom that is to come. For all these things we give thanks to you, and to your only-begotten Son and your Holy Spirit.*

After giving thanks, we beseech the Father to send the Comforter to consecrate the offering of the Son. The Comforter comes like *the voice of a light breeze* (3 Kingdoms [1 Kings] 19: 12), effects the Consecration* and gives Christ to us. All things are filled with the light of the Triple Sun of the Deity. And we are guests at the love feast of the Trinity.

We communicate in the holy Body of Christ and become the temple of the All-holy Trinity. For 'when one person of the Holy Trinity is within us, the Holy Trinity is within us'. The Christian's body becomes a 'foundation' of the Holy Trinity; anyone who receives Communion 'has Christ and His Father and the Comforter firmly established within him'.[42]

At the end of the Liturgy, the Christ-bearing person worships the Holy Trinity in gratitude: *We have seen the true Light; we have received the heavenly Spirit; we have found the true faith, worshipping the undivided Trinity; for the Trinity has saved us.*

iii. A concourse of heaven and earth

The presence of the triune God gives the eucharistic *synaxis* or assembly its true dimensions: it is a 'concourse' of heaven and earth. The space within which the Holy Anaphora is celebrated becomes the tabernacle ['dwelling'] of God among men (cf. Rev. 21: 3). Together with man, the entire creation glorifies God, because all things are called by God to an assembly in one place, up-

---

[42] St Athanasius the Great, *To Serapion of Thmuis 1*, 20, *PG* 26.577A; St John Chrysostom, *To the disgraced Theodore 1*, *PG* 47.278.

on the Altar before His throne (cf. Rev. 8: 3). God, who is the super-essential Good, 'is called *kallos* [beauty]...because He calls all things to Himself and assembles them together into one.'[43]

The Divine Liturgy is precisely this *synaxis*, this 'gathering together' of the entire cosmos* and its journey towards the Kingdom of God. The Fathers call the gathering of the faithful at the Divine Liturgy a con-course (*syn-odos*) because all the faithful and the Lord journey on a course together towards the Jerusalem on high. This *synaxis* shows that the raison d'être of the Church is the unity of the faithful. 'The Church came into being...so that we might be united. And this is demonstrated by our concourse.' St John marvels: 'What paradise is there like our concourse?' And he exhorts us: 'Let none of those who eat the holy Passover [of the Eucharist] pay any attention to Egypt [the vanity of this world], but rather to heaven, to the Jerusalem which is above.'[44]

The Divine Liturgy is the presence of Christ. On the Holy Table, 'the King of all is present'. Christ, who 'calls together and assembles the whole created world', gathers everything around the holy Altar, and 'by His divine providence binds intelligible and sensible creations tightly together, so that they are united both among themselves and with Him.'[45]

Beside Christ stands the Lady Mother of God. Even before Christ offered His Supper, the mystery of our salvation was cele-

---

[43] St Dionysius the Areopagite, *On the Divine Names*, 4.7, PG 3.701C. In the Greek text there is a play on the homophonic words καλόν (*kalon*), meaning 'good', κάλλος (*kallos*), meaning 'beauty', and καλῶ (*kalo*), meaning 'to call'.

[44] St John Chrysostom, *On 1 Corinthians*, 27.3, PG 61.228; *On Repentance*, 8.1, PG 49.336; *On Ephesians*, 23.2, PG 62.166; Cf. also St Cyril of Alexandria, *On John*, 12, PG 74.708B: 'In our holy concourses or gatherings, we also say this [Peace be unto all] to each other'; also PG 74.725C: 'It is therefore most appropriate that we perform our holy concourses in the church on the eighth day [Sunday]'.

[45] St John Chrysostom, *Homily on Isaiah 6*, 4, PG 56.140; St Gregory of Nyssa, *On Ecclesiastes*, 3, PG 44.649C; St Maximus the Confessor, *Mystagogy*, 1, PG 91.664D.

brated in the Mother of God, through the power of the Holy Spirit: 'Your womb became a Holy Table, for it held the heavenly Bread.' At the Divine Liturgy, the Queen of heaven is at the right hand of the King: 'Where Christ is, there the Theotokos* stands as well... For she is indeed His throne, and where the King is seated, there too is His throne.'[46]

The angelic world forms Christ's entourage. Christ proceeds to Golgotha *escorted by the angelic hosts*.[47] At the moment of the offering, the angels join us in glorifying God's goodness.

The choir of saints, too, participates in the Eucharist. That is why, during the Liturgy, 'the names of the saints are recited... which indicates that they are indissolubly conjoined in a sacred union with Christ, surpassing this world.' The eucharistic *synaxis* is the celebration of Christ's victory. All those who have accompanied Christ on His course are present with Him at this moment: 'When triumphal celebrations are held for a king, all those who have taken part in the victory are also acclaimed; so likewise here, for the celebration of the Divine Liturgy is a time of triumphal celebrations.'[48]

Also present at the Divine Liturgy are our departed brethren, for whom we ask God's mercy. Their commemoration* at the Liturgy brings 'much gain and great benefit' to their souls.[49]

Heaven and earth, angels and men, living and departed, join together in keeping festival and offering thanksgiving to the Lord for His love. 'Earth and sea, inhabited and uninhabited lands, will sing an eternal hymn; and they will give thanks in gratitude for the divine good things' which they have received.[50] All things give

---

[46] Matins* of Mid-Pentecost, Canon, ode 5; St Gregory Palamas, *Homily 53*, 21, *Oikonomou*, p. 157.

[47] Divine Liturgy, Cherubic Hymn.

[48] St Dionysius the Areopagite, *On the Church Hierarchy*, 3.3.9, PG 3.437C; St John Chrysostom, *On Acts*, 21.5, PG 60.170.

[49] St John Chrysostom, *On Philippians*, 3.4, PG 62.204.

[50] Ibid. *On Psalm 44*, 13, PG 55.203.

thanks: *To Him who sits upon the throne and to the Lamb be bless-ing and honour and glory and power for ever and ever!* (Rev. 5: 13).

6. The fruits of the Divine Liturgy

i. The Christian is incorporated into Christ

Through the Mystery of the Divine Eucharist, man receives the holy Body and precious Blood of Christ, and becomes 'one in body and in blood' with Him.[51] As Christ Himself said when He spoke of this Mystery for the first time, *he who eats my flesh and drinks my blood, abides in me and I in him* (John 6: 56).

Man receives Christ within him, and Christ receives man. Thus Christ becomes at once the home of man and at home in man. This is the supreme manifestation of Christ's love for man. St John Chrysostom tells us: 'It is needful to understand the mir-acle of the Mysteries: what it is, why it was given, and what is its profit. As St Paul says, we become one body and *members of His flesh and bones* (Eph. 5: 30)...so, in order to become one body with Christ not just through a feeling of love but in actuality, let us be mingled with Christ's flesh. This is achieved through the food which He has given us, desiring to show us the great love He has for us. This is why He mingled Himself with us and became one body with us, in order that we may be one with Him, as the body is attached to the head.'[52]

Through Holy Communion, the man of faith becomes one body with Christ, one 'compound', one 'mixture'. This happens not in some theoretical sense, but actually and existentially. Christ in His love for us 'was not content only to become man, to endure buffeting and be killed, but even mingled Himself with us. He changes us into His own Body, not in faith only but in reality.'[53]

---

[51] St Cyril of Jerusalem, *Mystagogical Catechesis 4*, 1, *PG* 33.1097A.
[52] St John Chrysostom, *On John*, 46.2–3, *PG* 59.260.
[53] Ibid. *On Matthew*, 82.5, *PG* 58.743.

On another occasion, St John hears Christ speaking to him: 'I am not simply joined with you; I am interwoven, I am eaten, I am attenuated little by little so that the mixing, the interweaving and the union can be greater. For things that are joined preserve their own boundaries, whereas I am interwoven with you. I do not want there to be anything between us. I want the two to be one.' Between Christ and the Christian there is no longer anything intervening. Everything dissolves in the light of His love: 'We and Christ are one.'[54]

Only a saint can speak this boldly. And that was how the saints did indeed speak:

> We become Christ's limbs, and our limbs become Christ:
> though I am a wretched man, my hand is Christ,
>   my foot is also Christ,
> though I am wretch, I am both Christ's hand and Christ's foot.[55]

The words of the saints are not well-turned phrases designed to impress us; they are the outpouring of hearts that overflow with Christ. Amidst this overflowing of Life and Light, the whole man flashes like lightning. All his limbs radiate light. And the world in which the saint lives and moves is full of the light of Christ. 'The light of Christ illumines all.'[56]

When we offer God bread and wine we are offering the world, and the world becomes Eucharist.[57] Through the descent of the Comforter *upon us and upon these Gifts here set forth*, man is sanctified and creation is renewed. All things are renewed: the world receives God's blessing, and man is made into Christ. The world becomes the house of God, and man becomes by Grace a *christ*, an anointed one.

---

[54] *On 1 Timothy*, 15.4, *PG* 62.586; *On Hebrews*, 7.3, *PG* 63.58.

[55] St Symeon the New Theologian, *Hymn 15*, 141–3, *SC* 156, p. 288.

[56] Liturgy of the Presanctified Gifts.*

[57] Cf. St Irenaeus, *Against Heresies*, 5.2.3, *SC* 153, p. 35.

So we experience a foretaste of the new age. In that day, 'when the Lord appears, He will be surrounded by the choir of His good servants; and when He shines, they will shine too.' The *Thean-thropos*,* the God-man, surrounded by the *synaxis* of saints will be radiant with divine beauty, 'God in the midst of gods, the fair one leading the chorus of the fair' (cf. Ps. 81: 1).[58]

ii. The Church is formed

When the faithful gather in a given place at a given time in order to celebrate the Divine Eucharist, their assembly reveals the mystery of the Church. The Church and the Divine Eucharist are the Body of Christ; they are Christ Himself. When we were incorporated into the Church through Baptism, Christ 'made us His own Body, and [through the Divine Eucharist] passed on to us His own Body'.[59]

The Mystical or Last Supper is the historical starting-point of the Divine Eucharist and of the Church. Christ's Supper is dominated by His sacrifice on the Cross. This is also the foundation on which the Church is built. The blood and water gushing from the Master's side when the soldier pierced it with a spear are symbols of the Mysteries of Baptism and the Eucharist. When Christ's side is pierced, we see the beginning of these two Mysteries and the creation of the Church: 'The soldiers pierced the Master's side with a spear, and blood and water poured forth together. This event was ordained by God as an image and inception of the Mysteries of the Divine Eucharist and Holy Baptism.' *There came out blood and water* (John 19: 34). 'The blood and the water are a symbol of Holy Baptism and the Divine Eucharist. From these two, the Church was born.'[60] The Mysteries of Baptism and the Eucharist

---

[58] St Nicholas Cabasilas, *On the Life in Christ*, 6 and 4, PG 150.649B, 624B.
[59] St John Chrysostom, *On Ephesians*, 3.3, PG 62.27.
[60] St Cyril of Alexandria, *On John*, 12, PG 74.677B; St John Chrysostom, *On John*, 85.3, PG 59.463.

begin from the Cross of Christ, and it is these very Mysteries that constitute the Church.

The Church is born of Christ and nourished on Christ: 'Those whom Christ begot — through Baptism — He nourishes with Himself.' This divine food builds up the Church and makes it into the Body of Christ: 'We Christians are nourished with the holy Body of Christ; we are mingled with this Body. And we have become the one Body of Christ.'[61] As St Paul writes, *because there is one bread, we who are many are one body, for we all partake of the one bread* (1 Cor. 10: 17). By partaking in the one Bread, in Christ, we Christians who are many form one body, the Church. Thus every eucharistic assembly is an assembly of the entire Church, because the Divine Eucharist is the mystery of Christ.

At His Incarnation, Christ 'took on the flesh of the Church' and 'came to His own home. He found the Church unclean, naked, covered with blood; and He washed her [with Baptism], anointed her [with oil and perfumes: holy Chrismation], nourished her [with Holy Communion] and clothed her in a garment the like of which it would be impossible to find. He Himself became the raiment of the Church, and holding her by the hand He took her up on high.'[62] He led her up to the heavenly Kingdom where the Divine Liturgy is celebrated.

---

[61] St John Chrysostom, *On Matthew*, 82.5, PG 58.744, 743–4.

[62] Ibid. *Homily before his Exile*, 2, PG 52.429; *On Psalm 5*, 2, PG 55.63.

I. THE PREPARATION FOR THE LITURGY

The rite of the divine service as a whole symbolises, through the mysteries celebrated in it, the entire dispensation [*economy*] of the condescension for our salvation of our true God and Saviour Jesus Christ.

(Theodore, Bishop of Andida, Protheoria, PG 140.421AB)

1. THE RITE OF THE *KAIROS*

The Priest who is preparing to celebrate the divine Mystery must be reconciled with everyone beforehand, and have nothing against anyone; he must guard his heart, as far as he can, from evil thoughts; from the evening before he should remain abstinent, and be vigilant until the time of the divine service.

The preparation of the celebrant

The priest is a minister of the mystery of man's salvation. Through his ministry, man is separated from sin and brought to God, for the purpose of the priestly ministry is 'to give the soul wings, to snatch it from the world and give it to God…to make Christ dwell in the hearts of the faithful through the grace of the Holy Spirit, and above all to deify man.' With the support of the celebrant, man is raised up to the 'blessedness above'.[1] The priestly ministry incarnates the prophetic proclamation: Brethren, *approach the eternal mountains* (Mica. 2: 9).

Through his ministry, the priest reveals the new life which Christ has brought us, which is Christ's own life. And because the Divine Liturgy is the Mystery through which Christ's life is offered to the faithful, it also lies at the heart of the priestly ministry.

The first prerequisites for a priest who is about to approach the holy Altar are forbearance and love. This is what Christ asks of His minister, as of course He asks of every Christian: *If you are*

---

[1] St Gregory the Theologian, *Homily 2*, 22 and *9*, 3, *PG* 35.432B, 824A.

offering your gift at the altar and there remember that your broth-er has something against you, leave your gift there before the al-tar and go; first be reconciled to your brother, and then come and offer your gift (Matt. 5: 23–4).

St John Chrysostom is amazed at Christ's love: 'The magnitude of His love for mankind! Christ regards the honour offered to Himself as inferior to love for our neighbour.' 'Let your worship of me be interrupted,' Christ says, 'in order that the love between you and your brother may be preserved.' By these words, the Lord wants to show us 'that He values love dearly, and considers it a sacrifice higher than any other. Without this sacrifice, He accepts no others.' In this way, Christ teaches us that 'the Holy Table does not accept those who harbour enmity among themselves'.[2]

In *The Spiritual Meadow*, the following story is told from the life of Bishop John of Amathous. The bishop had a deacon, and one feast day, when he was meant to be celebrating, the deacon lost his temper and insulted the bishop to his face. When the time came for them to carry out the Service of Preparation and put on their vestments, the deacon did not go to concelebrate because he was ashamed of what he had said to the bishop. Then the bish-op, like a good shepherd, went looking for the lost sheep, saying: 'Unless Deacon Epiphanios comes, there will be no Liturgy today.' When the deacon subsequently came, the good shepherd em-braced him and made a prostration* before him as if he were the one who was at fault. He then vested himself, and instructed that the fan* should be given to the deacon so that he would stand with him at the Divine Liturgy. After the Dismissal, he invited the deacon to a meal, and then sent him on his way in peace. The bishop's relatives grumbled about all this, but the man of God re-buked them, saying: 'Have you forgotten that when Christ was re-viled He did not return the abuse, and when He was struck he did not respond with blows? [cf. 1 Pet. 2: 23, Matt. 5: 39]… Believe me,

---

[2] *On Matthew*, 16.9, *PG* 57.250–1.

my children, when I offer the bloodless worship, before I begin the preparatory rite it is my practice to offer up prayers to God for myself and for you. But today, when I began the prayer, I omitted the prayer for myself and for you and propitiating God with tears I prayed for the deacon to be forgiven. And at once I saw divine Grace descend upon the Altar. So if you too want to be accounted worthy to see such a vision, you should offer the bloodless Sacrifice to God with genuine forgiveness; for there is no other way that leads so directly to Him.'[3]

My heart is ready, O God

Before he offers the eucharistic Sacrifice, the celebrant should sacrifice himself: 'No one is worthy of the great God who is at once Victim and High Priest, unless he has first presented himself to God as a living and holy sacrifice [cf. Rom. 12: 1]…or unless he has offered to God a sacrifice of praise and a *broken spirit* [Ps. 50: 19], the only sacrifice asked from us by Him who has offered everything for us.' This sacrifice requires that the celebrant should be pure in soul and body. The most pure God is pleased only with the sacrifice offered 'with clean hands and with a mind exalted and purified'.[4]

If a priest approaches the Holy Mysteries without having first sacrificed himself, he approaches, not the true Light but a burning fire (cf. Heb. 12: 29). As St Theognostus writes: 'You that have been accounted worthy of the divine and reverend priesthood should have first sacrificed yourself through the death of the passions and pleasures; only then should you dare to approach the

---

[3] John Eucratas and Sophronius the Sophist, *Leimonarion to palaion* [*The ancient Spiritual Meadow*], 3rd edn (Volos: Agioreitiki Bibliothiki, 1959), 'Concerning John, Bishop of Amathous in Cyprus', pp. 65–6. The fan (*ripidion*) was used in the old days by the deacon to keep flying insects away from the holy Cup. Its symbolism is related to the deacon because 'the *ripidia* and the deacons indicate the six-winged Seraphim' (St Germanus, *Contemplation*, PG 98.432D).

[4] St Gregory the Theologian, *Homily 2*, 95 and 4, 29, PG 35.497AB, 556B.

life-giving and terrible Sacrifice, if you do not want to be burnt like tinder by the divine fire.' We sacrifice ourselves through the death of the passions, that is, through repentance. This is why the saint admonishes the celebrant: 'Once you become whiter than snow [cf. Ps. 50: 9], shedding torrents of tears, and once you make your conscience white with the purity of your life, then approach the Holy Things as one who is holy.' 'For those who serve the all-pure God ought to be holy.'[5]

The evening before the Divine Liturgy, the celebrant makes ready his heart, alone, face to face with God. He banishes all feelings of rancour and every evil thought, purifies himself through abstinence and keeps vigil in prayer. The next morning, in church, he will ask for power from on high so that he can approach the holy Altar and say to the Lord: *My heart is ready, O God, I will sing and make melody in my glory* (Ps. 107: 2).

When the time has come for the divine mystagogy, the Priest and Deacon come out from the north door of the sanctuary into the nave of the church. After bowing to the bishop's throne, they go and stand before the Royal Doors* and make three bows,* each saying to himself: *God, have compassion for me, a sinner,[6] and have mercy on me.*

---

[5] *On the Priesthood*, 13 and 18, *Philokalia*, vol. 2, pp. 361, 362–3; St Cyril of Alexandria, *On Worship in Spirit and Truth*, 7, PG 68.492A.

[6] Luke 18: 13.

Then the Deacon says: *Master, give the blessing.*

Priest: *Blessed is our God, always, now and forever, and to the ages of ages.*

Deacon: *Amen.*

Priest: *Glory to you, our God, glory to you.*

Heavenly King, Comforter, the Spirit of truth, present everywhere and filling all things, the treasury of good and giver of life, come and dwell in us and cleanse us from every impurity, and save our souls, Gracious One.

Deacon: (the Trisagion prayers) *Holy God, Holy Mighty, Holy Immortal, have mercy upon us* (three times).

Glory to the Father and the Son and the Holy Spirit, both now and ever and to the ages of ages. Amen.

All-holy Trinity, have mercy upon us. Lord, be merciful to our sins. Master, forgive our transgressions. Holy One, visit us and heal our infirmities, for your name's sake. Lord, have mercy; Lord, have mercy; Lord, have mercy.

Glory to the Father and the Son and the Holy Spirit, both now and ever and to the ages of ages. Amen.

Our Father in heaven, hallowed be your name, your Kingdom come, your will be done on earth as it is in heaven. Give us today our daily bread and forgive us our sins, as we forgive those who sin against us. And do not lead us into temptation, but deliver us from the evil one.

Priest: *For yours is the kingdom and the power and the glory, of the Father, of the Son, and of the Holy Spirit, now and for ever, and to the ages of ages.*

Deacon: *Amen.*

The day without evening

When it is the appointed time for the Divine Liturgy, the celebrant, with the deacon beside him, 'takes *Kairos*'.*

Kairos[7] is the name given to the short rite that takes place in
front of the *iconostasis*.* This rite is the precursor of the Divine
Liturgy. It symbolises the time of Christ's Incarnation, and reminds us that *the time [kairos] is fulfilled, and the Kingdom of
God is at hand* (Mark 1: 15).[8] Thus the rite of the *Kairos* prepares
us to receive Christ the King and take part in the banquet of His
Kingdom.

According to God's pre-eternal counsel, at a particular moment in history 'He who is without beginning begins to be, and
the Word is made flesh'. The God of all time becomes a 'young
child'. The Ancient of Days comes into the world and makes all
things new — new life, new Kingdom, new time: 'When the time
came for Your appearance upon earth...the reign of Your eternal
Kingdom, which was without beginning, was made new.'[9]

The event of the Incarnation of the Word breaks through time
and renews it. The Timeless One is clothed in time; time plays
host to the One who is beyond time. The Lady Mother of God becomes the place within which 'nature and time are made new'.
Within renewed time, we experience the new Event, the victory
of love over time and death: 'We celebrate the death of death...
the inception of a new way of life which is eternal; and dancing
for joy we extol Him who is the Cause.'[10]

After the Resurrection of Christ, Life reigns instead of death,

---

[7] The rite of the *Kairos* is modern. Ancient manuscripts of the Divine Liturgy
begin with the Prayer of the Prothesis: *O God, our God who sent forth the
heavenly bread....* In the fourteenth century, the Diataxis of Patriarch Philotheos of Constantinople lays down that the priest who is going to serve says the
following prayer: *Lord, send forth your hand from the height of your dwelling
place...* (Trembelas, *Leitourgiai*, p. 1). See the prayers on pp. 99 and 42, below.

[8] Cf. St Germanus, *Contemplation*, PG 98.401A.

[9] Matins of Christmas: Lauds,* *Kontakion** and *Doxastikon** at Lauds.

[10] *Apolytikion*,* 2 July; Easter Canon, ode 7.

and eternity reigns within time. It is this victory of Christ that we celebrate in the Divine Liturgy, which is a continuous Easter: 'It is always Easter.' This is why the day of the eucharistic Mystery par excellence is the day of the Lord's Resurrection, the Lord's day: Sunday symbolises time transcended, because it is at once the first day of creation and the eighth day of the Kingdom. It is the 'day without evening, perpetual and unending. It is not that it does not yet exist, but that it is going to exist. No: it existed before the ages, it exists now, and it will exist to the endless ages.'[11]

'The day of salvation dawns' from the Table of Life. This is the eighth day, the day of the age to come which will manifest itself 'when this corruptible and transient time ceases to be'. The day of the Divine Liturgy is the day of the Kingdom which *is coming, and now is* (John 4: 23). For in the Liturgy, we live through past events and we give thanks for future events which have already been bestowed upon us: [for] *grant[ing] us your Kingdom that is to come, we thank You.*[12]

Just as the prophets were forerunners of Christ's coming in the flesh and prepared human beings to receive Him, so Christ Himself has become 'the forerunner of His spiritual presence. By His own teaching, He leads our souls forward to receive His manifest and divine advent. He accomplishes this advent ceaselessly as He changes those who are worthy from the flesh to the spirit by means of the virtues; and He will accomplish it for all to see at the end when He will manifest those things that were hitherto kept secret from all men.'[13]

What Christ has brought about by His Incarnation, we experi-

---

[11] St John Chrysostom, *On 1 Timothy*, 5.3, PG 62.530; St Basil the Great, *Hexaemeron*, 2.8, PG 29.52A; St Symeon the New Theologian, *Ethical Discourse 1*, 1, SC 122, p. 182.

[12] Cf. St John of Damascus, *Homily on the Dormition*, 3, 3, PG 96.757B; St Gregory of Nyssa, *On Psalm 2*, 5, PG 44.504D–505A; Divine Liturgy, Anaphora.

[13] St Maximus the Confessor, *Two Hundred Texts on Theology*, 2.29, PG 90.1137CD (*Philokalia*, vol. 2, p. 144).

ence sacramentally in the Divine Liturgy: He who *is* and who *was* reveals to us Him *who is to come* (Rev. 4: 8), since the Liturgy is the possibility for all rational creatures to experience 'the ineffable mystery of eternal well-being'[14] together with Christ.

The Divine Liturgy is a *synaxis*, a gathering: all the children of God are gathered in one place, the place where heaven and earth, the past, the present and the future all concelebrate. The *synaxis* of the Church extends 'not only to the whole world, but also to all ages'.[15]

Then the Priest and the Deacon say these *troparia** with compunction:

Priest: *Have mercy on us, O Lord, have mercy on us; for we sinners, casting away all excuse, offer you, as our Master, this supplication: have mercy on us.*

Deacon: *Glory to the Father...*

Lord, have mercy on us, for in you we have put our trust. Do not be very angry with us, neither remember our iniquities, but look on us now, as you are compassionate, and save us from our enemies; for you are our God, and we are your people; we are all the works of your hands, and we have called upon your name.

Priest: *Both now and for ever...*

Open the gate of compassion to us, O blessed Theotokos (as this is being said, the Royal Doors are opened by the Deacon); *hoping in you, may we not be confounded. Through you may we be delivered from adversities, for you are the salvation of the Christian people.*

---

[14] Ibid. 1.56, *PG* 90.1104C (*Philokalia*, vol. 2, p. 125).

[15] St John Chrysostom, *On Psalm 44*, 3, *PG* 55.203.

The Theotokos: The gate that faces east

The door through which Christ passed in order to come into the world was His love for man. It is this divine love that St Symeon the New Theologian addresses, asking that it may be for us too a door bringing Christ close to us: 'O divine love, where are you holding Christ? Where are you hiding Him?... Open even to us, unworthy though we are, a little door, that we may see Christ who suffered for us... Open to us, since you have become the Door to His manifestation in the flesh; you have constrained the abundant and unforced compassion of our Master to bear the sins of us all... Make your home in us, that you the Master may come and visit us in our lowliness, as you go before us to meet Him.'[16]

The door of love through which Christ passed in order to come into the world was opened by the Mother of God. Her holiness attracted divine mercy to the human race. Through her ministry in the mystery of the divine economy, the Mother of God became the 'Gate that faces east' (cf. Ezek. 46: 1, 12); the 'Gate that looks towards the east' from which Life dawned for men and scattered the darkness of death. On the day of her nativity, the Church keeps festival because the 'Gate that looks towards the east' is born; she 'awaits the entry of the great Priest, she who alone brings the one and only Christ into the world, for the salvation of our souls.'[17]

The Most Blessed Mother of God is the virgin Gate through which the light of divine compassion dawns: 'Through you, merciful one all-pure, the nature of mankind received mercy.'[18] This is the reason why, before beginning the Liturgy, we ask the Mother of God to open the gate of her motherly love, so that Christ may enter into us and we into Christ.

---

[16] *Catechesis 1, SC* 96, p. 232.

[17] St John of Damascus, *On the Birth of the Mother of God,* Homily 2, 7, PG 96.689D; Vespers,* 8 September.

[18] *Octoechos,** Tone 8, Wednesday Matins, Canon, ode 6.

Deacon: *Lord, have mercy* (twelve times). *Glory to the Father... both now...*

And the Priest and Deacon cross themselves and bow three times.

The Cross: the glory of Christ

When a Christian crosses himself, he is proclaiming Christ's victory over death and the Devil. The Cross 'has become a cause of great blessing and a wall of protection against every danger... The Cross has put death to death, rased to the ground the Devil's fortress...and delivered the whole world which was under condemnation.' The Cross has 'opened the gates of heaven' and 'set mankind at the right hand of God's throne'.[19]

Through the Cross, the love of the Triune God has been revealed to man: 'The Cross is the will of God the Father, the glory of the only-begotten Son, the exultation of the Holy Spirit. The Cross is the adornment of the angels, the security of the Church, the boast of the Apostle Paul, the wall which protects the saints, the light of the whole world.' That is why 'all believers constantly make the sign of the cross on the most notable part of the body, the forehead. In this way, they have it engraved upon them every day, and carry it around as if inscribed on a triumphal monument.'[20] 'Christians who believe in Christ make the sign of the cross upon themselves, not casually and disrespectfully, but with full attention, care, fear and trembling and all devout respect... For according to the respect each person shows to the Cross, so he receives corresponding strength and help from God.'[21]

---

[19] St John Chrysostom, *To the Jews and Pagans*, 10, and *Against the Jews*, 3.4; *PG* 48.827, 867.

[20] Ibid. *On the name 'cemetery'*, 2, *PG* 49.396–7, and *To the Jews*, 9, *PG* 48.826.

[21] St Symeon the New Theologian, *Homily 1*, 4, *Ta evriskomena* (Thessaloniki: Rigopoulos, 1969), pp. 31–2.

Glorify God in your body

We have already said that the celebrant prepares himself in spirit and in body: he fasts,* he keeps vigil, he prays. A similar preparation should be made by every Christian. The body, like the soul, needs to be prepared in order to take part in the eucharistic offering and to receive within itself the exalted Visitor who is Christ. The body, then, is not a passive spectator of the Divine Liturgy, but participates actively in its celebration.

St Paul says that our body is a temple of the Holy Spirit, and exhorts us to give glory to God in that temple: *So glorify God in your body and in your spirit, which are God's* (1 Cor. 6: 20). Indeed, in the Divine Liturgy the Christian's body becomes the place where the Lord is glorified. By our movements or by keeping still, by our words or our silence, we glorify the Lord.

At this time, the priest and deacon cross themselves and bow three times. There are two different sorts of bows or prostrations: the small bow referred to here, and the full prostration. In a small bow, we make the sign of the cross and bow before the Lord or the saints, bending from the waist. In a full prostration, also called 'bending of the knee', we fall to the ground. By this action of bending the knee, the creature humbly venerates the majesty of the Creator.

In his description of the Liturgy in the Kingdom, John the Evangelist says that when the Lamb, that is, Christ, had taken the sealed scroll, *the four living creatures and the twenty-four elders fell down before the Lamb, each holding a harp, and with golden bowls full of incense, which are the prayers of the saints; and they sang a new song* (Rev. 5: 8–9). According to the commentators, the four living creatures symbolise the angelic world, and the elders the Church triumphant.[22] So with the angels and the saints, we who still struggle on earth bow down before the Lamb, who by

---

[22] See Arethas of Caesarea, *Commentary on the Apocalypse* (Athens, 1845), pp. 57, 67, 70.

His sacrifice has raised us up to the throne of God. We fall to the ground, resting our forehead upon the earth, and ourselves become good earth fit to receive Christ (cf. Luke 8: 8).

The body cooperates in worshipping God. St Gregory Palamas, responding to the heretical Barlaam who contended that the operations common to soul and body are an impediment to prayer, writes: 'One might say to someone who suggested such things that a person who engages in prayer of the heart should neither fast nor keep vigil nor make prostrations...nor should he maintain a standing position, or do any such ascetic exercises.' Yet the saint continues, 'when we cultivate prayer, we certainly need the physical toil produced by fasting, vigil and the like.'[23]

Through physical toil, our prayer bears fruit: *Behold my humility and my toil, and forgive all my sins* (Ps. 24: 18), we say to Christ. And prostrations are par excellence an expression of toil and humility.

The Priest and Deacon, with their heads uncovered, then venerate the holy icons on the *iconostasis*.

As they venerate the icon of Christ, they say: *We venerate your most pure icon, loving Lord, asking forgiveness for our offences, Christ O God. For by your own choice you were well pleased to ascend the Cross in the flesh, to deliver those whom you had fashioned from the slavery of the enemy. Therefore with thanksgiving we cry to you: you have filled all things with joy, our Saviour, in coming to save the world.*

Venerating the icon of the Mother of God, they say: *You are a fountain of tenderness, O Theotokos: make us worthy of compassion. Look upon the people who*

---

[23] *In Defence of the holy Hesychasts*, 2.2.4 and 2.2.6, *Chrestou*, vol. 1, pp. 510, 512.

have sinned, and show your power as always; for hoping in you we cry, 'Hail', as once did Gabriel, the Chief Captain of the Bodiless Powers.

Venerating the icon of the Forerunner, they say: *The memory of the just is praised; but for you, O Forerunner, the testimony of the Lord sufficed. You were truly shown to be more venerable than the Prophets, for you were counted worthy to baptise in the streams Him whom you were proclaiming, therefore after your contest for the truth, rejoicing you announced to those in Hades the good news: God manifested in the flesh, taking away the sin of the world and giving us His great mercy.*

They then venerate the icon of the patron saint (or the feast day) of the church, reciting the corresponding *apolytikion.**

Through the icons, we see the Lord and the saints

As we prepare ourselves to participate in the divine service, we venerate the pure images of the Lord, the Most Holy Mother of God, the honoured Forerunner and the other saints. The icons bring to mind the mystery of the divine economy in its entirety, for 'what Holy Scripture is to the literate, the icon is to the illiterate, and what the word is to our hearing, the icon is to our sight'.[24]

According to the Church's hymnography, the first icon of the Lord was disclosed when He became incarnate, and the first iconographer was the Theotokos: 'The uncircumscribed Word of the Father became circumscribed, taking flesh from you, O Theo-

---

[24] St John of Damascus, *In Defence of the holy Icons*, 1.17, PG 94.1248C.

tokos; and He has restored the sullied image [that is, man] to its ancient glory, mingling it with the divine beauty. We therefore confess our salvation [through Christ's Incarnation], depicting it in action [through the holy icons] and recounting it in words.'[25]

The word of the Gospel and the 'word' of the holy icons help us to experience at first hand the mystery of the divine economy: 'While our physical eyes are looking at an icon, our intellect and the spiritual eyes of our heart are focussed on the mystery of the economy of the Incarnation.'[26] By means of the holy icons, we see the Lord and the saints. We converse with them: 'The holy Apostles saw the Lord with their physical eyes; others saw the Apostles, and others again saw the holy martyrs. But I too yearn to see them with my soul and body and to have them as a medicine against every ill... Because I am a human being and have a body, I long to see and communicate with holy things in a physical manner too.'[27]

The icons lead us to glorify God: 'When thoughts are choking me like so many thorns, I enter the church, the hospital of all our souls. There the beauty of the iconography attracts my eyes and delights my vision like a verdant meadow, and without my noticing it stirs my soul to praise God. I have seen the endurance of the martyr and the crowns he received in return, and eagerness to imitate him zealously burns like a fire within me. I fall down and worship God through the martyr, and gain salvation.'[28]

The church with its holy icons forms the space in which the Divine Liturgy is celebrated. There we coexist and dwell with the Mother of God and all the saints.

[25] *Kontakion* for the Sunday of Orthodoxy.
[26] St John of Damascus, *Against the Iconoclasts*, 13, *PG* 96.1360B.
[27] Ibid. *In Defence of the holy Icons*, 1.36, *PG* 94.1264BC.
[28] Ibid. 1.47, *PG* 94.1268AB.

After venerating the icons, the Priest and the Deacon go and stand before the Royal Doors. And the Deacon says: *Let us pray to the Lord. Lord, Have mercy.*

The Priest, bowing his head, says the prayer:

Lord, send forth your hand,[29] *from your dwelling-place on high, and strengthen me for this your service, so that, standing without blame before your dread Altar, I may offer the bloodless Sacrifice. For yours is the power and the glory to the ages of ages.*

Deacon: *Amen.*

The Priest gives the Dismissal.

Priesthood: a ministry of service

The celebration of the bloodless Sacrifice is the work of Christ the High Priest. He is the hand of God the Father which the priest asks the Lord to send from the throne of the Father: 'The Son is the all-powerful and mighty hand of the Father.' The priest as he stands before the holy Altar is the icon of Christ.[30] 'The one who changes the Gifts into the Body and Blood of Christ is not some human being, but Christ Himself who was crucified for us. The priest stands as a type of Christ, proclaiming those words [which Christ spoke at the Last Supper], but the power and grace belong to God.'[31]

At the Divine Liturgy, 'everything is performed by the Father, the Son and the Holy Spirit. The priest lends his tongue and offers his hand', so as to serve the great Mystery. In consequence, 'the

---

[29] Ps. 143: 7.

[30] St Methodius of Olympus, *On things generate*, 7, PG 18.341A. St Maximus the Confessor writes to a bishop: 'It has been given to you, holy Father, to bear the icon of Christ upon earth' (*Letter 30*, PG 91.624B).

[31] St John Chrysostom, *On the Betrayal of Judas*, 1.6, PG 49.380.

priest is only a servant... This is in fact what priesthood is — an office that serves the sacred [Mysteries of the Church].'[32]

The priest now asks Christ to strengthen him to perform His ministry of service. Indeed, Christ came into the world not to be served but to serve: *I am among you as one who serves* (Luke 22: 27). And the service that Christ offered man is the mystery of the divine economy of His Incarnation. This service, however, is continued by means of the Divine Liturgy. That is why, in this prayer, the Divine Liturgy is called Christ's service.

The Lord is among us *as one who serves*. Yet, Christ 'did not serve only in the present life, when He came and manifested Himself in the form of weak humanity...but also in the life to come, when He will come with power and manifest Himself in the glory of His Father,...then He will once more *gird Himself and have them sit at table, and will come and serve them*' (Luke 12: 37).[33]

* * *

A thirteenth-century manuscript records the following prayer said by a priest as he performs the rite of the *Kairos*:

'O God, our God, invisible to the Cherubim and incomprehensible to the Seraphim and unapproachable to all the powers of heaven, who in Your inexpressible love for mankind and unfathomable goodness have united Yourself to our poverty and lowliness, and have bestowed on us Your sinful and unworthy servants the rule of priesthood: as You are good and bounteous in mercy, do You Yourself strengthen me, O Saviour who loves mankind, as I prepare to make ready for the service of divine grace entrusted to me. For I come to stand before Your holy Altar which is fearsome and terrible, not trusting in my own power or purity, but trusting in the boundless ocean of Your compassion. For my sins will not triumph over the multitude of Your mercies.

---

[32] St John Chrysostom, *On John*, 86.4, *PG* 59.472; St Nicholas Cabasilas, *Comm. Liturgy*, 46, *PG* 150.469A.

[33] St Nicholas Cabasilas, *On the Life in Christ*, 4, *PG* 150.620B.

'Therefore I pray You, Master who loves mankind, clothe me, Your unworthy servant, with this priestly garment and grace of Your divine and All-holy Spirit. Enlighten the eyes of my mind that I may see the reflection of the brightness of Your grace; give clarity to my tongue to hymn You without fault; keep my intellect from wandering, free my mind from forgetfulness, preserve me entire in Your holiness and fulfil my petitions to You, holy Lord; receive my sacrifice as spotless incense and a divine burnt offering, and grant me the sweetness of Your beauty.

'Send down an angel of light to concelebrate and strengthen me, that I may rightly proclaim the word of Your true wisdom and become worthy of receiving Your heavenly and immortal Mysteries; and that, enlightened through them in soul and body, I may be accounted worthy to enjoy Your eternal good things with those who have truly loved and followed Your ordinances. For You have said, O Master, that whatever anyone asks in Your name, he will receive it freely from God Your coeternal Father. Therefore I too, a sinner, beseech Your Deity as I put on my priestly vestment: Give to me unto my salvation whatever I have asked of You, O Lord.

'For You love mankind, and are glorified together with Your Father who has no beginning, and Your All-holy and good and life-giving Spirit, now and ever and to the ages of ages. Amen.'[34]

---

[34] Trembelas, *Leitourgiai*, pp. 228–9.

After the Dismissal, the Priest and Deacon turn to the people and bow their heads, asking forgiveness. They then enter the sanctuary, each of them saying: *I shall go into your house; I shall worship toward your holy temple in fear of you.*[35]

They bow three times before the Holy Table; the Priest then kisses the Gospel Book and the Holy Table, while the Deacon kisses only the right hand edge of the Holy Table.

The celebrant enters heaven

The whole world is imaged in the form in which a church is built. The nave is an image of the earth and the sanctuary an image of heaven: 'The entire cosmos of beings created by God...is in a sense a church not made with hands, and with great wisdom it is imaged in the church that is built by human hands. As its sanctuary it has the world above which is assigned to the heavenly powers, while as its nave it has this world which is reserved for those whose lot is to live by the senses.'[36]

The celebrant now enters into the sanctuary, which symbolises heaven itself. There he will carry out his angelic ministry. 'That is why the priest has to be so pure, as if he were standing amidst the angelic powers in heaven itself.'[37]

God's love for mankind, which calls every Christian to sit with Him at the Table of Life, now calls the celebrant to enter into the Holy of Holies and venerate the holy Altar. But the celebrant's soul does not dare to approach the throne of God without fear: 'The holy and pure soul says, "Lord, I constantly offer You worship

---

[35] Ps. 5: 8.
[36] St Maximus the Confessor, *Mystagogy*, 2, PG 91.669AB.
[37] St John Chrysostom, *On the Priesthood*, 3.4, PG 48.642.

in the consecrated temple of Your glory, since I enjoy Your love for mankind and am guarded by Your right hand. For having Your fear ever with me, I will not permit it to be cast out through boldness engendered by Your love for mankind."[38]

The workshop of the gifts of the Holy Spirit

In the centre of the sanctuary is the holy Altar, which the Lord entrusts to the angelic powers to keep pure and holy. Abba Leontius relates in *The Spiritual Meadow*: 'One Sunday, I went to church to receive Communion. When I entered, I saw an angel standing to the right of the Altar...and I heard a voice saying, "Since this Altar was consecrated, it has been my task to remain in here."'[39]

The holy Altar is 'the border between heaven and earth'. It is 'the throne of glory and the dwelling-place of God, the workshop of the gifts of the Holy Spirit'.[40] It is the spring of Paradise from which flows the gift of the Master's love. 'In the Paradise of Eden, there welled up a spring which poured forth physical rivers. From the Holy Table, a spring wells up from which pour forth spiritual rivers. By this spring are planted...trees that reach to heaven. Trees that are always bearing fruit, ripe and imperishable.' 'From this sacred Table...wells up a spring which creates spiritual springs, and which waters souls and lifts them up to heaven.'[41]

During the Divine Liturgy, the priest discovers that 'this Table is full of spiritual fire; and just as springs gush with water, so too this Table has a sort of inexpressible flame', 'a flame that refreshes the holy'[42] ministers of Christ.

---

[38] St Athanasius the Great, *On Psalm 5*, PG 27.76A.

[39] John Eucratas, *Leimonarion* [*The Spiritual Meadow*], 4, PG 87iii.2856BC.

[40] St Germanus, *Contemplation*, PG 98.421C; St Symeon of Thessaloniki, *Consecration*, 111, PG 155.316D,C.

[41] St John Chrysostom, *On John*, 46.4, PG 59.261; St Gregory Palamas, *Homily 56*, 8, *Oikonomou*, p. 209.

[42] St John Chrysostom, *On the Incomprehensible*, 6.4, PG 48.756; *Octoechos*, *eirmos** of tone 1, ode 8.

At the Last Supper, the all-pure hand of Christ the Master became a terrible Altar higher than the heavens. At the Divine Liturgy, when the faithful draw near to receive Communion, they approach the all-pure hand of Christ, just as the twelve disciples did. For 'altars form an image of the hand of the Saviour. And we receive the Bread from the consecrated Table as the Body of Christ, as if we received it from His pure hand...since He Himself is Priest and Altar and Sacrifice.'[43]

The bloodless offering is being performed continuously, in many different times and places. But the presence of the one Christ does away with time and space. The Church invites us to run with longing to the one fountain of life: 'Let us all run together to the one Jesus Christ as to one temple of God, to one Altar.'[44]

---

[43] St Nicholas Cabasilas, *On the Life in Christ*, 3, PG 150.577D–580A.

[44] St Ignatius of Antioch, *Magnesians*, 7, PG 5.668C.

2. THE VESTING OF THE CELEBRANTS

Then the Priest and Deacon each take their *sticharion*,* face east and make three bows, saying: *God, have compassion for me, a sinner,*[1] *and have mercy on me.*

The Deacon approaches the Priest holding his own *sticharion, orarion** and *epimanikia,** and says: *Master, bless the sticharion and orarion.*

The Priest blesses them with the sign of the cross, saying: *Blessed is our God, always, now and for ever, and to the ages of ages.*

Deacon: *Amen.* And he kisses the Priest's right hand and withdraws to one side of the sanctuary to put on his vestments.

The vestments are holy and transmit holiness

When man lives outside the Church, he is naked of divine grace. His home is not the house of God, but the place of death. He is like the demoniac in the land of the Gadarenes: *He wore no clothes and he lived not in a house but among the tombs* (Luke 8: 27). Through Baptism, however, man is clothed in a garment woven by God: *As many as have been baptised into Christ have put on Christ* (Gal. 3: 27).

Having received the divine grace for himself at Baptism, the priest receives it again when he is ordained, in order to offer it to

---

[1] Luke 18: 13.

the world. Through the Mystery of priesthood, man becomes a steward of grace. This exalted ministry of the celebrant of the Holy Mysteries is imaged by the sacred vestments.

The sacredness of priestly vestments has been emphasised since Old Testament times. The Prophet Ezekiel says, *Let [the laity] not touch the garments in which [the priests] minister, for they are holy* (Ezek. 42: 14).

On the day of his ordination, the priest puts on for the first time 'the holy long tunic…and the hieratic clothing of the Holy Spirit'.[2] From that day forth, every time he prepares to celebrate he takes the sacred vestments one by one, blesses them with the sign of the cross, kisses them and puts them on. By these actions, he shows that the sacred vestments 'are holy, and they are sanctified by the Cross of Christ, and the wearing of them transmits sanctification'. This is why he who treats the sacred vestments with respect and kisses them 'performs a work of faith, and will be saved, just as those who touched the hem of Christ's garment were restored to safety', that is to say, cured (cf. Matt. 14: 36).[3]

The faithful treat the priest's vestments with reverence because they are sacred. By wearing priestly dress, the priest is reminding us that although he comes from this world, he does not belong to this world alone. He stands between man and God, a bridge by which our prayers arise to the Most High and the gifts of God come down.

The Priest takes his *sticharion*, blesses it with the sign of the cross and says: *Blessed is our God, always, now and for ever, and to the ages of ages. Amen.*

---

[2] Eusebius of Caesarea, *Church History*, 10.4, PG 20.849A.
[3] St Symeon of Thessaloniki, *On the holy Liturgy*, 83, PG 155.261C, and *Responses to Archbishop Gabriel*, 29, PG 155.880C.

> And he puts it on, saying: *My soul will rejoice in the Lord; for he has clothed me with a garment of salvation and enfolded me in a robe of gladness; he has set a crown upon my head as on a bridegroom, and adorned me with jewels as a bride.*[4] *Always, now and for ever, and to the ages of ages. Amen.*

Christ: the vestment from heaven

The celebrant is glad and rejoices because the Lord clothes him in *a garment of salvation* and *a robe of gladness*. He gives thanks to Christ who is *fair in beauty beyond the sons of men* (Ps. 44: 3) because He adorns him with His own beauty: *He has adorned me with jewels as a bride.* The adornment of the bride, of the soul, is the Bridegroom Himself, 'Christ, the vestment that came from heaven...the garment of incorruption'.[5]

Through Baptism, the Lord is offered to the baptised as clothing: 'Christ is the most befitting vestment for every saint. He is the garment of spiritual gladness which gives us strength and glory.'[6] So the *sticharion*, the vestment common to all three orders of the priesthood, symbolises the robe of light given at Baptism, the grace shared by all the faithful.

The priest is a member of the Body of Christ like every other Christian. The gifts of the Holy Spirit are offered to all Christians alike: 'Everything has been given to us clergy and to you laity alike, including even the greatest of good things', such as participation at the Table of the Eucharist.[7] This equality between the celebrant and the faithful is underlined by the *sticharion*.

---

[4] Isa. 61: 10.

[5] St Cyril of Alexandria, *On Isaiah*, 5.5, *PG* 70.1365D.

[6] Ibid. 5.1, *PG* 70.1144C.

[7] St John Chrysostom, *On 2 Thessalonians*, 4.4, *PG* 62.492.

Originally, the *sticharion* was always white in colour; it was a symbol of purity, and also of the angelic height of the priestly ministry. The *sticharion* 'indicates the shining raiment of the angels, for angels have often appeared dressed in shining garments, for example, the angel who appeared at the tomb of the Lord dressed in a white raiment [cf. Matt. 28: 3]. The *sticharion* also represents the undefiled purity of the priestly order.' By 'the angel-like whiteness of [his] outer garments', the celebrant reveals his 'soul's inner beauty'.[8]

The celebrant, like an angel *in shining garments* (Luke 24: 4), waits for the faithful at the holy Altar — the tomb of Christ that is the source of Life — so as to invite them to the Supper of the Resurrection, the Supper of the Divine Eucharist.

The Priest then takes the *epitrachelion*,* makes the sign of the cross over it and kisses the cross on the garment's neck, and puts it on, saying:

Blessed is God, who pours out his grace upon his priests, like myrrh upon the head, which runs down upon the beard, upon the beard of Aaron, which runs down to the fringe of his raiment:[9] *always, now and for ever, and to the ages of ages. Amen.*

The epitrachelion, symbol of Grace

The *epitrachelion*, the stole, is the symbol of the grace of the priesthood, and of the priest's participation in the priesthood of

---

[8] St Symeon of Thessaloniki, *Church Building*, 33, *PG* 155.712A; St Theognostus, *On the practice of Virtues, Contemplation and the Priesthood*, 18, *Philokalia*, vol. 2, pp. 362–3.

[9] Ps. 132: 2.

Christ. The priest 'uses it at every rite he performs', because 'it symbolises the performative grace of the Holy Spirit'.[10]

The grace given to the priest is like the special myrrh, the symbol of priestly blessing, with which the Jewish High Priest was anointed (cf. Ex. 30: 25–30). Just as somebody who is anointed with myrrh 'has a joyful countenance, and is filled with fragrance and spreads joy to all who see him',[11] so too does the priest: the true Light is reflected in his face, and his presence brings spiritual joy to the faithful.

The verse of the psalm recited by the priest as he puts on his *epitrachelion* (*like myrrh upon the head, which runs down upon the beard…*) means: 'Once the Church has gathered together and there is harmony, at that very moment the anointing of the Holy Spirit is given…first upon the head of the Church, which is Christ, then on the beard which gives the Church's face its dignity and signifies the Apostles. Finally, the anointing extends spreads over the whole body, meaning all who belong to the Church and have put on Christ.'[12] The divine grace, like myrrh, comes down from the head of the Church, Christ, to the 'beard' which is the celebrant as successor to the Apostles, and reaches to the hem of the garment which is the faithful.

The priest is a link between God and the faithful. In other words, he becomes the conduit through which divine grace reaches the faithful. This reality is what the *epitrachelion* calls to mind: the neck symbolises Christ, and the fringes at the bottom symbolise the souls which God has entrusted to the priest. Through the priest, the faithful receive the grace of Christ.

The *epitrachelion* also shows 'that the priest is below the head, which is Christ, and that he should perform the services under His direction. He must submit himself humbly to Christ's yoke,

---

[10] St Symeon of Thessaloniki, *Church Building*, 39, PG 155.712D–713A.

[11] St John Chrysostom, *On Psalm 132*, PG 55.385.

[12] St Athanasius the Great, *On Psalm 132*, PG 27.524B.

and perform his sacred tasks together with Him. He should do nothing without Christ.'[13]

The priest celebrates the Mystery of the Divine Liturgy, which is the mystery of Christ, together with Christ Himself: 'With Him he performs His Mysteries.'[14]

The Priest then takes the *zone** (girdle) and blesses it, and says as he puts it on:

Blessed is God, who girds me with power and has made my way blameless:[15] *always, now and for ever, and to the ages of ages. Amen.*

The symbolism of the girdle

According to the prayer said by the priest, the girdle symbolises, first, the power of God which gives the celebrant strength in the divine mystagogy, and secondly, the purity and sobriety with which he should be adorned. The girdle, 'in that it is placed round the waist, signifies the strength [that the priest receives] from God... It also signifies sobriety and modesty, inasmuch as it is placed around the loins'[16] — which are regarded as the centre of our desires and thus calls to mind their mortification.

Like the priest, every Christian should be 'girded' in order to partake at the Lord's Table. Just as the Hebrews ate the first Passover girded, in order to be ready for the journey that would take them to the Promised Land (cf. Ex. 12: 11), so, too, we Christians 'should eat [the Passover, that is, Christ] girded, so as to be

---

[13] St Symeon of Thessaloniki, *Church Building*, 39, PG 155.713A.
[14] Ibid.
[15] Ps. 17: 33.
[16] St Symeon of Thessaloniki, *On the holy Liturgy*, 81, PG 155.260A.

ready for our exodus, our departure from this life... [For] being girded is the sign of a soul that is in a state of watchfulness.'[17]

Along with the celebrant, all of us prepare ourselves to partake at the Lord's Table. Wakeful and with the lamps of our soul alight, we await the Lord at His holy assembly, in accordance with His commandment: *Let your loins be girded and your lamps burning, and be like men who are waiting for their master to come home from the marriage feast, so that they may open to him at once when he comes and knocks. Blessed are those servants whom the master finds awake when he comes; truly, I say to you, he will gird himself and have them sit at table, and will come and serve them... Therefore you also must be ready* (Luke 12: 35–40).

The Priest then makes the sign of the cross over the *epimanikia* (cuffs). When putting on the right cuff, he says: *Your right hand, Lord, has been glorified in strength; your right hand, Lord, has shattered enemies, and by the greatness of your glory you have crushed the adversaries.*[18]

And putting on the left cuff, he says: *Your hands have made me and fashioned me; give me understanding and I will learn your commandments.*[19]

The priest acts as the hand of Christ

The symbolism of the cuffs relates to the creation of man and the divine economy.

As he puts the cuff on his left wrist, the priest says: *Your hands*

---

[17] St John Chrysostom, *On Ephesians*, 23.2, PG 62.166.

[18] Ex. 15: 6–7.

[19] Ps. 118: 73.

have made me and fashioned me, 'for it is through the hands of the Father, namely the Son and the Holy Spirit, that man comes to be "in the image and likeness* of God"' (cf. Gen. 1: 26).[20]

The all-holy hands of God — the Word and the Holy Spirit — created man. But instead of friendship with God, man chose subjection to the Devil. And he remained captive to the Devil until the right hand of the Most High *shattered enemies* and *crushed the adversaries*. Christ not only crushed the forces of the enemy, but also raised man up to heaven: 'the right hand of God, that made all things that are…Itself raised up man — who was united with It [through the divine Incarnation] — to Its own height, making him to be what It is by nature, namely Lord and King [cf. Acts 2: 36].'[21] The new man, like the first-formed man, is a creature shaped by the hands of God.

The same hands that created and formed man also perform the eucharistic Mystery. The cuffs signify 'that Christ with His own hands carries out the holy Sacrifice of His own holy Body and Blood'.[22] The hand that gives God's peace and blesses the Gifts which are offered is that of Christ the High Priest.

Before Christ was taken up into heaven, He gave His Apostles, and through them the bishops and priests, 'the creative grace of the Holy Spirit, through which the recreation and regeneration of human beings was to be performed, both of those in existence and of those who would exist in the future, even to the end of the ages… He entrusted them with carrying out His own task.'[23] The priest acts as the hand of Christ. 'When you see the priest giving you the Holy Mysteries,' says St John Chrysostom, 'do not think that it is the priest doing this. Believe that the hand stretched out is that of Christ.'[24]

---

[20] St Irenaeus, *Against Heresies*, 5.6.1, *SC* 153, p. 73.

[21] St Gregory of Nyssa, *Against Eunomius*, 5, *PG* 45.697B.

[22] St Symeon of Thessaloniki, *Church Building*, 42, *PG* 155.713CD.

[23] Theophanes, *Letter 3*, 6, *PG* 150.336C–337A.

[24] *On Matthew*, 50.3, *PG* 58.507.

The right hand of the Most High extends within time that is 'without evening' and beyond infinite space. It reaches every believer and offers him His peace. It offers His holy Body and His most pure Blood.

The Priest then takes the *epigonation*,* if he holds the appropriate ecclesiastical rank; he blesses and kisses it, and says: *Gird your sword on your thigh, O Mighty One, in your beauty and your splendour; and proceed prosperously and reign, for the sake of truth and meekness and justice, and your right hand shall guide you wondrously:*[25] *always, now and for ever, and to the ages of ages. Amen.*

Gird on Your sword, O Mighty One

The *epigonation* is a rhomboid of stiff material which is hung from the girdle, with a cross or an icon of the Resurrection embroidered upon it. Originally it was an episcopal vestment, but later it was also granted to priests of a certain rank.

When a bishop-elect is being ordained, he puts on the *epigonation* for the first time to confirm his betrothal to the Bride, the Church, for the *epigonation* 'is the sign of the victory of Christ the Bridegroom, through the Cross and the Resurrection'. More specifically, the *epigonation* signifies 'victory over death and the incorruption of our nature, as well as the greatness of God's power over the tyranny of the Devil... That is why it is shaped like a sword... This is further shown by the words said as the *epigonation* is put on: *Gird Your sword on Your thigh, O Mighty One.*'[26]

---

[25] Ps. 44: 4–5.
[26] St Symeon of Thessaloniki, *On Ordinations*, 203, PG 155.412BC; idem, *Church Building*, 41, PG 155.713BC.

According to St Nikodimus of the Holy Mountain, in the verse of the psalm that is recited as the *epigonation* is attached to the girdle, 'David summons Christ to the war against the Devil, that He may grant us triumph and victory over the Devil and liberate us who were enslaved by his tyranny... Gird on Your sword, he says, in Your beauty and Your splendour; that by Your sword You may terrify Your enemies, and by the beauty of Your soul and the splendour of Your virtues You may attract Your friends to You.'[27]

The *epigonation* reminds us of the victory of Christ the High Priest, and the words of the psalm confirm that symbolism. Christ reigns in the souls of those who join with Him at His eucharistic Supper, radiant with His beauty.

The Priest then takes the *phelonion** (chasuble) and blesses it, and puts it on saying: *Your priests, Lord, will clothe themselves with righteousness, and your holy ones will rejoice with gladness:*[28] *always, now and for ever, and to the ages of ages. Amen.*

Priests, clothe yourselves in righteousness, in Christ

The *phelonion* is the symbol of divine righteousness, that is, a symbol of Christ, *whom God made our wisdom, our righteousness and our sanctification* (1 Cor. 1: 30). 'Priests, clothe yourselves in righteousness...' says St Gregory the Theologian, 'in the great and spotless garment which is Christ, our adornment.'[29]

Before the Word became incarnate, 'righteousness was not to

---

[27] *Ermeneia eis tous 150 psalmous* [*Commentary on the 150 Psalms*], vol. I, 2nd edn, (Thessaloniki: Orthodoxos Kypseli, 1979), pp. 633–4.
[28] Cf. Ps. 131: 9.
[29] *Homily 5*, 30, PG 35.704A.

be found upon earth'. When Christ became man, righteousness descended from heaven 'and made its first appearance among men in true and perfect form'. We who were formerly under indictment 'became friends of God and righteous through His death'. When we participate in the sacred Mysteries, 'Christ causes His own righteousness and life to rise in our souls'.[30]

The righteousness of God is His love for mankind. It is this that made us His friends through the death of Christ. And for that reason the *phelonion*, which symbolises divine righteousness, 'also signifies the Passion of Christ our Saviour, and the priest imitates Him as he puts it on. That is to say, he imitates Christ who through His Passion and death on the Cross accomplished true righteousness... That is why the priest says as he puts it on, *Your priests, Lord, will clothe themselves with righteousness, and Your holy ones will rejoice with gladness*. For indeed, the righteousness that came through the Cross has brought us joy.'[31]

The priests of the Lord clothe themselves in righteousness — in Christ — and are filled to overflowing with divine rejoicing.

As the Deacon vests himself, he says the same words as the Priest when putting on the *sticharion* and the cuffs. He then takes the *orarion*, kisses it and places it over his left shoulder, saying: *Holy, holy, holy, Lord of Sabaoth, heaven and earth are full of Your glory.*[32]

---

[30] St Nicholas Cabasilas, *On the Life in Christ*, 1, *PG* 150.508C.

[31] St Symeon of Thessaloniki, *Church Building*, 43, *PG* 155.716AB. In this paragraph the Greek word *dikaiosyni*, rendered here in English as 'righteousness', also has the meaning of justice.

[32] Cf. Isa. 6: 3.

The deacon, minister of the Mysteries of Jesus Christ

The clerical order of the diaconate has its beginnings in apostolic times (cf. Acts 6: 3–6), and the deacons' task is to be of service during the celebration of the Mysteries. St Ignatius the Godbearer calls the deacons 'servants of the Church' and 'ministers (*diakonoi*) of the Mysteries of Jesus Christ'. And he admonishes the faithful, 'Let everyone respect the deacons as they would Jesus Christ.'[33]

Diaconal dress consists of the *sticharion*, the cuffs and the *orarion*. The last is the vestment peculiar to the deacon, and it is first mentioned by the Council of Laodicaea (fourth century). The word *orarion* 'is derived from the Latin *os* [genitive *oris*], meaning mouth... So *orarion* means a cloth for wiping the mouth; for as the deacon gave the faithful to drink from the holy Cup,... those who came to drink from the holy Cup would immediately wipe their mouths on the *orarion*.'[34]

The *orarion* also 'signifies the spiritual quality of the angels', for the ministry of the deacon imitates the liturgical ministry of the angels. That is why the deacon recites the thrice holy angelic hymn as he puts on the *orarion*: *Holy, holy, holy, Lord of Sabaoth.* Indeed, 'the deacons with their linen *oraria* like delicate wings symbolise the angelic powers which run hither and thither'[35] as *ministering spirits sent forth to serve* (Heb. 1: 14).

The priest carries out the high-priestly work of the Lord, and the deacon reminds us that the clerical ministry should be adorned with our Master's humility. It is in this sense that the *orarion* 'reminds us of the humility of the Lord, who washed the feet of the disciples and wiped them dry' (cf. John 13: 4–5).[36]

---

[33] *Trallians*, 2–3, PG 5.676B–677A.

[34] St Nikodimus of the Holy Mountain, *Pedalion* [*The Rudder*], 6th edn (Athens: Astir, 1957), pp. 429–30.

[35] St Symeon of Thessaloniki, *On Ordinations*, 173, PG 155.381C; St Sophronius of Jerusalem, *Homily comprising the whole of Church History*, 7, PG 87iii.3988AB.

[36] St Isidore of Pelusium, *Letters*, 1.136, PG 78.272C.

Then the Priest and Deacon both go and wash their hands, each saying:

I will wash my hands in innocency and I will encircle your altar, Lord; that I may hear the voice of your praise and tell of all your wonderous works. Lord, I have loved the beauty of your house, and the place where your glory dwells. Destroy not my soul with the ungodly, nor my life with men of blood. In their hands are iniquities; their right hand is filled with bribes. But I have walked in my innocence; redeem me, O Lord, and have mercy on me. My foot has stood in uprightness; in the churches I will bless you, O Lord.[37]

I will wash my hands in innocency

One who lives in sin and does not repent is not able to glorify the Lord. He is a *land* that is *foreign* to God. Just as the Jews were unable to sing *the Lord's song in a foreign land* (Ps. 136: 4), so likewise one who is embroiled in the passions cannot sing in praise of God's wondrous works. 'If the law of Moses enjoined silence upon those who were captives and had become slaves of men in a foreign country, how much more should those be silent who are slaves of sin and live a life foreign to God.' Indeed, 'sin is alienation from God'.[38]

The celebrant who serves the Lord is aware that he has wounded God's love many times by the way he lives. And though he has received remission of sins through confession, he feels unworthy to sing in praise of the wondrous works of God. The celebrant's spiritual sensitivity is expressed in the Anaphora Prayer: 'Who is

---

[37] Ps. 25: 6–12.

[38] St John Chrysostom, *On Romans*, 6.6, *PG* 60.440; St Gregory of Nyssa, *Against Eunomius*, 2, *PG* 45.545B.

able to tell of Your mighty works? Or to make known all Your praises? Or to recount Your wonderful works at all times?'[39]

We must approach the holy Altar with 'purified minds'. This purity is symbolised by the washing of the hands. 'Having our conscience clear, and a pure mind and heart which are the hands of our soul, let us approach the Holy Table with fear and with sobriety.' Whatever work we do, we do with our hands. So, 'because the hands are a symbol of every action, by washing them we suggest that all our actions are pure and blameless'.[40]

Referring to the practice among Christians of his time of washing their hands when they came into church, St John Chrysostom asks: 'Do we wash our hands when we come into church, but not our heart? Is it the hands that speak? It is the soul that utters the words of prayer, and that is what God is looking at... To pray with an impure heart is the greatest of evils.' 'Those who come to the all-holy celebration of the service should have purged their souls of every last fantasy, so as to approach with a soul that is as pure as the sacred service itself, insofar as that is possible. Thus they will be illumined ever more brightly by the divine epiphanies'[41] of the eucharistic Mystery.

The work of cleansing our soul is performed by Christ, if we desire it, just as He did at the Last Supper when He girded Himself with a towel and washed the feet of the disciples. On that occasion He made it clear to the Apostle Peter, who out of pious deference for Christ did not accept to be washed by Him: *If I do not wash you, you have no part in me* (John 13: 8). At the eucharistic Supper, there is a place with Christ only for those who have accepted, with awe, that the Master should perform within them the washing of mind and heart. 'If anyone is not washed and

---

[39] Liturgy of St Basil.
[40] Matins of Holy Monday, Lauds; St Germanus, *Contemplation*, *PG* 98.424C; St Cyril of Jerusalem, *Mystagogical Catechesis 5*, 2, *PG* 33.1109A.
[41] *On John*, 73.3, *PG* 59.399–400; St Dionysius the Areopagite, *Church Hierarchy*, 3.3.10, *PG* 3.440AB.

cleansed by the grace of Christ from the pollution of sin and wrongdoings, he will have no share in the life which Christ offers and will never taste of the Kingdom of heaven. For those who have not been purified are not allowed to enter the heavenly dwelling-places, but only those with a pure conscience and love for Christ.'[42]

To each Christian who approaches to partake in the Divine Liturgy and of Holy Communion, the Lord says: *If I do not wash you, you have no part in me*. Which is to say: If you do not first come to me with the repentance of the Prodigal Son so that I can receive you back into my House, you cannot participate at the Table of the royal wedding, the Divine Liturgy. We have therefore to come to the Mystery of the washing of the soul, that is, the sacrament of confession.

In this way, pure in soul and body, we can gather round the holy Altar to hear the angelic hymns of praise and add to them our own thanksgiving. We can recount the works of God's love. Acknowledging the debt we owe for God's ineffable benefactions, 'we offer Him the Divine Eucharist and receive Communion, giving thanks because He has delivered the human race from error, and brought us back to Himself when we had strayed far from Him, giving thanks because when we were without hope and were in the world without God, He made us His brethren and heirs' (cf. Eph. 2: 12; Rom. 8: 17).[43]

With souls full of gratitude, we recount the works of God's love and wisdom which have performed 'great and wondrous things': 'Through death came life, and through sin, justice. Through the curse came blessing, and through dishonour, glory.'[44] Giving thanks for all these things, we approach the throne of Grace.

---

[42] St Cyril of Alexandria, *On John*, 9, PG 74.117B.

[43] St John Chrysostom, *On 1 Corinthians*, 24.1, PG 61.199.

[44] St Gregory of Nyssa, *On the Song of Songs*, 8, PG 44.948C.

3. THE SERVICE OF PREPARATION
OF THE EUCHARISTIC GIFTS

The Deacon then goes to the holy Prothesis,* and prepares the sacred vessels.* He places the holy Paten* on the left and the holy Chalice* on the right, and the other implements beside them.

The Chalice and the Paten

The two basic holy vessels that are used for the Divine Liturgy are the Chalice and the Paten. The wine that is offered is poured into the Chalice, and the bread that is offered is placed on the Paten.

The symbolism of the Chalice, the holy Cup, was revealed by Christ Himself when He called His sacrifice on the Cross a *cup* which the Father had given Him to drink (cf. John 18: 11). After Christ's Crucifixion, the cup of death became *a cup of blessing* (1 Cor. 10: 16) and of salvation for man (cf. Ps. 115: 4). The Paten is also connected to Christ's most pure Passion: 'The Paten is the bier on which the Body of the Lord is laid.' At the same time, 'it symbolises heaven — which is why it is round — and holds the Master of heaven'.[1]

In apostolic times, the holy vessels were made of glass or some cheap metal, or even of wood. With the passage of time, and especially once the persecutions ceased, Christians began giving silver or gold vessels for use in the churches. This was of course an

---

[1] St Germanus, *Contemplation*, PG 98.397B; St Symeon of Thessaloniki, *On the holy Liturgy*, 85, PG 155.264C.

expression of devotion to Christ. But in addition to showing such devotion, Christ calls us to love His brethren. He asks us to set our hearts on fire with love, to make them wholly radiant and golden and offer them to Him: 'For God does not need golden vessels, but golden hearts', as St John Chrysostom says. If you want to show your love for God and to honour His sacrifice, 'offer your soul, for which He sacrificed Himself. Make that golden. Otherwise, if the vessel is golden whereas the soul remains worse than a leaden or earthenware pot, what is the profit in that?... The Church is not a goldsmith's or a mint, but a festival of angels.' In order to take part in this angelic festival, our souls must be purer and shine more brightly than the holy vessels. For 'those [vessels] do not participate in the Christ who is within them; they have no feeling. But we do participate in Him. Now, while you would not tolerate the use of a dirty vessel, would you approach with a dirty soul?'[2]

The table at the Last Supper was not made of silver, nor was the cup used by Christ made of gold, but 'all those things were holy and terrible, because they were filled with the Holy Spirit'.[3] What makes the liturgical vessels holy and terrible is not the precious materials of which they are made, but the grace of the Holy Spirit which sanctifies them. This is why, before new vessels are used, the Church consecrates them with a special service in which the bishop anoints the holy Chalice and Paten with chrism, the symbol of the gifts of the Holy Spirit. Then the bishop prays: 'O Master, Christ our God, send forth Your Holy Spirit upon this new Chalice, and bless it and sanctify it and perfect it.'[4]

The holy vessels are primarily blessed and sanctified however by being used in the Mystery of the Divine Eucharist. Referring to the practice of his time for the concelebrating priests to each

---

[2] *On Matthew*, 50.3, PG 58.508; *On Ephesians*, 3.4, PG 62.28–9.

[3] St John Chrysostom, *On Matthew*, 50.3, PG 58.508.

[4] *The Great Euchologion*, 'Service of the Consecration of a new Paten and Chalice', (Athens: Astir, 1980), pp. 482–3.

carry a Chalice at the Great Entrance, St Symeon of Thessaloniki writes: 'The faithful should kneel before the priests and because of the holy vessels, even if some of those that the priests hold are empty. For all the sacred vessels are sanctified, since the precious Gifts are consecrated within them.'[5] All of us, ministers of Christ and faithful alike, revere and honour the sacred vessels, knowing that the very sight of them sanctifies us.

> Then both the Priest and the Deacon bow three times before the holy Prothesis, each saying to himself: *God, have compassion for me, a sinner, and have mercy on me* (three times).
>
> Priest: *Make ready, O Bethlehem; for Eden has been opened to all. Prepare yourself, O Ephratah; for the tree of life has blossomed from the Virgin in the cave. For her womb is shown to be a spiritual paradise, in which is the divine plant: eating of this, we shall live, and not die like Adam. Christ is born, to raise up the image which before was fallen.*[6]

'Make ready, O Bethlehem'

The priest and deacon, standing before the holy Prothesis, are ready to begin the celebration of the bloodless Sacrifice. There the faithful bring the fruits of their labours — bread and wine — which are placed before God. From the *prosphora** the celebrant chooses the oblation bread that will be used for the Liturgy.

---

[5] *Church Building*, 78–9, PG 155.729BC. St Symeon adds: '[the priests] hold these vessels in honour of the divine Gifts, and in order that all may be sanctified, both those who see them and those who touch them'.

[6] *Apolytikion* for the Forefeast of Christmas.

According to its liturgical symbolism, the holy Prothesis signifies Bethlehem and the cave where Christ was born; that is why the icon of the Nativity is usually depicted in the apse above it. And just as Bethlehem is close to Jerusalem and the Holy Sepulchre of the Lord, so the holy Prothesis is near the holy Altar. Its position in the corner of the sanctuary signifies 'the poverty of Jesus' first coming, and the poor place and insignificant cave' where He was born.[7]

Bethlehem was the place where *God appeared in the flesh* (1 Tim. 3: 16). This is why the liturgical appearance of Christ begins at the holy Prothesis.

The Priest takes the *prosphora* and the lance* and raises them level with his forehead. With great fear and compunction, he lifts his eyes to heaven and says: *You have redeemed us from the curse of the law by your precious Blood; nailed to the Cross and pierced by the lance, you have poured forth immortality to man. Our Saviour, glory to you.*[8]

You have redeemed us from the curse of the law

In the previous *troparion*, the priest referred to Christ's nativity. Now he refers to His Crucifixion. Christ was born in order to be crucified: *For this purpose I have come to this hour* (John 12: 27), the hour of the Passion and the Cross.

By His sacrifice on the Cross, Christ redeemed man from the curse of the law and bestowed on him the freedom of the Holy Spirit: 'When Christ died,...that was when we acquired freedom

[7] St Symeon of Thessaloniki, *Consecration*, 137, *PG* 155.348A.
[8] *Apolytikion* of Holy Friday.

and adoption.' 'For the Father accepted the reconciliation, the Son effected it and the Holy Spirit became a gift to those who had already been established as friends. The Father set us free, the Son was the ransom with which we were set free and the Holy Spirit is freedom itself.'[9]

When the celebrant lifts up the *prosphora*, this recalls Christ lifted up on the Cross and reveals the love which He offers us. The bread of the holy Prothesis reveals 'the surpassing riches of God's goodness, that the Son of God became man and gave Himself as a sacrifice and an offering...*for the life* and salvation *of the world*' (John 6: 51).[10]

> Deacon: *Master, give the blessing.*
> Priest: *Blessed is our God, always, now and for ever, and to the ages of ages. Amen.*

The offering of bread and wine

Through the Divine Liturgy, God offers man His life. But because He does not wish that the divine gift should be accomplished only as grace, He accepts some offering from man so that 'the gift of grace should appear as a payment, and His immeasurable mercy should also have some element of justice'.[11] Thus the Divine Liturgy is God's offering to man, and man's offering to God.

The rite of the Prothesis or preparation, which now begins, is man's offering to God. The celebrant receives the *prosphora* offered by the faithful and selects the one that will be dedicated and consecrated through the Mystery of the Divine Eucharist.

---

[9] St Nicholas Cabasilas, *On the Life in Christ*, 1 and 2, PG 150.520B, 532CD.

[10] St Germanus, *Contemplation*, PG 98.397A.

[11] St Nicholas Cabasilas, *Comm. Liturgy*, 4, PG 150.380A.

The Divine Liturgy is an icon of the life of Christ. Christ was born and dedicated to God as the firstborn and the first-fruits of the new creation: His most holy Mother and Joseph brought Christ *to Jerusalem to present Him to the Lord* (Luke 2: 22). That is why the bread and wine 'are not immediately placed on the Altar to be sacrificed. This will happen later, once they have been dedicated to God and have thus become, and come to be called, precious Gifts.'[12] The Service of Preparation symbolises Christ's birth and His reception in the temple by St Symeon.

Food is what maintains our physical life. So it is not accidental that we offer it to God, especially in the Mystery of the Divine Eucharist. 'God commanded those to whom He would give eternal life — His life-giving Body and Blood — to offer first the provisions required for our temporal life.'[13]

At the Last Supper, Christ offered His holy Body and Blood in the form of bread and wine. By this act, He instructed us also to use bread and wine — two of the basic staples of human nourishment — at the Divine Liturgy. The offerings of the Jews were also foodstuffs (produce of the earth, animals, etc.), but they included foods used to feed animals as well as humans. Bread and wine are used exclusively for human nourishment.

Christ described Himself as *the Bread of life* and *the true Vine* (John 6: 48, 15: 1). 'He calls Himself *the Bread of life* because He is the stuff of our life, both our present life and that which is to come.' Christ is the food that came from heaven, the food of the Kingdom: 'So since through Christ we have been summoned to the Kingdom of heaven...there is now no Old Testament manna for us... There is the Bread of heaven, namely Christ, who gives us food for a life that is long'[14] and eternal.

---

[12] St Nicholas Cabasilas, *Comm. Liturgy*, 2, PG 150.376D.

[13] Ibid. 4, *PG* 150.377D–380A.

[14] St John Chrysostom, *On John*, 46.1, *PG* 59.258; St Cyril of Alexandria, *On John*, 3.6, *PG* 73.517CD.

In the precious Gifts lie our hope and surety of resurrection. 'Just as the vine cutting embedded in the earth bears fruit in its season and the grain of wheat falling on the earth and decomposing is then raised up with manifold increase...and then [as wine and bread] receive the word of God and become the Eucharist, which is the Body and Blood of Christ; so also in the same manner our bodies, being nourished by the Divine Eucharist, and laid in the earth, and suffering decomposition there, will be raised up at the appointed time, granted resurrection by the Word of God.'[15]

At the Divine Liturgy, in offering the bread and wine we offer our entire life to God, like the widow in the Gospel who *put in all the living that she had* (Luke 21: 4) when she offered the two copper coins. In return, God offers us His entire life, 'so that we may receive Life in return for life, the eternal in return for the temporal'. God asks one thing only: that we should make our offering with a pure intention, so that it is acceptable. 'We should be grateful to the Creator for all things, offering the first and choicest gifts of His own created things, with a pure intention, unfeigned faith, firm hope and ardent love.'[16]

Bread and wine, symbols of unity

The gifts that man offers to God, the bread and wine, symbolise the unity of the Church.

St John Chrysostom talks about the symbolism of the bread. Starting from the Apostle's words, *Because there is one bread, we who are many are one body* (1 Cor. 10: 17), he poses the question: 'What is the *Bread*?' And he answers: 'The Body of Christ. And what do those who partake of it become? The Body of Christ. Not several bodies, but one body. Just as the bread, while it is made

---

[15] St Irenaeus, *Against Heresies*, 5.2.3, SC 153, p. 37.
[16] St Nicholas Cabasilas, *Comm. Liturgy*, 4, PG 150.380A; St Irenaeus, *Against Heresies*, 4.18.4, SC 100, p. 607.

up of many grains, is one bread, so that the grains are nowhere apparent, even though they are there...in the same way, we are united with each other and with Christ. For it is not that you are nourished by one body, and the other person by another; we are all nourished by the same Body. That is why St Paul adds, *For we all partake of the one bread* [1 Cor. 10: 17].'[17]

Some ancient liturgical prayers also express that unity of the faithful which is underlined by the use of the bread, such as this early one that has come down to us from the fourth century: 'As this bread was scattered upon the mountains and was gathered and became one, do You likewise gather Your holy Church from every nation and every country and town and village and household and make one living catholic Church.'[18]

The wine too is a symbol of the unity of the faithful: it is a mixture made from the pressing of many grapes gathered from different vines.

Man's offering of bread and wine to the Creator also expresses the unity of the entire creation in a movement of gratitude. We approach the holy Altar, and the world which we hold in our hands, the world which we are, comes with us.

Man, and man alone, was created to participate in the intelligible and the sensible world. He is a *micro-cosm*. And the entire cosmos is an image of man: it is a *macro-anthropos*, man writ large. Man and the cosmos join together in glorifying their common Father and Creator. The entire creation ministers at the Mystery of Love that is offered up.

[17] *On 1 Corinthians*, 24.2, *PG* 61.200.

[18] *Euchologion* of St Serapion of Thmuis 13/1, Prayer of Offering; R. J. S Barrett - Lennard, ed. and tr., *The Sacramentary of Sarapion of Thmuis* (Alcuin Club – GROW Joint Liturgical Studies no. 25: Bramcote, Nottingham: Grove Books, 1993), p. 26. Cf. also *Didache*, 9.4, *ANF* 7, p. 380; and p. 6, above.

The Priest then takes the *prosphora* and makes the sign of the cross over it three times with the lance, saying each time: *In remembrance of our Lord and God and Saviour, Jesus Christ.*

And the Deacon adds: *Always, now and for ever, and to the ages of ages. Amen.*

Celebrating the remembrance of Christ

The Divine Liturgy is celebrated in two ways: in word and in action. In the words of the readings* and prayers, we hear Christ Himself or hear about Him. In the actions performed, we see Him. 'We could say that we *see* the great poverty of Him who is rich, the coming to earth of Him who occupies every place, the reproaches heaped on the Blessed One, the Passion of Him who is passionless. How much He loved, and how much He was hated! How great He was, and how He humbled Himself! We see what He suffered and what He did in order to prepare this Table before us.'[19]

Through word and action, the Divine Liturgy is the *anamnesis* of Christ's life: *In remembrance of our Lord and God and Saviour Jesus Christ*, says the priest three times while making the sign of the cross on the *prosphora* with the lance.

The first time the Mystery was celebrated, Christ took the bread in His hands, and when He had given thanks to the Father He broke it and gave it to the disciples, saying: *This is my body which is given for you* (Luke 22: 19). Then He called His holy Blood *my blood of the new covenant which is shed for many* (Matt. 26: 28). 'By these words, He signifies that he is going to die.' Thus 'by the Holy Mysteries, He reminds the disciples that He will be slaughtered, and as they sit at the table He speaks about the Cross.'[20]

---

[19] St Nicholas Cabasilas, *Comm. Liturgy*, 1, PG 150.373C.
[20] St John Chrysostom, *On Matthew*, 82.1, PG 58.738, 737.

Before Christ was crucified, He celebrated the Divine Liturgy (cf. Luke 22: 19–20) — the remembrance of His Passion on the Cross. And He commanded us to celebrate it in the same way: to recall those things that seem 'to betoken weakness, namely the Cross, the Passion and death'. Why, we may ask, when Christ said, 'This is my Body, this is my Blood', did He not add '...which raised the dead, which healed lepers', but only '...which is broken for you, which is poured out for your sake'? Why does He not recall His miracles, but rather His Passion? 'Because the Passion was more necessary than the miracles... His Passion is the very cause of our salvation...whereas the miracles took place in order that it might be believed that the Lord is truly the Saviour.'[21] Miracles are a confirmation of Christ's divinity; the holy Passion offers us salvation and Christ the Saviour.

The Priest then thrusts the lance into the right side of the seal* and cuts along it, saying: *Like a sheep he was led to the slaughter.* And as he cuts along the left hand side: *And as an unblemished lamb before the shearer is dumb, so he does not open his mouth.* Then as he cuts across the upper side: *By reason of his humiliation judgement was denied him.* And the lower side: *Who shall declare his generation?*

Deacon: *Master, take away.*

And the Priest takes out the Lamb,* saying: *For his life is taken away from the earth.*[22] And he places the Lamb on the Paten.

---

[21] St Nicholas Cabasilas, *Comm. Liturgy*, 7, *PG* 150.384AC.
[22] Isa. 53: 7–8.

A narrative of the Passion in actions

The celebrant now removes the Lamb from the *prosphora* and places it on the Paten, reciting the prophecy of Isaiah that refers to the Passion of Christ. We could say that the priest is 'writing the Passion of Christ on the Lamb' with the lance, for that which the priest now does is 'a narrative in actions of the saving Passion and death of Christ'.[23]

When the Apostle Philip approached the chariot belonging to the minister of the Queen of the Ethiopians, the minister was reading the words of Isaiah that the celebrant has just recited. On that occasion, the Apostle, *beginning with this scripture, told him the good news of Jesus* (Acts 8: 32–5). Now the celebrant, using those same words of Isaiah, begins the good news of Christ's eucharistic Sacrifice.

i. Like a sheep He was led to the slaughter

These words from the Prophet Isaiah refer to the Passion of Christ. When Christ 'offers Himself as a sacrifice and an offering to God for our sins, He is called *the Lamb of God* [John 1: 29] and *sheep* [Isa. 53: 7].'[24] He is the unblemished Lamb that is sacrificed for the lost sheep which is man (cf. Matt. 18: 12).

Christ's sacrifice on the Cross was prefigured in the Jewish Passover with the slaughter of the sheep. The Jews used a sheep as the sacrificial victim 'because of its innocence, and because fleece was the covering of our ancient nakedness [that is, the nakedness of the first-formed humans after their disobedience]. Moreover, Christ, the victim who was sacrificed for our sake, is and is called a garment of incorruption' (cf. Rom. 13: 14).[25] When the Master was stripped naked on the life-giving Cross, He became a garment of incorruption for man.

---

[23] St Nicholas Cabasilas, *Comm. Liturgy*, 6, PG 150.381A.
[24] St Basil the Great, *On Psalm 28*, 5, PG 29.296B.
[25] St Gregory the Theologian, *Homily 45*,13, PG 36.640C.

ii. As an unblemished lamb before its shearer is dumb

Christ's silence during the Passion indicates that He accepted His Crucifixion willingly: *I lay down my life, that I may take it again. No one takes it from me, but I lay it down of my own accord* (John 10: 17–8). By His own will, Christ 'endured the Cross for us. For He Himself offered Himself, as a holy victim, to God the Father.'[26]

Christ is silent before the High Priests and before Herod (cf. Matt. 26: 63, Luke 23: 9). He is also silent before Pilate: *Jesus gave him no answer* (John 19: 9). But Pilate interprets His silence as contempt for his own person; 'for he in no way understood the mystery of Christ's silence'.[27]

iii. By reason of His humiliation judgement was denied Him

Christ's silence and humility resulted in His being deprived of justice: *judgement was denied him*. And the unjust sentence passed upon Him led Christ to the Cross.

In becoming human, Christ *emptied Himself, taking the form of a servant, and humbled Himself* and *became obedient unto death, even death on a cross* (Phil. 2: 7–8). From His Father's throne, Christ trod the way of humiliation and arrived at the Cross. 'As was the exaltation Christ enjoyed, so correspondingly great was the humiliation that He endured... Truly, it is something momentous that Christ became a slave! It is something altogether inexpressible. Yet for Him to undergo death in addition is something greater still. But there is even something much greater and more wonderful than this. What is that?... Death on a cross...a death shameful and accursed. For it is said: *cursed be every one that hangs on a tree* [Deut. 21: 23, Gal. 3: 13]'.[28]

Christ is love. From the height of the Cross, He showed the heights of love and the depths of humility.

---

[26] St Cyril of Alexandria, *On John*, 5.1, *PG* 73.721A.

[27] Ibid. 12, *PG* 74.640C.

[28] St John Chrysostom, *On Philippians*, 7.3, *PG* 62.232.

iv. Who shall declare His generation?

By the word *generation*, the Prophet Isaiah means the mystery of Christ's generation before the ages. It is asked: 'Who is able to express, even in the smallest part, the mode of existence of the Only-begotten? What tongue can tell of the Son's ineffable generation from the Father?' That Christ was begotten of the Father, 'we know and believe. But the mode of His generation is a mystery inaccessible to any mind.'[29]

v. For His life is taken away from the earth

The action of taking out the Lamb from the *prosphora* and placing it on the Paten recalls Christ's words, *And I, when I am lifted up from the earth, will draw all men to myself* (John 12: 32).

Christ's sacrifice was offered for the entire world. St John Chrysostom writes: 'Why was Christ slaughtered on a tall cross and not in an enclosed space with a roof?... Because the nature of the air was purified when Christ, the Lamb, was sacrificed on high. The earth too was purified, for blood dripped upon it from His side... That was why Christ was sacrificed outside the city and outside the walls, so that you might learn that His sacrifice was for all men... His offering was for the entire earth.'[30] The Passover lamb was sacrificed by the Jews secretly, and exclusively for themselves. Christ opens His arms on the Cross in order to embrace and sanctify the whole world: 'Stretching out Your hands upon the Cross, Merciful One, You brought together the nations which had grown distant from You, to glorify Your abundant goodness.'[31]

---

[29] St Cyril of Alexandria, *On John*, 5, PG 73.712CD.

[30] *On the Cross and the Thief 1*, 1, PG 49.400.

[31] *Octoechos*, Wednesday Matins, Tone 1, *kathisma*.* Cf. Holy Saturday Matins, *Engomia*,* stasis* 1: 'Of old, they sacrificed the lamb in secret; but when You were sacrificed beneath the open sky, forbearing Saviour, You purified the whole creation.'

> Deacon: *Sacrifice, Master.*
> The Priest sacrifices — that is, he makes a deep vertical cut in the underside of the Lamb — saying: *The Lamb of God, who takes away the sin of the world, is sacrificed for the life and salvation of the world.*[32]
> Deacon: *Crucify, Master.*
> And the Priest makes another cut in the Lamb, horizontally across the vertical cut so forming a cross, saying: *When you were crucified, O Christ, the tyranny was destroyed; the power of the enemy was trampled. For it was not an Angel or a man, but you the very Lord who saved us: glory to you.*[33]

The Lamb of God is sacrificed

In words and actions, the priest continues the narrative of Christ's Passion: *The Lamb of God is sacrificed.* 'The true Lamb, the unblemished victim, is led to the slaughter for the sake of us all, in order to remove the sin of the world...to abolish death... and to become the beginning of every good thing for the human race...the source of eternal life, the foundation for our reformation in the likeness of God, the beginning of reverence and righteousness, the path to the Kingdom of heaven... Because we lived amidst many sins and were therefore in the debt of death and corruption, the Father gave His Son as a ransom for us... One died for the sake of all, that we all might live in Him.'[34]

When the Lord was crucified, the tyranny of the Devil was shattered and the 'knowledge of God' took root. Now 'the consubstantial Trinity is worshipped, the uncreated Godhead, the

---

[32] John 1: 29 and 6: 51.

[33] *Octoechos*, Friday Matins, Tone 1, *kathisma*. Cf. Isa. 63: 9.

[34] St Cyril of Alexandria, *On John*, 2, PG 73.192B–D.

one true God, the Creator and Lord of all. The virtues are culti-
vated, the hope of resurrection has been given us by the Resurrection of Christ, the demons tremble before human beings, who
had previously been subservient to them. And what is most amaz-
ing: all this has been achieved through the Cross, the Passion and
death.'[35]

* * *

The Athonite Elder Paisios († 12.7.1994) of blessed memory
once related: 'Something happened to me when it was my duty to
assist the celebrating priest. At the words *the Lamb of God is sacrificed*, I saw the Lamb on the Paten writhing like a lamb being
slaughtered. How could I ever dare approach there again! That is
why the priests should not cut up the *prosphora* before hand.
When they say those words, that is when they should take the
holy lance and cut the *prosphora*.'

That experience so shook the Elder that he was never willing
to receive the grace of priesthood himself.

---

[35] St John of Damascus, *On the Orthodox Faith*, 4.77, PG 94.1108CD–1109A.

> The Deacon says: *Pierce, Master.*
> And the Priest pierces the Lamb with the lance on the right side, saying: *One of the soldiers pierced his side with a lance, and at once there came out blood and water; and he who saw it has borne witness, and his witness is true.*[36]

There came forth blood and water

At the moment the celebrant pierces the Lamb with the lance, he is representing the Roman soldier who used his lance to pierce Christ's holy Body on the Cross, and *there came out blood and water.* It is recorded of St Theodosius the New that when he reached this point at his first Liturgy, he was so shaken that he asked to retire from the priesthood.[37]

Christ's side 'poured forth blood mixed with water. God ordained this event as a sort of image and inception of the mystical blessing [that is, the Divine Eucharist] and Holy Baptism. For Baptism does indeed belong to Christ and was instituted by Him, and the power of the Mystery of the Divine Eucharist grew forth from His holy Body.'[38]

The two Mysteries originate from Christ and create the Church: 'That blood and that water symbolise Holy Baptism and the Divine Eucharist. From these two Mysteries, the Church was born... So Christ created the Church from His side, exactly as He created Eve from Adam's side [cf. Gen. 2: 21–2]'. 'As Eve was created while

---

[36] John 19: 34–5.

[37] Cf. Archim. G. Paraskevopoulos, *Ermineftiki epistasia epi tes theias Leitourgias [Interpretation of the Divine Liturgy]* (Patras, 1958), p. 32.

[38] St Cyril of Alexandria, *On John*, 12, *PG* 74.677B. Cf. Introduction, p. 25, above.

Adam slept, so was the Church created from the side of Christ [the new Adam] at His death.'[39]

At the moment of supreme pain and death came supreme joy and life: 'You were pierced in the side in order to pour forth streams of life for me.' The Master's side gives life to man: 'From Your side pierced with a spear, O Saviour, You drop life upon "Life" [that is, upon Eve, cf. Gen. 3: 20] who exiled me from life, bringing me to life along with her.'[40]

From the life-bearing side of Christ, the Church — the rational Paradise of God — is born and given life.

The Deacon pours sufficient wine and water into the Chalice, saying: *Bless, Master, the holy union.*
And the Priest blesses, saying: *Blessed is the union of your holy things, always, now and for ever, and to the ages of ages. Amen.*

Sober inebriation

The wine and water which the deacon pours into the Chalice symbolise the blood and water which came forth from Christ's side.

St John Chrysostom stresses that 'the foundation for the good things of our salvation [that is, the Eucharist] is accomplished through wine.' But evil intent, says the saint, can turn wine into a cause of drunkenness. At the Divine Liturgy, however, 'the spiritual Cup does not cause drunkenness,...it does not paralyse man's strength, but increases it... This is a new mode of inebria-

---

[39] St John Chrysostom, *Baptismal Catecheses*, 3.17, *SC* 50, p. 161; *Encomium on Maximus*, 3, *PG* 51.229.
[40] Holy Friday Matins, Beatitudes; Holy Saturday Matins, *Engomia*, stasis 1.

tion: it adds to our strength... For it pours forth from the spiritual rock',[41] which is Christ (cf. 1 Cor. 10: 4).

This inebriation tears man away from material things and leads him into a divine state: 'An "ecstasy" takes place, a movement from things material to something divine.' The eucharistic Cup causes 'sober inebriation': an inebriation that produces a state of vigilance and makes man a partaker of eternal life. 'For whoever has tasted of that inebriation exchanges the fleeting for the immortal, and extends his stay in the house of the Lord *unto length of days* [Ps. 22: 6].'[42]

There we express our gratitude to our Lady the Mother of God, because it was from her that Christ, who offers us the wine of salvation, sprang forth: 'As a vine uncultivated, O Virgin, you have brought forth the most beautiful cluster of grapes, which pours forth for us the wine of salvation, making glad the souls and bodies of us all. Whence we bless you as the cause of good things, ever crying with the angel: Hail, thou who art full of grace.'[43]

The Priest takes in his hands the same *prosphora*, or a second one, and with the lance cuts around the small triangular part of the seal, saying: *In honour and memory of our most blessed and glorious Lady, Theotokos and Ever-Virgin Mary; at whose prayers, Lord, accept this sacrifice at your Altar above the heavens.*

---

[41] St John Chrysostom, *On Genesis*, 29.3, PG 53.265; *Against Drunkards*, 2, PG 50.436.

[42] St Gregory of Nyssa, *On Song of Songs*, 5, PG 44.873B; *On the Ascension*, PG 46.692B.

[43] Matins, 15 January.

Taking this particle with the lance, he places it on the right hand side of the Lamb, saying: *At your right hand stood the Queen, arrayed in a garment of inwoven gold; adorned in various colours.*[44]

The Queen stood at Your right hand

During the rite of the *Kairos*, the celebrant asked the Most Blessed Mother of God to become the gate leading to Life. Now, through the celebrant, we ask for her all-holy intercessions that our offering may be acceptable.

The Lady Theotokos is the immaculate Altar on which the eucharistic Sacrifice is offered. She is the place where her only-begotten Son rests throughout the Holy Mysteries.[45] 'For where else should Christ, that new victim, be for ever present if not in her from whom He was born,...since there could be no place holier than her?'[46]

The Lady Mother of God is the bond linking heaven and earth: she stands between man who offers a *sacrifice of praise* (Heb. 13: 15) and God who receives the offering. From Christ, the head of the body which is the Church, comes *every perfect gift* (Jas. 1: 17); and through the Mother of God, who is the neck of the body, the divine gift reaches the faithful, the members of the body. 'The Mother of Jesus, who directly bears the head which is Christ, is a mediator between the head of the Church and the body, and in a way a link joining the two like a neck... In consequence, just as the head [Christ] is the only way that leads to the Father..., so this

---

[44] Ps. 44: 10.

[45] Cf. Liturgy of the Presanctified Gifts, Prayer after the Entrance: 'Invisible King... Look upon us, Your unworthy servants, who stand about this holy Altar as if around Your throne upon the Cherubim, on which Your Only-begotten Son, our God, rests through the terrible Mysteries here set forth...'.

[46] Theophanes, *Theotokos*, p. 146.

sacred neck [the Mother of God] is also a way, the only way, that leads everyone to the head of all [Christ].'[47]

By her ministry in the divine economy, the Lady Theotokos became the benefactress of the entire creation. Heaven and earth, humans and angels have been blessed by her divine motherhood. The Virgin 'caused light to dawn even for the angels, and made it possible for them to become wiser and purer than before, to know God's goodness and wisdom better... In this way, the Virgin created *a new heaven and a new earth* [Rev. 21: 1]. Or rather, she is herself the new earth and new heaven.'[48]

There are two reasons why we regard the Mother of God as a new earth and new heaven. First, because she held within her 'Him whom the vast expanse of heaven cannot contain'. Secondly, because of her purity. It is therefore clear 'that which the Prophet David calls the "heaven of heaven" and which, he stresses, alone befits the one and only God, saying, *the heaven of heaven for the Lord* [Ps. 113: 24], is the Blessed Virgin'.[49]

If, however, the Virgin was the 'heaven of heaven' while she lived on earth, her position in heaven is analogous. The Most Holy Mother of God is the Queen of heaven. That is why in heaven her dormition was a celebration. It was a celebration presided over by Christ Himself. St John of Damascus says, addressing Christ: 'Come down, O Lord, come down, to repay to Your Mother, to whom You are so indebted, all that You owe her for nuturing You... Call Your Mother with a sweet whisper, "*Come, my fair one, thou who art close to me* [S. of S. 2: 10]... You gave me what was yours; come and enjoy what is mine... Come and reign with me who was humbly born of you and humbly lived with you."'[50]

---

[47] Theophanes, *Theotokos*, pp. 128–32. Cf. John 14: 6: *No man comes to the Father except through me.*

[48] St Nicholas Cabasilas, *On the Dormition*, 4, *PO* 19.498.

[49] Annunciation, Little Vespers; St Nicholas Cabasilas, *On the Dormition*, 4, *PO* 19.499.

[50] *On the Dormition, Homily 3*, 4, *PG* 96.760AB.

Heaven's joy knew no bounds when it received its Queen. One of the Church's hymnographers celebrates the event: 'The angelic powers greet you, O Theotokos, with sacred hymns and shining lamps for the most radiant feast, as if they were saying: *Who is she who is coming up, shining white, who looks forth like the dawn, fair as the moon, exquisite as the sun?... The King has brought you into his chamber* [S. of S. 8: 5, 6: 10, 1: 4]... You have reached even the royal throne of your Son; you see Him with your eyes. You rejoice and stand at His side... You bless the world, you sanctify all things.'[51]

As the celebrant places the particle for the Theotokos to the right of the Lamb and recites the verse of the psalm, *At Your right hand stood the Queen*, he reveals the honour that Christ gives to His most holy Mother: 'Making you shine with the radiance of the Spirit, your Son placed you at His right hand, All-pure Lady, like a queen in golden raiment.'[52]

From the seal of the same *prosphora*, or a third one, the Priest then cuts out the first of the nine small triangular particles impressed upon it and places it on the left hand side of the Lamb, saying:

In honour and memory of the supreme Commanders, the Archangels Michael and Gabriel, and of all the Bodiless Powers of heaven.

---

[51] St John of Damascus, *On the Dormition, Homily 1*, 11, PG 96.716D–717B.
[52] *Octoechos*, Tone 6, Sunday Matins, Canon, ode 8.

Holy angels assist the priest

The heavenly powers also minister in the work of the divine economy, and that is why the celebrant places to the left of the Lamb a particle in their honour.

Before the Incarnation of the Word, the angels were dimly aware of the mystery of Christ. When the Word became man, *God was manifested in the flesh* and *seen by angels* (1 Tim. 3: 16). 'When He put on flesh He then became visible to angels...for before that time to them also was His essence invisible.'[53] The *mystery of the divine economy which from the beginning of the ages has been hidden in God* (Eph. 3: 9) was manifested first to the holy angels. They then revealed it to human beings: 'First the angels were initiated into the divine mystery of Jesus' love for mankind, then the grace of knowledge passed through them to us.'[54]

The Archangel Gabriel visited the priest Zachariah to announce the future birth of the Forerunner, who according to the words of the Prophet was to be a *messenger before the face of the Lord* (Matt. 11: 10, Mal. 3: 1). The same Archangel visited the Mother of God to announce to her that 'the divine mystery of the inexpressible Incarnation of God the Word would be accomplished in her'.[55] Again, an angel visited Joseph to tell him that the Virgin had conceived of the Holy Spirit, and was carrying the Saviour of the world (cf. Matt. 1: 20).

Finally, when Christ was born in Bethlehem, an angel of the Lord visited the shepherds, since they were pure of soul (living as they did in peace and quiet),[56] and announced to them the joyful news. *And suddenly there was with the angel a multitude of the heavenly host, praising God and saying: Glory to God in the highest* (Luke 2: 13–4).

---

[53] St John Chrysostom, *On John*, 15.2, PG 59.98.
[54] St Dionysius the Areopagite, *On the Heavenly Hierarchy*, 4.4, PG 3.181B.
[55] Ibid.
[56] Cf. ibid.

Now, in the liturgical Bethlehem — the holy Prothesis — where the mystery of the Incarnation of the Word is celebrated, angels of the Lord appear to celebrants who, like the shepherds, are pure of soul. There was one Elder 'who was pure and holy, and while he was solemnising the Proskomide he saw holy angels standing to his right and left'.[57]

At every Divine Liturgy, *a multitude of the heavenly host* (Luke 2: 13) is present, glorifying God as once they did in Bethlehem. The story is told of the holy Bishop Niphon that during the Great Entrance he saw a multitude of angels accompanying the priest, 'joyfully singing ineffable hymns. And when the priest placed the precious Gifts on the Holy Table, the angels covered the Altar with their wings. Then two Cherubim came and stood on the celebrant's right, and two Seraphim on his left.'[58]

During the Holy Anaphora, 'angels stand around the priest, all the ranks of heavenly powers sing praises in a loud voice, and the space around the Altar is filled in honour of the One [Christ our Master] who is being sacrificed.'[59]

At the Divine Liturgy, mysteries are performed which the holy angels *long to look into* (1 Pet. 1: 12). They are present as ministers and servants, but only the priest can celebrate the divine mystagogy: 'When the pure and worthy priest...enters the sanctuary to celebrate the Divine Liturgy, he is invisibly surrounded by a great host of bodiless and divine angels, who serve him throughout the Divine Liturgy with great reverence. But although the holy angels serve the priest at the Divine Liturgy, they themselves are not able to celebrate the Liturgy on their own without a priest... So the priest is like some major dignitary of the King's, while the angels are like His soldiers and servants.'[60]

---

[57] John Eucratas, *Leimonarion* [*The Spiritual Meadow*], 199, *PG* 87iii.3088A.

[58] *Enas asketes Episkopos* [*An ascetic Bishop*], 3rd edn (Oropos, Attica: Paraklitou Monastery, 2000), p. 214.

[59] St John Chrysostom, *On the Priesthood*, 6.4, *PG* 48.681.

[60] Anonymous Hesychast, *Niptiki Theoria* [*Neptic Contemplation*] (Thessaloniki: Orthodoxos Kypseli, 1979), pp. 197–8.

The Priest then cuts out the further eight corresponding particles, saying:

Of the honoured and glorious Prophet, Forerunner and Baptist, John; of the holy, glorious Prophets Moses and Aaron, Elias, Elisha, David, Jesse, Isaiah and Jeremiah; of the Three Holy Youths, the Prophet Daniel and all the holy Prophets.

Of the holy, glorious and all-praised Apostles Peter and Paul, of John the Theologian, of the Twelve, the Seventy and all the holy Apostles.

Of our Fathers among the Saints, great Hierarchs and Ecumenical Teachers, Basil the Great, Gregory the Theologian and John Chrysostom, Athanasius and Cyril and John the Merciful, Patriarchs of Alexandria, Nicolas of Myra, Spyridon of Trimythous, Gregory Palamas, Dionysios of Aegina, Nectarios of Pentapolis, the holy God-bearing Fathers of the seven Councils and all the holy Hierarchs.

Of the holy Protomartyr and Archdeacon Stephen; of the holy glorious Great Martyrs, George the victorious, Demetrios the myrrh-streaming, Theodore the Recruit and Theodore the General. Of the Hieromartyrs Ignatius, Polycarp, Haralambos, Eleftherios and Kosmas the Aetolian. Of the holy martyrs Thekla, Katherine, Barbara, Irene, Euphemia, Kyriaki, Marina, Paraskevi and all the Holy Martyrs.

Of our venerable and God-bearing Fathers, Anthony, Euthymios, Sabas the Sanctified, Arsenios, Paisios, Poemen, Sisoes, Ephrem and Isaac the Syrians, Maximus the Confessor, John of Damascus, Symeon the New Theologian, Dionysios of Olympus, John the Russian, Seraphim of Sarov, Nicolas Planas, Arsenios the Cappadocian; of the Athonite Fathers Peter, Athanasios,

Maximus, Nikodimus, Silouan and Sabas; of the venerable women Mary of Egypt, Theoktisti, Synklitiki, Macrina, and all our venerable Fathers and Mothers.

Of the holy and glorious Wonderworkers and Unmercenary Physicians, Cosmas and Damian, Cyrus and John, Panteleimon and Hermolaos, Sampson and Diomedes, Mokius and Anicetus, Thalellaius and Tryphon, and all the holy Unmercenary Saints.

Of the holy and righteous Forebears of God, Joachim and Anna, Zacharias and Elizabeth, Joseph the Betrothed, of (the names of the saints of the day and of the church, if they have not already been commemorated) *and of all the Saints, at whose intercessions visit us, O God.*

Of our Father among the Saints John Chrysostom, Archbishop of Constantinople. (If the Liturgy of St Basil is being celebrated, he is commemorated instead.)

The assembly of the saints

At the Divine Liturgy, the assembly of saints is present together with Christ, and the faithful experience the communion of saints made manifest.

After placing the Lamb which is being offered on the Paten, the celebrant cuts out pieces in honour and in memory of all the saints. 'This reveals the indissoluble bond of the transcendent and sacred union of the saints with Christ.'[61] 'Because the saints have struggled together with Christ, they enjoy greater glory and exaltation through this terrible Mystery, through communion in this saving Sacrifice. And indeed, the more we commemorate

---

[61] St Dionysius the Areopagite, *Church Hierarchy*, 3.3.9, PG 3.437C.

them, the more they reconcile us with Christ and unite us with Him.'[62]

The Church is 'the assembly of the saints', and the Divine Liturgy is par excellence the Mystery that assembles the entire Church into 'a godly way of common life', a 'unified and single accord'.[63] In the Liturgy, we are with all the saints.

The choir of saints has fulfilled the purpose of the divine economy. 'God the Word took flesh, preached, worked miracles, suffered and died in order for human beings to move from earth to heaven, and become heirs of the heavenly Kingdom.' The choir of saints is the proof that the Kingdom of God has already been given to us: 'Through the myriads of members it has sent like colonists to heaven, [the Church] has truly inherited the very Kingdom of heaven.'[64]

We give thanks to the Lord for the good things He has bestowed on the saints, because we regard them as our own family, and we feel that the gifts God has given them are ours as well. And together with the saints, we give thanks to the Giver, offering gifts of our own.

At the Divine Liturgy we live the mystery of the Church, because each eucharistic community is the *one flock* which offers its gifts to the *one Shepherd* (John 10: 16) 'with one mouth and one heart' (cf. Acts 4: 32 and Rom. 15: 6). We are nourished on the holy Body of Christ, on Holy Communion, and the Church is made manifest as the Body of Christ. 'With this we are nourished, with this we are mingled, and we have become the one Body of Christ.'[65] Communion in the holy Body of Christ creates the communion and unity of the Church: 'As we partake of the holy Body of Christ, so we too become the Body of Christ.'[66]

[62] St Symeon of Thessaloniki, *On the holy Liturgy*, 94, *PG* 155.281C.
[63] St Isidore of Pelusium, *Letters*, 2.246, *PG* 78.685A; St Dionysius the Areopagite, *Church Hierarchy*, 3.3.1, 5, *PG* 3.428B, 432B.
[64] St Nicholas Cabasilas, *Comm. Liturgy*, 49 and 10, *PG* 150.480CD, 388C.
[65] St John Chrysostom, *On Matthew*, 82.5, *PG* 58.743–4.
[66] Nicholas of Methoni, *To those who hesitate*, *PG* 135.512C.

Communion in divine Love creates the communion of the love of the saints. In this way, the life of every saint is constantly extended within time. For before passing through the gate of death, the saints partook of the food which is the medicine of immortality. And through death, they entered into Life.

Then the Priest cuts out a small particle, saying: *Remember, O Master, Lover of mankind, every bishopric of the Orthodox, our Archbishop* [name], *the honoured order of presbyters, the diaconate in Christ and every order of clergy and of monastics, our brothers and fellow celebrants, priests and deacons, and all our brethren whom, through your compassion, you have called to your service, most loving Master.* And places it below the Lamb. He then commemorates the Bishop who ordained him, if he is still alive, and then commemorates those whose names he has among the living, taking out particles and placing them in the same way below the Lamb.

Then from another part of the seal the Priest cuts further particles for the departed, saying: *For remembrance and forgiveness of sins of the blessed founders of this holy house.* He then commemorates the Bishop who ordained him, if he is dead, and commemorates those whose names he has among the departed. And he concludes by saying: *And of all our Orthodox fathers and brethren who have fallen asleep in communion with you, Lord, Lover of mankind, in the hope of resurrection to eternal life.* And he places particles for those he has commemorated on the Paten. Likewise the Deacon also commemorates those he wishes from the living and the dead, as the Priest cuts out particles for them.

Finally the Priest says: *Remember me also, Lord, your unworthy servant, and forgive all my offences, both voluntary and involuntary.*

And taking the sponge,* he draws in together all the particles on the Paten, so that everything is safe and nothing will fall.

Remember, O Master, Lover of mankind

When the celebrant takes out a particle of the *prosphora* for a brother who is living, 'because it is placed near the eucharistic Bread, when that becomes the Body of Christ in the course of the Liturgy, the particle too is immediately sanctified. And when it is placed in the Chalice, it is united with the holy Blood. That is why it transmits divine grace to the soul of the one for whom it is offered. So a spiritual communion takes place [between that person and Christ]. If [the person commemorated] is among the godly, or those who have sinned but then repented, that person receives the communion of the Holy Spirit invisibly in his soul.'[67]

Once the celebrant has commemorated the living, he goes on to commemorate the departed — those who are unable to help themselves, and who look to us to show them our love.

The first way in which the departed are helped is by the prayers of the saints, which reach even to hell. In the life of St Macarius the Egyptian, it is recounted that the saint once encountered the skull of a pagan priest in the desert, and heard a voice coming from it, saying, 'Whenever you have compassion upon those in hell and pray for them, they receive a little comfort.'[68]

The second way in which they are helped is by the Divine

[67] St Symeon of Thessaloniki, *Church Building*, 103, PG 155.748D–749A.
[68] Palladius, *Sayings of the Fathers*, 38, PG 65.280B.

Liturgy. Our brethren who have fallen asleep are not deprived of the sanctification which Holy Communion conveys to the living. For 'Christ gives of Himself to the departed too, in a way known to Him'. In the Divine Liturgy, the souls of the departed 'receive remission of sins through the prayers of the priests' and by the grace of the precious Gifts which have been sanctified.[69]

St John Chrysostom writes: 'Not by accident did the holy Apostles decree that the departed should be commemorated in the presence of the awesome Mysteries. They knew that there is much to be gained from that, much benefit. When all the people stand with their hands raised [in prayer], when the entire priesthood is present and the terrible Sacrifice [that is, Christ] is in their midst, how is it possible for God not to bow to our supplications on their behalf?' Therefore 'let us never tire of helping those who have departed and offering the Divine Eucharist for them. For here before us lies Christ, the propitiation of the whole world.'[70]

During the time when the priest is commemorating the living and departed brethren, each of the faithful may also commemorate his family and those dear to him. On the Holy Mountain, the celebrant rings a little bell so that those present can commemorate whomever they wish at the same time he is cutting out particles on their behalf.

When the priest has finished commemorating the living and the departed, he beseeches Christ to remember also his own unworthiness.

Commemoration at the Divine Liturgy is one of the greatest gifts we can receive or offer to our brethren. Christ is before us, crucified, and we take courage from the example of the thief on the Cross and beseech Him: 'Remember us, Lord, in Your Kingdom' (cf. Luke 23: 42).

---

[69] St Nicholas Cabasilas, *Comm. Liturgy*, 42 and 45, PG 150.457C, 464D.
[70] *On Philippians*, 3.4, PG 62.204; *On 1 Corinthians*, 41.5, PG 61.361.

God in the midst of gods

In the Lamb and the particles assembled on the holy Paten, we have an image of the Church. Close to Christ and His holy Mother, in the company of the angels and saints, we experience the reality of the eucharistic Ecumenical Council of the Church: 'We see Christ Himself and the whole of His one Church, having in its midst Him who is the true Light... His Mother is to the right... The saints and angels to the left, while below we have the entire devout assembly of the faithful. And this is the great mystery: God in the midst of humans, or rather *in the midst of gods* [Ps. 81: 1], those who are being led to deification by Him who is truly God by nature, who became flesh for their sake. This is also the Kingdom which is to come, the polity of eternal life: God with us, seen and partaken of.'[71]

At the Divine Liturgy, we see upon the Paten the 'assembly of God', which 'the Son assembled together through Himself'.[72] Christ has assembled us together into the Liturgy of His Kingdom.

Then the Deacon takes the censer* and says to the Priest: *Master, bless the incense.* And the Priest blesses it, saying the Prayer of the Incense:

We offer incense to you, Christ our God, as a fragrance of spiritual sweetness. Accept it on your Altar above the heavens and send down upon us in return the grace of your All-holy Spirit.

---

[71] St Symeon of Thessaloniki, *On the holy Liturgy*, 94, *PG* 155.285AB.

[72] St Irenaeus, *Against Heresies*, 3.6.1, *SC* 211, p. 69.

When the soul becomes a censer

The Lord almighty says through His Prophet Malachi: *From the rising of the sun until its setting my name is glorified among the nations, and in every place incense is offered to my name, and a pure sacrifice* (Mal. 1: 11). 'When was this prophecy fulfilled, and incense offered to God in every place...and a pure sacrifice?' asks St John Chrysostom; and he gives the answer: 'Only after the coming of Christ.' The pure sacrifice is the Divine Eucharist. When one compares the Jewish sacrifice with the offering of the Eucharist, one realises that 'this alone could truly be called a pure sacrifice. For it is not offered with smoke and the stench of meat, nor with the blood of animals and atonements, but with the grace of the Holy Spirit.'[73]

The incense which the celebrant now uses is a prefiguration of the descent of the Holy Spirit on the Gifts which are offered: 'The fragrant smoke signifies the fragrance of the Holy Spirit.' As the celebrant censes, he 'honours God by the offering of incense and by its fragrance, and indicates that whatever he does, he does together with the Holy Spirit.'[74] 'As the incense catches fire and burns and gives off fragrant smoke, it signifies the grace of the Holy Spirit...who brilliantly illumines our senses and at the same time makes them fragrant with a spiritual fragrance. He illumines, because He is Light and is seen by the pure in heart. He gives off a pleasant scent because He is the Tree of Life, which crucifies [that is, puts to death] the will of the flesh, and makes the whole world fragrant.'[75]

St John Chrysostom urges us to set our soul on fire with divine zeal, so that through prayer the soul itself may become a censer: 'Just as incense is good and fragrant even on its own, but displays

---

[73] *Against the Jews*, 5.12, PG 48.903.

[74] St Germanus, *Contemplation*, PG 98.400C; St Symeon of Thessaloniki, *On the holy Liturgy*, 95, PG 155.285C.

[75] St Symeon the New Theologian, *Ethical Discourse 14*, 3, SC 129, p. 430.

its fragrance properly when it comes in contact with fire, so it is with prayer. It is good even on its own, but it becomes even better and more fragrant when it is offered up with a warm and ardent soul, when the soul becomes a censer and is burning with fierce fire... First set your heart on fire by your eagerness, and then pray.'[76]

In the Liturgy of St James, the celebrant beseeches Christ to count him worthy to stand at the holy Altar with soul and body fragrant: 'Master Lord Jesus Christ, Word of God, who willingly brought Yourself to God the Father as an unblemished sacrifice on the Cross, who are the coal in two natures which was carried in tongs to touch the lips of the Prophet and took away his sins: touch also the senses of us sinners, cleanse us from every stain and present us in purity at Your holy Altar so as to offer to You a sacrifice of praise. Receive also this incense from us Your unworthy servants as a sweet-smelling fragrance; make fragrant the stench of our souls and bodies; and sanctify us by the sanctifying power of Your All-holy Spirit.'[77]

Deacon: *Let us pray to the Lord. Make firm, Master*. The Priest censes the star* and places it over the Lamb, saying: *The star came to rest over the place where the Child was, with Mary His Mother.*[78]

Deacon: *Let us pray to the Lord. Glorify, Master*. The Priest censes the first veil* and covers the Lamb and Paten with it, saying: *The Lord is King, he is clothed with majesty; the Lord has clothed and girded himself with power; for he has established the world, which will not be shaken.*[79]

[76] *On Psalm 140*, 3, *PG* 55.430–1.
[77] Prayer of the Incense, Liturgy of St James.
[78] Cf. Matt. 2: 9, 11.
[79] Ps. 92: 1.

The Lord is King, He is clothed with majesty

Before Christ became man, 'mankind was enslaved to the Devil, to sin and death... The Devil would deceive us, sin would slay us and death would bury us.'[80] Christ became incarnate in order to free us from the tyranny of the Devil and sin and give us the freedom of the Holy Spirit: 'The human race was subjugated to the tyranny of Satan, since as a result of the Fall it strayed far from the Kingdom of God; that was why the only-begotten Son of God came to earth, to subdue our race under His own sceptre once more; and so it happened.' Thus was fulfilled the prophecy of the Psalmist: *The Lord is King, He is clothed with majesty.* For '"God's majesty" is the name given to the salvation of the human race.'[81]

The Lord has clothed and girded Himself with power, the Psalmist adds. What is the power that Christ the King put on and girded Himself with when He became incarnate? It is His all-holy Body that became the garment which Christ put on. The Psalmist 'calls the Body of Christ itself His "clothing"'. When He clothes and girds Himself, this symbolises 'the destruction of the hostile powers [of the Devil] which Christ accomplished, having assumed in a way the form of a warrior'. Christ's all-holy flesh became for Him a garment, clothing and a girdle. 'With this clothing and this girdle He overcame the powerful Devil. He snatched the prisoners out of his hands and freed them, binding the Devil himself in chains. And for us who have been saved, the flesh of the Saviour became *the power of God* [1 Cor. 1: 18].'[82]

Christ was victorious, and *established the world* — that is, the Church — upon the true and unshakable rock which is Himself. The Church leaps for joy over Christ's victory and makes festival

---

[80] St John Chrysostom, *That there is one Lawgiver for the Old and the New Testament*, 3, PG 56.402.

[81] St Athanasius the Great, *On Psalm 92*, PG 27.408A.

[82] St John Chrysostom, *That there is one Lawgiver for the Old and the New Testament*, PG 56.403; St Athanasius the Great, *On Psalm 92*, PG 27.408A; St Nicholas Cabasilas, *On the Dormition*, 7, PO 19.502–3.

in honour of His Kingdom. And that world-wide celebration is the Divine Liturgy.

Deacon: *Let us pray to the Lord. Cover, Master.*
The Priest censes the second veil and covers the Chalice with it, saying: *Your virtue, O Christ, has covered the heavens, and the earth is full of your praise.*[83]
Deacon: *Let us pray to the Lord. Shelter, Master.*
The Priest censes the third veil, the *Aer,** and covers both the Paten and the Chalice with it, saying: *Shelter us in the shelter of your wings; drive away from us every enemy and adversary;*[84] *bring peace to our lives; Lord, have mercy on us and on your world, and save our souls, for you are good and the lover of mankind.*

Your virtue, O Christ, has covered the heavens

The celebrant covers the Gifts which are being offered 'with the sacred covers... Similarly, the power of God incarnate was covered at first, until the time of His miracles.' The Gifts remain covered from this moment up to the recitation of the Creed. This covering reminds us of the fact 'that Jesus was not known to all from the beginning, and that even though He became incarnate, He did not come forth from the hiddenness of His divinity and His providence... He is known only to the extent that He reveals Himself.'[85]

For the first thirty years of His earthly life, Christ remained in obscurity. And when later they said to Him, *Show Yourself to the*

---

[83] Hab. 3: 3.
[84] Cf. Ps. 16: 8.
[85] St Nicholas Cabasilas, *Comm. Liturgy,* 11, *PG* 150.389D; St Symeon of Thessaloniki, *Church Building,* 80, *PG* 155.729C.

world, Jesus replied: *My time has not yet come* (John 7: 4, 6). For Christ's time is the time of His Sacrifice.[86]

* * *

God's virtue, which has covered the heavens, is His love for mankind. And the greatest proof of this love are the gifts offered to us by Baptism and the Eucharist. What can compare with these great gifts? 'That humans should become gods and sons of God, that human nature should be honoured with God's honour, that our clay should be raised to such a height of glory as to be equal in honour with the divine nature, equal to God... This is God's virtue which has covered the heavens.'[87]

As the celebrant covers the precious Gifts, he says these prophetic words which were fulfilled when Christ became man. And he asks for the Lord's protection and mercy for the whole world.

Deacon: *Bless, Master.*

The Priest takes the censer and censes the holy Prothesis, saying three times: *Blessed is our God, who has been thus well-pleased. Glory to you.*

The Deacon concludes each time: *Always, now and for ever, and to the ages of ages. Amen.*

The blessing of God and the blessing of man

The book of Genesis says that God blessed creation, man and time (cf. Gen. 1: 22–8, 2: 3). Having received God's blessing, man should

---

[86] Christ says through St John Chrysostom, 'My time has come when the hour of the Cross comes' (*On John*, 48.2, PG 59.271).

[87] St Nicholas Cabasilas, *On the Life in Christ*, 1, PG 150.505B.

have repaid the gift by glorifying His holy name. But sin not only prevented him glorifying his Creator; it also turned God's blessing into a curse. Once again, however, the loving Father did not abandon His creature, but sent into the world His Blessing, Christ: 'Eve, through the sickness of disobedience, brought in the curse. But You, Virgin Theotokos, have caused blessing to flower for the world.'[88]

Christ, the Blessing of the Father, has set us free from the curse, *becoming a curse for us* (Gal. 3: 13). St John Chrysostom says: 'Just as [Christ] humbled Himself in order to exalt you and died in order to make you immortal, so He became a curse in order to fill you with His blessing.'[89]

At the Divine Liturgy, we receive Christ, the fullness of every blessing, and give thanks to the Giver by blessing. But the blessing that we celebrate is a new gift of God. For 'he who blesses God gains something himself, making himself more glorious, without giving anything to Him. When God blesses, however, He makes us more glorious... So in both cases, the gain is ours.'[90]

Christ desires that our life should be one continuous Liturgy, so that He can offer us His blessings. Hence 'let us take care to live in such a way, and so show such zeal for virtue, that those who see us will offer up hymns of blessing to God our Master. Since He is good and loves mankind, He wants to be glorified by us — not because He is adding something to His glory, since He lacks nothing, but so that we may give Him opportunities to favour us with yet more of His love.'[91]

We begin every service and sacrament by blessing God because it is through them that we receive His grace. We receive His grace even more at the Divine Liturgy, since we receive Christ Himself, the blessing of God the Father. It is this blessing addressed to God

---

[88] *Octoechos*, Tone 4, Monday Matins, Canon, ninth ode, *eirmos*.
[89] *On Psalm 44*, 4, *PG* 55.188–9.
[90] St John Chrysostom, *On Psalm 113*, 5, *PG* 55.311.
[91] Ibid. *On Genesis*, 29.7, *PG* 53.271.

that the Apostle Paul is indicating when he calls the Cup of the Eucharist the *cup of blessing* (1 Cor. 10: 16).

Through her ministry in the mystery of the Incarnation of the Word, our Lady the Mother of God became the instrument whereby the Holy Trinity is glorified: 'In you, Immaculate One, the mystery of the Trinity is hymned and glorified.'[92] In a similar way, the celebrant becomes the instrument whereby the Threefold Sun of the Godhead is glorified through his ministry in the Mystery of the eucharistic Incarnation of the Word: he censes three times, and each time blesses the name of God the Father, who was well pleased to bestow His benefactions on man through the Son in the Holy Spirit. Even before the Liturgy begins, man experiences the love of God and spontaneously blesses and glorifies Him. And when the celebration of the Mystery begins, man enters into the *blessed Kingdom of the Father, and of the Son, and of the Holy Spirit.*

The Deacon takes the censer and says: *For the holy and sacred offering of the precious Gifts, let us pray to the Lord.*

With a contrite heart, the Priest says the Prayer of the Offering:

God, our God, who sent forth the heavenly Bread, the food of the whole world, our Lord and God Jesus Christ, as our Saviour, and Redeemer and Benefactor, to bless and sanctify us; bless this offering, and receive it on your Altar above the heavens. In your goodness and love for mankind remember those who have offered it, and those for whom they have offered it; and

---

[92] 8 September, Matins, Canon, ode 6.

as we celebrate your divine Mysteries keep us without condemnation. For sanctified and glorified is your all-honoured and majestic name, of the Father, the Son and the Holy Spirit, now and for ever, and to the ages of ages. Amen.

The Priest then gives the Dismissal.

From the Father through the Son in the Holy Spirit

Christ is the heavenly Bread, the 'Bread of eternal life' (cf. John 6: 41, 54). The fact that communion in the Bread of life bears fruit in the form of eternal life 'is clear proof that the Bread is from heaven, that is, from God the Father'.[93]

Christ has assured us: *My Father gives you the true Bread from heaven* (John 6: 32). Symbolic of the heavenly Father's assent to the offering of His Son is the veil which the celebrant puts over the Gifts, which is called the *Aer*. This assent is revealed also by Christ's words to Pilate: *You would have no power over me if it had not been given you from above* (John 19: 11). The words *given from above* signify the Father's assent to the Passion of the Son, and at the same time signify that the Son voluntarily accepts His sacrifice on the Cross.[94]

Through the Service of Preparation, the Church is preparing us for the mystery of trinitarian theurgy, the triune action of God: Christ is offered, the Father gives His assent and the All-holy Spirit — symbolised by the incense — prepares for the entry of the great King. Everything takes place 'from the Father, through the Son, in the Holy Spirit'.[95]

---

[93] Service of Preparation for Holy Communion, Canon, ode 1; St Cyril of Alexandria, *On John*, 4.3, *PG* 73.596A.

[94] Cf. St Cyril, ibid. 12, *PG* 74.641AB.

[95] Ibid. *On John*, 10.2, *PG* 74.336A.

The Deacon censes the holy Prothesis; then he censes the holy Altar all round in the form of a cross, and
the sanctuary and the people, saying in a low voice the
troparia:

With your body, O Christ, you were in the tomb,
with your soul in Hell as God, in Paradise with the
thief, and on the throne with the Father and the Spir-
it, filling all things, yet yourself uncircumscribed.

Glory to the Father...

How life-giving has your tomb become, O Christ;
truly lovelier than Paradise and more radiant than any
royal bridal chamber, the source of our resurrection.

Both now...

Rejoice, sanctified divine tabernacle of the Most
High; for through you, O Theotokos, joy was given to
those who cry: Blessed are you among women, all-im-
maculate Lady.[96]

And he puts the censer in its place.

The entire church is censed

It is a very ancient practice to cense the holy Altar, the sanctuary
and the entire church before the beginning of the celebration of
a sacrament or some other service.[97] This is also done before the
Divine Liturgy.

According to St Symeon of Thessaloniki, the celebrant first
censes 'the holy Prothesis and the Holy Table in the form of a
cross, and then the entire sanctuary. In this way, he indicates that
the transmission of God's gifts begins from within the holy sanc-

---

[96] Compline, Bright Week.

[97] Cf. St Dionysius the Areopagite, *Church Hierarchy*, 3.2, PG 3.425B.

tuary, and from there passes to the rest of the church. Some celebrants also cense the entire church and the people. This is also referred to by St Dionysius, who says that before the Divine Liturgy the whole church is censed, starting and finishing with the holy Altar. For God is the beginning and end of good things, and the Altar is God's throne and His place.' By censing in this manner, the celebrant 'indicates the grace, gift and fragrance of the Holy Spirit which is poured out upon the world from heaven through Jesus Christ, and which through Christ has ascended again to heaven.'[98]

The *troparia* recited by the celebrant as he censes refer to the Resurrection of Christ, the mystery that we experience in every Liturgy. The first *troparion* in particular brings us into liturgical space and time. Christ, who is with us, is the uncircumscribed God who fills all things. For this reason, the space of the Divine Liturgy is infinity, and its time is eternity. It is into this space and time we are welcomed when the celebrant censes us.

The censing at this point recalls the custom among Eastern peoples of receiving their guests by anointing their heads with fragrant oil (cf. Luke 7: 46). Christ, through the celebrant, receives us into His house, where we are invited to the eucharistic Supper.

As the *apolytikion* of *Matins** is being sung, the Deacon holds up his *orarion* and bows his head to the Priest, saying: *It is time for the Lord to act.*[99] *Holy Master, give the blessing.*

The Priest places his right hand on the Deacon's head, saying: *Blessed is our God always, now and for ever, and to the ages of ages.*

---

[98] *On the holy Liturgy*, 96, *PG* 155.288C–289A.
[99] Ps. 118: 126.

Deacon: *Amen. Pray for me, holy Master.*

Priest: *May the Lord direct your steps into every good work.*[100]

Deacon: *Remember me, holy Master.*

Priest: *May the Lord God remember you in his Kingdom*[101] *always, now and for ever, and to the ages of ages.*

Deacon: *Amen.*

The Priest bows three times and says in a humble voice: *Glory to God in the highest, and on earth peace; goodwill toward men* (three times). Then:

Lord, you will open my lips, and my mouth will proclaim your praise (twice).

Lord, Lord, open to us the door of your mercy.[102]

And so they begin the Divine Liturgy.

Time for the Lord to act

While we are preparing to begin the Divine Liturgy, Christ's time (*kairos*) is drawing near. The deacon reminds us of this when he addresses the celebrant and says: *It is time for the Lord to act.* It is time to yield our place to the Lord, so that He Himself may become the celebrant of the service of our offering, and accept it, and through it that He may be given to us.

When it was suggested to Christ that He should go up to the feast of Tabernacles, He answered: *My time is not yet fully come* (John 7: 8), His time meaning 'the moment of the Cross and death'.[103] This is the time in which we live during the Divine Liturgy.

---

[100] Cf. 2 Tim. 2: 21.

[101] Cf. Luke 23: 42.

[102] Luke 2: 14; Ps. 50: 17; cf. Luke 13: 25.

[103] St John Chrysostom, *On John*, 48.2, PG 59.271.

Christ's time, His *kairos*, is also His glory which is to come, of which the Jewish feasts were the type and prefiguration. Thus Christ says: 'I am not coming to this [Jewish] feast...because nothing in it delights me. I am waiting instead for the time of the true festival, which is not yet come. Then, when my time comes, I shall be with my disciples, rejoicing in the radiance of the saints, and I will shine with supreme brightness in the glory of the Father.'[104] The Divine Liturgy prefigures this time of the Kingdom of God which is to come.

May the Lord direct your steps into every good work, says the priest to the deacon. The supreme good work is the Divine Liturgy, through which God — the principial Good — works our salvation. Christ told us: *My Father is working still, and I am working* (John 5: 17). Through the Liturgy, God continues His work of creation: He recreates man and the world. The Divine Liturgy is the Lord's work, His act: *It is time for the Lord to act.*

---

[104] St Cyril of Alexandria, *On John*, 4.5, PG 73.644A.

II. THE DIVINE LITURGY

O Lord our God…take away the veils of hidden meaning which shroud this sacred rite, reveal it to us in shining clarity, and flood our spiritual eyes with Your infinite light.

(Liturgy of St James, Anaphora prayer)

1. THE LITANY OF PEACE AND THE ANTIPHONS

The Priest, lifting up the Gospel Book, and making the sign of the cross with it over the *Antimension*,* proclaims in a clear voice: *Blessed is the Kingdom of the Father, and of the Son, and of the Holy Spirit, now and for ever, and to the ages of ages.*
Choir [of chanters]: *Amen.*

The Liturgy transforms earth into heaven

At Christ's Incarnation, the mystery of the triune God was revealed to man. 'Because the rites performed in the Divine Liturgy are a sacramental initiation into the Incarnation of the Lord, it is necessary for the Holy Trinity to shine forth and be proclaimed from the very beginning of the Liturgy.'[1] This is why the priest begins with the trinitarian doxology: *Blessed is the Kingdom of the Father, and of the Son, and of the Holy Spirit.* The Divine Liturgy is the revelation of the blessed Kingdom of the triune God.

The Liturgy, as a manifestation of the Kingdom, is at the same time the mystery of Christ's presence, for that is what the Kingdom is. 'What is the Kingdom of God?' asks Christ, through St John Chrysostom. And He replies: 'It is my presence.' It is the actual presence of Christ that is celebrated in the Divine Liturgy. Throughout the Liturgy, Christ 'appears in the Mysteries themselves'.[2]

---

[1] St Germanus, *Contemplation*, PG 98.401B.
[2] *On Matthew*, 41.2, PG 57.447; *On the Incomprehensible*, 4.4, PG 48.733.

It is Christ's presence in the sacrament of the Eucharist that 'transforms earth into heaven... For that which is most precious in heaven is shown to you on earth below...the Lord Himself, the Lord of angels and archangels.' The place in which Christians gather to give thanks to the Lord is 'a place of angels, a place of archangels, the royal palace of God, heaven itself'.[3]

'Before the Word of God became man, the Kingdom of heaven was as far from us as heaven is from the earth. But when the King of heaven came to us and was well-pleased to unite Himself with us, then the Kingdom of heaven came near to us all [cf. Matt. 4: 17].'[4] By His Incarnation Christ opened the door of the Kingdom, and by means of the Divine Liturgy we go through that door. In the Divine Liturgy, we have a foretaste of the good things of the Kingdom, for the Divine Liturgy is the Banquet of the Kingdom, and those who partake of it are transported by death 'from one Banquet to another Banquet, from that which is still veiled to that which is already revealed'.[5]

Those who partake in the Liturgy are journeying towards the Kingdom which is beginning to be revealed.

The Cross is the symbol of the Kingdom

As the priest blesses the Kingdom of God, he makes the sign of the cross over the Holy Table with the Gospel Book. The first words of the Divine Liturgy are a doxology, and the first act is the making of the sign of the cross. The Divine Liturgy is the Kingdom of God, and it is through the Cross that we are able to reach the Kingdom.

The Cross is the proof that Christ is the only true King. The thief who was crucified on Christ's right speaks theology from the height of the Cross: 'The Cross is the symbol of the Kingdom.

---

[3] St John Chrysostom, *On 1 Corinthians*, 24.5 and 36.5, PG 61.205, 313.

[4] St Gregory Palamas, *Homily 31*, 6, PG 151.392C.

[5] St Nicholas Cabasilas, *On the Life in Christ*, 4, PG 150.625A.

I call Christ 'King' precisely because I see Him crucified. For it is the mark of a king to die for the sake of his subjects. As Christ said, *The Good Shepherd gives up his life for His sheep* [John 10: 11]; hence the good king sacrifices his life for his subjects. He sacrificed His life, and that is why I call Him 'King': *Remember me, Lord, in your Kingdom* [Luke 23: 42].'6

*   *   *

Before Christ was crucified, 'a cross signified a death sentence, but now it has become an object of honour. Previously it was the symbol of condemnation, but now it is the foundation of our salvation.' Through the Cross, we have found the way that leads to the Kingdom: 'On account of the Cross, we no longer wander in the wilderness because we have come to know the true way. We no longer remain outside the palace of the King, because we have found the door.' The Kingdom of God has been bestowed on us through the Cross. The Cross 'has opened Paradise which was closed... For Christ said [to the thief], *Today you will be with me in Paradise* [Luke 23: 43].'7

The Cross of Christ is not only the road leading to Paradise and the door by which we can enter; it is also 'the beautiful paradise of the Church'. It is the tree of new and incorruptible life which nourishes the faithful:

> The wood in former times brought bitterness into Eden,
> but the wood of the Cross has blossomed with sweet life.
> For Adam ate, and fell into corruption;
> but we delight in the flesh of Christ
> and live and are mystically deified,
> receiving the eternal Kingdom of God.8

---

6 St John Chrysostom, *On the Cross and the Thief*, 1.3, PG 49.403.

7 Ibid. 1.1, 2, *PG* 49.399–401.

8 Sunday of the Veneration of the Cross, *sticheron** at Vespers; *Octoechos*, Tone 8, Wednesday Matins, *kathisma*.

Christ is King of the Kingdom that has come and is coming. It came through the Cross, and it is coming with the Cross. For when the end comes, *then will appear the sign of the Son of man* (Matt. 24: 30), that is, the Cross. When the light of this world is extinguished once and for all, the sign of the cross will shine like a new sun. And just as 'before a king enters a city, the soldiers will take up banners and lift them upon their shoulders to herald his entry', so it will be at the Second Coming: 'When the Lord descends from heaven, He will be preceded by hosts of angels and archangels bearing the Cross upon their shoulders, and they will announce to us His royal entry.'[9]

The Cross of Christ is the road, the door and the herald of the Kingdom of God.

The faithful conclude with the Amen

The faithful set their seal on the doxology pronounced by the priest by singing *Amen*.[10] With this response, the faithful accept the truth expressed in the celebrant's proclamation, and pray that they may taste the good things of the Kingdom of the Trinity.

The faithful 'conclude with *Amen*, and thus make everything that the priest says their own'. This ending to every pronouncement of the priest signifies that what 'is lacking in the perfection of the priests is completed by the action of the people, and God accepts *the least with the greatest* [Ps. 113: 21] in one unity of spirit. For the congregation also believe that their prayers are accepted when they join them to the prayers of the priests.'[11]

---

[9] St John Chrysostom, *On the Cross and the Thief*, 1.4, PG 49.404.

[10] *Amen* is a Hebrew word meaning 'indeed', 'let it be so'. St Jerome compares the singing of the *Amen* with thunder from heaven (*On Galatians*, PL 26.355B).

[11] St Nicholas Cabasilas, *Comm. Liturgy*, 15, PG 150.401AB; St Cyril of Alexandria, *On 1 Corinthians*, P. E. Pusey, ed., *Sancti patris nostri Cyrilli Archiepiscopi Alexandrini in D. Ioannis Evangelium*, vol. 3 (Oxford, 1872), p. 296. Cf. *PG* 74.893B.

With the assent of the faithful, the priest's blessing ascends to the Altar above the heavens. The faithful actively participate in the Divine Liturgy, which at every moment confirms its name: it is a work of the people.[12]

Deacon:[13] *In peace, let us pray to the Lord.*
Choir: *Lord, have mercy [Kyrie eleison].* And so after each petition.

The Mystery of the peace of God

Immediately after the blessing of the Kingdom of God, our Mother Church teaches us the way of liturgical prayer: *Let us pray to the Lord in peace.*

The road that leads to the Divine Liturgy is peace of soul. Without this peace, we cannot take part in the Liturgy: 'Without tranquillity of thoughts, the human intellect cannot explore hidden mysteries.' Real participation in the eucharistic Mystery is proportionate to our inner peace: 'The more the heart ceases to be disturbed by recollections of external things, the more the intellect is astounded by understanding divine meanings.'[14]

True peace of soul, however, is to be had at the heavenly Altar where the Holy Anaphora is celebrated: 'True peace is from

---

[12] The Greek word *leitourgia* is a compound of *leitos*, meaning 'common' or 'public', and *ergon* meaning 'work'. So *leitourgia* means a common work, a work of the people. Thus the designation *Liturgy* cogently manifests the fact that the faithful actively participate in the eucharistic Mystery, and that without their presence and consent the priest is unable to celebrate.

[13] When there is no deacon concelebrating in the Divine Liturgy, the deacon's words, except for those that are addressed by him directly to the priest, are spoken by the priest. For this reason, in the commentary special distinction is not always made with regard to whom is saying the petition.

[14] St Isaac the Syrian, *Homily 5* and *Homily 4*, *Asc. Hom.*, p. 45 and pp. 35–6. The translations here are adapted to the Greek text.

above.' And we approach the Altar *in peace*. St Basil writes: 'Seek peace… Acquire a calm mind and a state of soul untroubled and undisturbed…that you may acquire the peace of God *which passes all understanding* [Phil. 4: 7] as the guard of your heart.'[15]

* * *

The fact that man has been created in the image of God means that human nature has been created 'peaceable, free from strife and faction, bound to God and to itself by love'. The peace which man received as a gift from God was enjoyed by living a virtuous life close to Him. For 'nothing gives such peace to our soul as knowledge of God and the acquisition of virtue'.[16] Sin, however, brought confusion and trouble to man and to the world. 'For evil by its nature is dispersive, unstable, multifarious and divisive.' Through sin, man became an enemy both to himself and to God. Once man had reached that point, Christ alone was able to help him and give him peace. 'Christ is the only one who can reconcile us with God, the only one who gives peace of soul.' It was for precisely this reason that 'in His love for man God became man so that He might unite human nature to Himself and stop it from acting evilly towards itself, or rather from being at strife and divided against itself'.[17]

The peace that Christ brought by becoming human is acquired through repentance: 'From her unceasing tears, the soul receives peace in her thoughts. And from peace in thoughts she is raised to the limpid purity of the intellect. And through this limpidity of the intellect a man comes to see the mysteries of God.'[18] Tears of

[15] St Basil the Great, *On Psalm 33*, 10, *PG* 29.376BC.
[16] St Maximus the Confessor, *Various Texts on Theology, the Divine Economy, and Virtue and Vice*, 1.46, *PG* 90.1196B (*Philokalia*, vol. 2, p. 174); St John Chrysostom, *On Psalm 4*, 11, *PG* 55.57.
[17] St Maximus, ibid. 1.49, *PG* 90.1197A (*Philokalia*, ibid.); St Nicholas Cabasilas, *Comm. Liturgy*, 44, *PG* 150.464B; St Maximus, ibid. 1.47, *PG* 90.1196C.
[18] St Isaac the Syrian, *Asc. Hom.*, 18, p. 96.

repentance are the beginning of the road. They form the first rung of the ladder that takes us up to contemplation of the divine Mysteries. The second rung is peace of soul.

When we approach Christ in repentance, He sends us to the place where His peace reigns: *Go in peace* (Luke 7: 50). He sends us into the church, which is the 'impregnable palace of [God's] peace'. There our soul, guided by Christ the High Priest, occupies itself with the contemplation of God in the Holy Spirit; that contemplation which is 'peaceful and free from any disturbance'.[19]

The Divine Liturgy is the Mystery of the peace of God: 'This Mystery is a Mystery of peace.' For the Divine Liturgy is our encounter with Christ, who is 'the true peace' for man.[20]

> Deacon: *For the peace from on high and for the salvation of our souls, let us pray to the Lord.*

Christ is our peace

Having instructed us in the first petition how we should pray, the Church now teaches us what we should first ask for: the peace of God and the salvation of our souls. That is what Christ taught us when He said, *Seek first the Kingdom of God and His righteousness* (Matt. 6: 33), for '*the salvation of our souls* means the Kingdom of God, and the *peace from on high* means righteousness'. The righteousness of God is virtuous life, the life that man scorned when he fell, and that has been given us anew as a gift from Him *who became for us...righteousness from God and sanctification* (1 Cor. 1: 30).[21]

---

[19] St Maximus the Confessor, *Mystagogy*, 23, PG 91.697D.

[20] St John Chrysostom, *On Matthew*, 50.3, PG 58.508; *Octoechos*, Doxastikon for the sixth Sunday Matins Gospel.

[21] St Nicholas Cabasilas, *Comm. Liturgy*, 12, PG 150.393C.

As the angels heralded at His birth, *Glory to God in the highest and on earth peace, goodwill among men* (Luke 2: 14), Christ brought true peace to the earth. The angels guarded well the place assigned to them 'and are at peace with God, for they heed His will in all ways and remain steadfast in righteousness and sanctity. We wretched humans, on the other hand, exalted our own desires in opposition to the will of the Master and assumed an attitude of enmity towards Him. This enmity was annulled by Christ, for He is our peace and through Himself He united us with God the Father, putting sin to flight... So Christ became peace and goodwill for us.'[22]

The reconciliation of earth with heaven came about through Christ: *Now in Christ Jesus you who were once far off have been brought near through the blood of Christ. For He is our peace, who has made the two one and has broken down the dividing wall of enmity...that He might create in Himself one new man in place of the two, so making peace, and reconciling both to God in one body through the Cross, thereby slaying enmity. And He came and preached peace to you who were far off and peace to those who were near* (Eph. 2: 13–7).

Christ became human, and offered human beings the peace of God. On the Holy Table 'Christ lies slaughtered. For whom was He slaughtered, and why?' asks St John Chrysostom. And he answers: 'In order to make peace between heaven and earth, to make you a friend of the angels, to reconcile you with the God of all. To make you a friend, you who were an enemy and adversary... This Sacrifice took place in order that you might be at peace with your brother.'[23]

Through the grace of Christ's peacemaking Sacrifice, we are able to overcome the obstacles that separate us from the Kingdom

---

[22] St Cyril of Alexandria, *On Luke*, 2, PG 72.493CD–496A.
[23] *On the Betrayal of Judas*, 1.6, PG 49.381-2.

of peace: 'Once we recover from the inebriation of the passions and rise up against the wiles and tyranny of the Devil...we will then receive invisibly within us the irenical presence of Christ, the gentle King of peace.' When man attains the realm of dispassion, his intellect, 'the temple mystically built by peace, becomes in spirit the dwelling-place of God'.[24]

God's peace transforms man into a temple. And God comes to dwell in man: *His abode has been established in peace, and His dwelling-place in Zion* (Ps. 75: 3).

> Deacon: *For the peace of the whole world, for the stability of the holy Churches of God, and for the union of all, let us pray to the Lord.*

The peace of the whole world

All believers have the Lord as their common Father and are members of His spiritual family, the Church. With the eyes of love we embrace our brethren, however distant they may be, and petition the Lord for them. 'That is what the eyes of love are like: distance is no object to them, nor do they grow weak with the passage of time.' Love is a 'spring of fire' and 'imitates the path of flame' — in other words, it imitates the swift movement of flame.[25] Love courses over the entire world; it extends through the whole of time.

In the same petition, we ask the Lord to grant the fruits of His peace: the stability of the local Churches, the union of all in His

---

[24] St Maximus the Confessor, *Letter 43*, PG 91.640AB; *Two Hundred Texts on Theology*, 1.53, PG 90.1104A (*Philokalia*, vol. 2, p. 125).

[25] St John Chrysostom, *Letter 36*, PG 52.630; St John Climacus, *Ladder of Divine Ascent*, 30.18, PG 88.1160B; St John Chrysostom, *Letter 222*, PG 52.734.

truth. Peace bears fruit in the *stability of the holy Churches*. In God's peace, the ship of the Church sails on an even keel towards the calm haven of the Kingdom. That is why in the Liturgy of St Basil we ask: 'Remember, O Lord, Your holy catholic and apostolic Church, and give it peace… Speedily bring to an end the uprisings of heresies by the power of Your Holy Spirit… Grant us Your peace and love, O Lord our God.'[26]

The fruit of peace is unity in Christ. Peace 'is the power that unites all, the power that engenders and produces concord and unity among all'. The unifying power of peace is stressed also by St Paul: Brethren, preserve *the unity of the Spirit in the bond of peace* (Eph. 4: 3). Indeed, 'it is not possible for the unity of the Spirit to exist amidst enmity and dissension… St Paul writes this because he wants believers to be bound together. Not simply to be at peace, not simply to love, but to be all one, one soul.'[27]

Confusion and tumult, particularly as interior states, distract our mind. 'A mind that is agitated cannot possibly be united with God… Just as peace unifies the many, so tumult changes the one into many', that is to say, it fragments a person. Peace unites us among ourselves, and also unites us with God. That is why we ask the Lord: 'Lord, You have given us peace, concord among ourselves. Give us also the peace that is indivisible unity with You, so that being at peace with Your Holy Spirit, whom You placed within us when first You created us, we may be inseparable from Your love.'[28]

It is in this bond of peace through love that St John Chrysostom bids us be bound to one another and to God. 'This bond is a good bond. In this bond let us bind ourselves, both to one another and to God.' This bond does not constrict those it binds, it does

---

[26] Liturgy of St Basil, prayer after the Consecration.

[27] St Dionysius the Areopagite, *Divine Names*, 11.1, PG 3.948D; St John Chrysostom, *On Ephesians*, 9.3, PG 62.72–3.

[28] St Nicholas Cabasilas, *Comm. Liturgy*, 12, PG 150.396A; St Isidore of Pelusium, *Letters*, 1.122, PG 78.264C.

not put pressure on them. On the contrary, it lets them feel freer than the 'free', and 'brings them bountiful ease'.[29]

Bound together in peace and love, the faithful reach the spaciousness of God's love through the Divine Liturgy.

One who seeks peace is searching for Christ

Living as we do in the world, we often see the 'sea of life surging', but we do not feel the presence of Christ, the Lord of peace. Our life is like a journey travelled in pitch darkness. Within us, contrary winds blow strongly. We are battered by waves and have no sense of consolation, whether divine or human. So we experience what St Gregory the Theologian describes: 'The voyage at night; no beacon anywhere; Christ is asleep [cf. Mark 4: 37–8].'[30]

In this state, we come to the house of God. There we feel that 'the Church of Christ is tranquil peace'. And when the Divine Liturgy begins, we ask with all our might for peace from above, peace in our souls, peace for the world. In seeking peace however, we are in reality seeking Christ Himself: 'One who seeks peace is searching for Christ, for He is peace.'[31]

---

[29] *On Ephesians*, 9.3, PG 62.73.

[30] *Octoechos*, Tone 6, Canon, *eirmos* of the 6th ode; *Letter 80*, PG 37.153C.

[31] *Apostolic Constitutions*, 2.20, PG 1.637A; St Basil the Great, *On Psalm 33*, 10, PG 29.376C.

Deacon: *For this holy house, and for those who en-*
ter it with faith, reverence and the fear of God, let us
pray to the Lord.

The church is heaven on earth

Every time we cross the threshold of the house of God, 'we are entering a heavenly palace... In its interior, peace reigns, and it is
filled with inexpressible mysteries.' There, within the divine
palace, the mystery of the Kingdom of God is celebrated. 'All mortal flesh falls silent' in reverence and awe, so that the mystery of
God's Word may be heard.[32]

In God's house, when the Divine Liturgy is taking place, everything is illumined by the light of Christ. He is the lightning that
comes from the east and shines as far as the west (Matt. 24: 27).
And the firmament of the liturgical heaven — the house of God —
is radiant with the light of Christ: 'The light of Christ shines upon all.'[33]

All people and all things are illumined by Christ, and the souls
of all are filled with tranquillity and joy. For the light of Christ,
though blinding like lightning, is at the same time comforting
like a cool breeze: 'Gladsome light of holy glory'.[34] This Light
changes the church into a calm haven for the soul.

St John Chrysostom writes: 'Just as a calm and sheltered harbour provides great security to the ships moored there, so does
the temple of God: when people enter it, it snatches them away
from worldly affairs as from a storm, and gives them the capacity to stand and listen to God's words in calm and security. This

---

[32] St John Chrysostom, *Homily on Isaiah* 2, 1, *PG* 56.109; cf. Cherubic Hymn, Holy Saturday.
[33] Liturgy of the Presanctified Gifts.
[34] Hymn at the lighting of the lamps, Vespers.

place is the bedrock of virtue and the school of spiritual life... You need only set foot on the threshold of a church and at once you are liberated from the cares of daily life. Go on into the church, and a spiritual dew will envelop your soul. The stillness there moves you to awe, and teaches you how to live spiritually. It elevates your thoughts and prevents you from remembering things or matters belonging to the present life. It transports you from earth to heaven. And if there is such great gain from simply being in a church when no service is going on, then how much benefit will people derive from being present...when the holy Apostles proclaim the Gospel, Christ stands in our midst, God the Father receives the Mysteries that are performed and the Holy Spirit gives His own joy!'[35]

The church is the paradise of the Master's presence. St John stresses this point: 'What paradise can compare with our gathering? Here there is no serpent to plot against us [as the Devil did against the first-formed humans (cf. Gen. 3: 1–13)], but Christ who initiates us into the mysteries.'[36] By His presence, Christ changes the church into paradise and brings us into His mysteries.

*   *   *

The church building bestows all these gifts on us because it is the house of God. It is 'a heaven on earth, in which the heavenly God dwells and walks about'. Through the rite of Consecration, a church becomes heaven: 'Today Your unapproachable glory has come upon Your temple built on earth, making it heaven.' After the rite of Consecration, 'we no longer call [the church] simply a house, but holy, because it has been sanctified by the Holy Father, through the All-holy Son, in the Holy Spirit, and is the House of the Holy Trinity'.[37]

---

[35] *Rebuke of those who are absent*, 1, PG 51.145.

[36] *On Repentance*, 8.1, PG 49.335–6.

[37] St Germanus, *Contemplation*, PG 98.384B; Canon for the Consecration of a Church, ode 1; St Symeon of Thessaloniki, *Consecration*, 128, PG 155.336B.

Man is a Christ-bearing temple

As a special blessing, man was given by his Creator the capacity to become His temple: 'Among all sensible things, mankind alone is able to be God's true temple and altar.' This capacity was given to man anew by Christ when he was re-created: 'Every Christian believer at the present time [since Christ's Incarnation] is a house and temple of God, because he has Christ dwelling within him.' So all our life must be lived as if the Lord Himself were living in us. 'So that we are His temples, and God Himself is within us.'[38]

In God's holy house, the faithful receive the sanctifying gift of the Comforter and are changed into the blessed material of which the Church is built. 'For the Church is nothing other than the house built out of our souls.' We faithful are 'stones in the Father's temple, prepared for the edifice that God the Father is building'.[39]

One of the Apostolic Fathers describes the following vision that he saw: Six young men, helped by many others, were building a gigantic tower upon the waters. The construction of the tower was so perfect that it was impossible to make out the joins between the stones. Then the Church, in the form of a venerable lady, appeared and interpreted the vision: 'The tower that you see being built is I, the Church... It is built upon the waters, because our life has been saved and will be saved through water [at the Flood and in Holy Baptism]. The tower is founded upon the word of the All-mighty... The six young men are angels... And the stones are the Apostles, bishops, teachers and deacons who have lived in holiness before God. Some are still alive, some have already fallen asleep. They were always in agreement among them-

---

[38] St Nicholas Cabasilas, *On the Life in Christ*, 5, PG 150.629C; St Cyril of Alexandria, *On Worship in Spirit and Truth*, 10, PG 68.656C; St Ignatius of Antioch, *Ephesians*, 15, PG 5.657A.

[39] St John Chrysostom, *On Ephesians*, 10.2, PG 62.78; St Ignatius of Antioch, *Ephesians*, 9, PG 5.652B.

selves and at peace. That is why the stones in the building fit perfectly together, and it looks as if it is one single block of stone.'[40]

* * *

Through Holy Communion, the entire human being becomes
a 'Christ-bearing temple', and every member of his or her body is
a part of Christ's temple. The eucharistic Table 'makes us to dwell
in Christ, and Christ in us. For He says: [he] abides in me, and I in
him [John 6: 56]... Christ is for us both dweller and dwelling. So
we should count ourselves blessed on account of our Dwelling,
and again blessed because we have become the dwelling of such
a Dweller.'[41]

St Maximus the Confessor says that man is a 'mystical church'.
The body is the nave, the soul is the sanctuary and the spiritual
intellect is the altar. 'On the altar of his intellect, man invokes the
silence of the Godhead, which is amply hymned...[summoning It]
through another, eloquent silence which speaks volumes. So far
as is attainable for a human being, he joins himself with the Godhead through mystical theology; he becomes such as befits one
counted worthy of God's indwelling and marked by His dazzling
radiance.'[42]

The church faces east 'so that we turn our gaze to Paradise', in
imitation of the Paradise of Eden which was planted in the east
(Gen. 2: 8). As we sail the sea of life, we are journeying towards the
Light that knows no evening. Christ is the Light that illumines
the righteous during their earthly journey. 'So they attain to eternal life shining with that Light with which they have lived the entire time.'[43]

We hasten towards the Jerusalem which is above. Where — for

[40] Hermas, The Shepherd, 1, vision iii. 2–5, ANF 2, pp. 13–4.
[41] St John Chrysostom To the disgraced Theodore, 1.1, PG 47.277; St Nicholas
Cabasilas, On the Life in Christ, 4, PG 150.584BC.
[42] Mystagogy, 4, PG 91.672BC.
[43] St Athanasius the Great, To the prefect Antiochus, 37, PG 28.620B; St Nicholas
Cabasilas, On the Life in Christ, 4, PG 150.624B.

the saints — *night shall be no more; they need no light of lamp or sun, for the Lord God will be their light* (Rev. 22: 5). There, where God is the temple of the saints, definitively and irrevocably: *I saw no temple in the city, for its temple is the Lord God almighty and the Lamb* (Rev. 21: 22).

Deacon: *For our Archbishop* [name], *for the honoured order of presbyters, for the diaconate in Christ, for all the clergy and the people, let us pray to the Lord.*

He who presides in the place of God

The first time the eucharistic Mystery was celebrated, the celebrant was the author of our salvation, Christ our Master. After His Ascension, His place at the eucharistic synaxis was taken by the twelve Apostles, and thereafter by the bishops whom they had ordained. As time went on and the local Churches multiplied, presbyters began to celebrate the Divine Liturgy on the instruction of the bishops. This continuity is unbroken, and thus it is that the celebrant of every Liturgy is the successor of Christ.

This continuity is seen particularly in the person of the bishop who sits '...on the throne of Christ, so as to care for His Church and govern it with piety'.[44] In his person we see Christ: 'We should look upon the bishop as the Lord Himself.' The presence of the bishop at the Divine Liturgy or his assent to its celebration is an assurance that the Mystery is genuine: 'The eucharistic Mystery performed by a bishop, or by one who has received permission from him, is the Mystery that should be considered valid.'[45]

In early Byzantine times, when the Divine Liturgy began with

---

[44] St Clement of Rome, *Homily 3*, 60, *PG* 2.149B.
[45] St Ignatius of Antioch, *Ephesians*, 6, *PG* 5.649AB; *Smyrnaeans*, 8, *PG* 5.713B.

what is now the Little Entrance,* the first liturgical act was the entry of the bishop into the church. The bishop would then put on his episcopal vestments in the middle of the church, as is often done today. The vesting of the bishop represents the Incarnation of the Word. As 'the Word of God, being without flesh, clothed Himself in holy flesh from the Holy Virgin', so the bishop clothes himself in his sacred vestments which 'signify the Incarnation of Christ, and the [marks] of His Incarnation'.[46]

The bishop is the envoy of the Lord, 'whom Christ, the Master of the household, sends out to administer His affairs'. He comes into the house of God to perform Christ's work: to bring back the lost sheep into the one flock of the Church. The *omophorion*,* the vestment distinctive to the bishop, symbolises 'the salvation and recall of the sheep that had strayed' (cf. Matt. 18: 12). That is why he says as he puts it on: 'Taking upon Your shoulders, O Christ, the nature that had gone astray, You ascended and brought it to God the Father.'[47]

The entry of the bishop into the church, his reception by the faithful who are already gathered and his vesting in the middle of the church underline the special significance of the bishop's presence at the Divine Liturgy. This liturgical practice reveals to us that the bishop is the living image of Christ our Master, the *blessed one who comes in the name of the Lord* (Matt. 21: 9). And the faithful gathered in the church are the Israel of grace which receives the Messiah.

During the Divine Liturgy, the bishop is 'he who is seated before in the place of God' and the presbyters are 'in the place of the council of the Apostles'.[48] The Divine Liturgy is the Mystical Sup-

---

[46] St Hippolytus of Rome, *On Christ and Antichrist*, 4, PG 10.732B; St Symeon of Thessaloniki, *On the holy Liturgy*, 79, PG 155.256B.

[47] St Ignatius of Antioch, *Ephesians*, 6, PG 5.649A. St Symeon of Thessaloniki, *On the holy Liturgy*, 82, PG 155.260C; Ascension, First Canon, ode 7.

[48] St Ignatius of Antioch, *Magnesians*, 6, PG 5.668A (in place of the reading *topos*, 'place', some editions have *typos*, 'type, figure', so that the meaning would be: 'the bishop [or the presbyters] seated form a figure…').

per itself, at which together with Christ and the Apostles (whom we see in the persons of the bishop and presbyters), all the faithful are present.

The faithful are aware of the grandeur of the priestly ministry and the dangers risked by celebrants. And because they know the power of communal prayer, they pray to Christ for the bishop. St John Chrysostom says: 'If someone from the congregation commanded you to pray privately for the salvation of the bishop, every one of you would shrink from it, believing the burden to be beyond your powers. But when all of you together hear the deacon directing you and saying, "Let us pray for the bishop…", you do not shrink from carrying out his commission, but zealously raise your prayer, because you know the power of your gathering.'[49]

The faithful rely on this power of communal prayer, and dare to petition the Lord for those who stand 'near to the blessed and pure nature':[50] *Lord, have mercy* upon our father the bishop, upon Your presbyters and deacons.

Deacon: *For this city, for every city, country, and for the faithful who dwell in them, let us pray to the Lord.*

Christians sustain the world

The love that is of God is universal and ecumenical: it embraces all people, all places, all times. 'Perfect love…loves all men equally.'[51] It is this love that our holy Church imitates, and she desires

---

[49] *On the Obscurity of the Old Testament*, 2.5, PG 56.182.

[50] St John Chrysostom, *On the Priesthood*, 3.5, PG 48.643.

[51] St Maximus the Confessor, *Four Hundred Texts on Love*, 1.71, PG 90.976B (*Philokalia*, vol. 2, p. 60).

that we believers should live in the same way. The overflowing of this love is our prayer for the city in which we live, for every city and country.

Christian believers 'live in their own homelands, but as temporary visitors... They live on earth, but behave as if they are in heaven... They love all and are persecuted by all... In a word, what the soul is to the body, Christians are to the world. The soul is diffused through all the members of the body, as Christians are in all the cities of the world... Christians sustain the world.'[52]

Since Christians are the soul of the world, they should rejoice in people's joy and suffer with their suffering. They should love people more than their parents according to the flesh love them. For 'the saints occupy the place of father, surpassing all fathers according to the flesh in their love and care for the people'.[53]

* * *

St John Chrysostom showed this paternal love for the cities to which he was father, such as Antioch. His homilies *On the Statues* are proof of his love for that city.

Early in the year 387, rampaging mobs of Antiochenes reacted to a heavy tax imposed by the Emperor Theodosius by smashing statues of the emperor. In punishment Theodosius deprived the city of all its privileges, and threatened to raze it to the ground. Many notable citizens were killed, estates were confiscated; fear and terror spread everywhere. Some who were in a position to do so fled, but the majority were dragged off to prison, tortured and put to death.

Flavian, the bishop of the city, an old man and in ill health, decided to set off for Constantinople, despite the hard winter, and attempt to mollify the emperor's anger. The priest John, as he then was, remained in Antioch, and the people turned to him.

---

[52] *Epistle to Diognetus*, 5–6, PG 2.1173B–1176C.
[53] St John Chrysostom, *Commentary on Isaiah*, 7.3, PG 56.80.

'The market place was empty and the church was full', the saint relates.[54] The terrified multitude was consoled by its holy father.

When, subsequently, a court was set up by the emperor's legates to try those responsible for the rampage, many hermits 'left their huts and caves and converged from all around, like angels who had descended from heaven. The city then looked like heaven, because those holy men were to be seen everywhere, and by their very appearance gave solace to those who were suffering.' When finally it was learnt that Bishop Flavian's mission had been successful and the emperor had pardoned the people, St John celebrated the salvation of the city together with the bishop and the faithful: 'Blessed be God who has granted us to celebrate today this holy feast with great joy and gladness... Let us thank God who loves mankind, and let us wonder at His power, His love for man, the wisdom and care that He has shown to the city.'[55]

That is how the saints loved, and continue to love, the city and place that had been entrusted to their care, and every city and country. We try to imitate them always, but especially at the Divine Liturgy.

> Deacon: *For favourable weather, an abundance of the fruits of the earth, and temperate seasons, let us pray to the Lord.*

Let creation rejoice

With this petition, we ask the Lord to extend the blessing of His love to the air, the earth, the whole of creation. We ask that all creation should follow the path appointed to it by the Creator.

---

[54] *On the Statues*, 4.1, *PG* 49.59.
[55] Ibid. 17.1 and 21.1, *PG* 49.172–3, 211.

The visible world was created by God as a kingdom for man. Man is 'king of things on earth and subject to a King in heaven'. The very sight of the world and our life in it gives man 'great enjoyment, and moves him to offer grateful thanks' to God.[56] He receives the world from God as a blessing, and offers it back as thanksgiving. Man, therefore, is king and priest of God's world.

Man's peaceful coexistence with God and with the world was disrupted by the disobedience of the first-created humans. The earth that was created *very good* (Gen. 1: 31) became corruptible. Man ceased to be king and priest of the world and was made subject to corruption and death. His relationship with himself, the world and God changed. Man, who had been ruler of the world, became its slave: 'He became lower than those things to which he had been created to be superior.'[57]

'When all of the created world which God had brought out of non-being into existence saw Adam leave Paradise, it no longer wished to be subject to the transgressor. The sun did not want to shine by day, nor the moon by night, nor the stars to be seen by him. The springs of water did not want to well up for him, nor the rivers to flow. The very air itself thought about contracting itself and not providing breath for the rebel. The wild beasts and all the animals of the earth saw him stripped of his former glory and, despising him, immediately turned savagely against him. The sky was moving as if to fall justly down on him, and the very earth would not endure bearing him upon its back.' But God's love for man intervenes in this truly cosmic catastrophe: 'He restrains everything by His own power and compassion and goodness, suspends the assault of all creation and straight away subjects all of it once again to fallen man. He wills that creation serve man for whom it was made, and like him become corruptible, so that when again man becomes spiritual, incorruptible and immortal,

---

[56] St Gregory the Theologian, *Homily 38*, 11, *PG* 36.324A; St John Chrysostom, *On Genesis*, 13.4, *PG* 53.109.

[57] St Maximus the Confessor, *Ambigua*, *PG* 91.1356A.

then creation, too, will be freed from its slavery...and, together with man, be made new, and become incorruptible and wholly spiritual' (cf. Rom. 8: 20–1).[58]

God's compassionate intervention limited the consequences of man's rebellion. Man and the cosmos then had to wait for the blessed coming of the Lord.

* * *

As long as God's peace was absent, the world ceased to be a cosmos,* an adornment of God: 'When it ceased to be at peace, it also ceased to be a cosmos.'[59] But with the coming of Christ, divine peace returned to the world and the world became once again God's adornment. The created world too is invited to the festival of the new creation: 'Let creation be glad, let nature dance... Dance, you mountains, for Christ is born!'[60] In Christ Jesus, the cosmos and man coexist in peace.

The fact of the divine economy of Christ, however, not only means the return of man and creation to their state prior to the Fall. It is also man's — and through him creation's — ascent to the place *where Christ is seated at the right hand of God* (Col. 3: 1).

The Divine Liturgy is the Mystery whereby the peace of Christ is spread throughout creation. That is why we now petition God that every catastrophic disruption in nature may cease, that the earth may give her fruits to man, and the whole world may be at peace in accordance with God's command: 'The heavens, under His direction, move peacefully and are subject to Him. Day and night pursue the course that He ordained... The sun, the moon and the clusters of stars...follow the orbits appointed for them...

---

[58] St Symeon the New Theologian, *Ethical Discourse 1*, 2, *SC* 122, p. 190; tr. Fr A. Golitzin, St Symeon the New Theologian: *On the Mystical Life*, vol. 1 (Crestwood: St Vladimir's Seminary Press, 1995), p. 29.

[59] St Gregory the Theologian, *Homily 6*, 14, *PG*35.740C.

[60] Feast of the Annunciation, *Doxastikon* at Lauds; Feast of the Nativity, Lauds.

The seasons of spring, summer, autumn and winter follow one another in peaceful succession.'[61]

This is the blessing that we ask the Lord to extend: 'Grant us temperate and beneficial weather; send gentle rains upon the earth that it may bear fruit.'[62]

> **Deacon:** *For those who travel by land, air or water, for the sick, the suffering, for those in captivity and for their safety and salvation, let us pray to the Lord.*

Those who are weary and heavy laden

In this petition, we pray to Christ for all those who travel by sea, by land or by air. We pray for the sick, the weary, those in captivity. For everyone, we ask of the Lord that the troubles in their lives may become a path to His Kingdom.

Christ invites those who are weary and heavy laden to come to Him and be given rest. He invites them into the church and to the Divine Liturgy, because 'in the house of God is joy for those who are in distress, gladness for those who sorrow, comfort for those who are tormented, rest for those who are weary. For Christ says, *Come unto me all you who are weary and heavy laden, and I will give you rest* [Matt. 11: 28]. What is more welcome than these words? What is more delightful than this invitation? When the Lord invites you to the church, He is inviting you to a festival. He is asking you to rest from your labours... What inexpressible care, what a heavenly invitation!'[63]

---

[61] St Clement of Rome, *To Corinthians I*, 20, *PG* 1.248C–253A.

[62] Liturgy of St Basil, Prayer after the Consecration.

[63] St John Chrysostom, *Homily on Isaiah 1*, 1, *PG* 56.98.

The suffering and weary among us who accept Christ's invitation experience His fatherly love and presence. We experience what St Gregory the Theologian affirms: 'The soul that is afflicted is close to God.'[64] This presence of Christ is pre-eminently given to us in the Divine Liturgy.

Deacon: *For our deliverance from all affliction,*[65] *wrath, danger and constraint, let us pray to the Lord. Help us, save us, have mercy on us, and keep us, O God, by your grace.*

For our deliverance from affliction

When man first tasted sin and the pleasure that accompanies it, he tasted at the same time the bitterness of suffering and pain: 'Because of the pleasure that illogically invaded human nature, pain also gained entrance as a logical consequence... For the pleasure that is foreign to our nature is certainly followed, in the natural order of things, by pain.'[66]

God permitted man to taste pain in order to heal the wound caused him by sin: 'Immediately after the sin of our forefathers, God allowed death and pain, not to punish those who had sinned but rather to offer a medicine to those who had fallen sick.' What looks to us like a punishment is actually a divine therapy: 'It sounds like a penalty and a punishment when you hear, *In the sweat of your brow shall you eat bread* [Gen. 3: 19]. In reality, how-

---

[64] *Homily 17,* 5, PG 35.972B.

[65] Cf. Ps. 33: 5.

[66] St Maximus the Confessor, *Various Texts on Theology, on the Divine Economy, and Virtue and Vice,* 4.35, 37, PG 90.1320AB (*Philokalia,* vol. 2, p. 244).

ever, it is an admonition, a corrective chastisement, a medicine for the wounds caused by sin.'[67]

That is how the saints accepted the afflictions and tribulations in their lives: as a medicine from God. A medicine that heals the illness of sin and restores to man his health of soul. That is why they call afflictions the source of virtue: 'Amidst afflictions and troubles, the commandments of God are fulfilled.' The saints therefore exhort us: 'Endure your afflictions. For in the midst of afflictions virtues grow and are nurtured, like roses in the midst of thorns.' In the sight of the Lord, 'the afflictions that we endure for His sake are more precious than any prayer and sacrifice. And the odour of the sweat that is induced by our afflictions is superior to all perfumes.'[68]

Through afflictions, we are freed from sins, 'and if we have done some good, we make that good shine more brightly'.[69] In that way we progress towards the Kingdom of God which we must enter *through much tribulation* (Acts 14: 22). Yet *for the moment all discipline seems painful rather than pleasant; later it yields the peaceful fruit of righteousness to those who have been trained by it* (Heb. 12: 11). At the beginning, we experience the pain of affliction, but if we accept the temporary pain with patience, we go on to enjoy the *peaceful fruit*. The peace of Christ enters into our life.

The Apostle Peter posits the question: 'What is the benefit of patiently enduring the punishment for some wrong that we have done?' Then he goes on to answer: 'What has value and is pleasing to God is when we suffer and endure even though we are doing good. For Christ suffered for our sake, and left us an example so that we could follow in His footsteps' (cf. 1 Pet. 2: 20–21). If we endure without complaint the afflictions in our lives, we become imitators of the original victim of injustice, of Christ.

---

[67] St Nicholas Cabasilas, *On the Life in Christ*, 1, *PG* 150.513C; St John Chrysostom, *On Priscilla and Aquila*, 1.5, *PG* 51.194.

[68] St Isaac the Syrian, *Asc. Hom.*, 41, p. 205; St Neilos the Ascetic, *Chapters of Exhortation*, 92, *PG* 79.1257A; St Isaac the Syrian, *Asc. Hom.*, 6, p. 60.

[69] St John Chrysostom, *On Psalm 141*, 3, *PG* 55.446.

The saints loved afflictions because they knew that, if they accepted them without complaint, those afflictions would become the door to the Kingdom of God. But they also knew that while afflictions grant the Kingdom to those who are spiritually strong, they can lead the weak into despair. The petition to be delivered from afflictions evidently concerns the weak and not the strong.

The Elder Paisios used to say that 'one who is spiritually healthy thoroughly enjoys his sickness. It's the one who is [spiritually] sick that suffers.' There is a story about the Elder Philaretos, abbot of Konstamonitou Monastery, that one of his monks found him one day sitting on his stool looking dejected. 'What's the matter, Elder?' the monk asked him. And the Elder replied: 'Not a single temptation today, my child. God has abandoned us!'

St John Chrysostom considers that the only real calamity is sin. All the other ills that befall man he regards as calamities in name only: 'Names of calamities with no substantial reality.'[70] And yet in this petition, St John enjoins us to ask God to deliver us from afflictions. For it is better for us to be deprived of the crowns given to the warriors, than for affliction to lead us into despair, better to recognise our spiritual weakness and await everything from the Lord's great mercy.

* * *

In the heavenly Liturgy described by John the Evangelist in the Book of Revelation, a great throng from every nation and race takes part. All stand, dressed in white, before the throne of God and of the Lamb. One of the presbyters explains to the Evangelist who the people dressed in white are: *These are they who have come out of the great tribulation; they have washed their robes and made them white in the blood of the Lamb. Therefore are they before the throne of God, and serve Him day and night... The Lamb in the midst of the throne will be their shepherd, and He*

---

[70] *On the Statues*, 5.2, PG 49.70.

will guide them to springs of living water; and God will wipe away every tear from their eyes (Rev. 7: 14–7).

The *great tribulation* is this life. As the faithful go through the valley of afflictions, they partake in the Divine Liturgy. Through the grace of Christ's all-holy Blood, they whiten the robe of their soul, and arrive at the heavenly Altar clothed in white. There in their midst is the Lamb, Christ. His love shepherds them, and transforms the tears of the great tribulation into a torrent of the water of life.

That we may be delivered from wrath

The arrogance of the person who sins and does not repent draws down upon him the wrath of God. When we speak of the 'wrath of God', we should not of course have in mind some passion on God's part, but rather the punishment of the person. 'Even when God punishes, He remains dispassionate. For He does not act out of anger, but out of concern and great love for mankind.'[71] God knows that it is in the best interests of a proud person for him to be devoid of any good thing or any virtue: 'The wrath of God is the suspension of gifts of grace — a most salutary experience for every self-inflated intellect that boasts of the blessings bestowed by God as if they were its own achievements.' Through the instructive punishment of His anger, God 'leads the proud person to humility and decency'.[72] The person gains knowledge of his own weakness, cleanses his heart from the abscess of conceit, and receives the grace of God once more.

In this petition, we ask God that we may recognise our weakness and humble ourselves, before He abandons us in order to teach us a lesson.

---

[71] Cf. St John Chrysostom, *On Psalm 7*, 6, *PG* 55.90; *To the disgraced Theodore*, 4, *PG* 47.281.

[72] St Maximus the Confessor, *To Thalassius*, 52, *PG* 90.492A (*Philokalia*, vol. 2, p. 211, §§ 10 and 9).

That we may be delivered from danger

Every day, we learn about new life-threatening dangers and constantly hear about the natural disasters, wars, accidents and crimes that happen all over the world. This knowledge leads us into uncertainty, worry, anxiety, and we feel insecure in our very homes. A constant fear pervades the soul of modern man; he does not know from whom or when he is going to be in danger or what form that danger will take.

In this troubled world, we experience peace of mind and security only when we approach God with the trust of a little child. This is what Abba Isaac urges us to do: 'Approach God with the mind of an infant, and walk before Him in that manner, that you may be counted worthy of that paternal care that fathers show to their small children. It has been said that *the Lord preserves infants* [Ps. 114: 6]. An infant [that is, one who has the simplicity and trust of a small child] goes up to a snake and picks it up and puts it around his neck, and it does him no harm... On a freezing cold day he sits naked and suffers nothing, because his tender body, thanks to the hidden providence of God, is swaddled with another, invisible garment, that protects his every limb lest harm from any source come near them.'[73]

We beseech the Lord to show us how to avoid every danger, to grant us, that is to say, the trust that a small child has in its father.

That we may be delivered from constraint

In this petition, we ask the Lord first of all to deliver us from those circumstances that 'constrain' us, that *of necessity* force us into a particular state, force us even onto the path of God. For it is God's desire 'that nothing leading to sanctification should come about of necessity and by force, but through the free incli-

---

[73] *Asc. Hom.*, 72, p. 351.

nation of the soul.' Without freedom, there is no spiritual life: 'Anything that is brought about through force is not virtue.'[74]

We are also asking to be delivered from various material 'necessities' or 'needs'. Modern man is especially aware of these, for although he lives in a society that satisfies his material requirements as never before, his life is a drama of endless 'needs'. He satisfies one, and two new ones appear.

Our various 'needs' place a restriction on human freedom. St John Chrysostom says: 'The more you need, the more you limit your freedom... Let us get rid of this terrible slavery, and finally become free. Why do we invent all kinds of endless bonds for ourselves?' And he goes on: 'It is truly desirable and expedient to cut away everything that binds us, and seize the heavenly city.'[75]

In this petition, we ask the Lord that the bonds of slavery to all the needs which constrain us may be cut. With the Psalmist we ask Christ: Lord, *deliver me from my necessities* (Ps. 24: 17).

Let not your hearts be troubled

The Divine Liturgy is the presence of the risen Christ. We come together in church and gather round the life-giving tomb – the holy Altar – longing to see Him, to hear Him, to touch Him (cf. Luke 24: 39), and to become, like the disciples, guests with Him at His table (cf. John 21: 13).

But, sadly, we are not myrrh-bearers who run to the Master's tomb with our hearts aflame with divine love and desire. It is not the boldness of love that brings us to God's house but fear of the dangers that threaten us. Often we form a gathering of frightened and anxious disciples, a gathering of believers who have closed the doors of their hearts to the supra-rational love of myrrh-bearing souls and whose hopes for the heavenly Kingdom

---

[74] St Methodius of Olympus, *Symposium of the ten Virgins*, 3.13, PG 18.81C; St John of Damascus, *On the two Wills in Christ*, 19, PG 95.149B.
[75] *On John*, 80.3, PG 59.437–8.

barely flicker. The myrrh-bearers in every age shut their eyes to dangers, while those of little faith shut their hearts to hope.

In this assembly, Christ appears. Like a bridegroom He comes forth from the tomb and comes among us. *The doors being shut* (John 20: 19), He enters into our hearts. His presence dissolves our fears, His love give us His peace: *Let not your hearts be troubled nor afraid... my peace I give to you* (John 14: 1, 27).

Deacon: *Commemorating our all-holy, pure, most blessed and glorious Lady, Theotokos and Ever-Virgin Mary, with all the Saints, let us entrust ourselves and one another and our whole life to Christ our God.*
Choir: [*All-holy Theotokos, save us.*] *To you, O Lord.*

Let us entrust ourselves to Christ our God

The saints know from their own experience that 'the soul which in faith has surrendered itself to God, once and for all time, and has liberally tasted of His help, will not take thought for itself again but falls silent in awe-struck wonder.' Entrusting our lives totally to God, however, is not something that is achieved easily. It becomes a reality 'when our hearts do not censure us...when we disdain our own concerns so as to concern ourselves with the things of Christ'. For this reason we ask the help of the Lady Mother of God and all the saints, and that is what is meant here by the word *commemorating*: 'calling to our aid, beseeching'.[76]

There is also another reason why we beseech the Theotokos for her aid. The act of entrusting our lives to the Lord is something

---

[76] St Isaac the Syrian, *Asc. Hom.*, 52, p. 253; St Nicholas Cabasilas, *Comm. Liturgy*, 14, PG 150.400A.

analogous to her own dedication to God. The Mother of God, at the age of three, was dedicated to the Lord in order to become His living throne, and in a similar way every believer is offered to the Lord in order to become His dwelling-place. On the day of her Entry into the Temple, the Virgin went 'to be dedicated as a dwelling for the ruler of all'. At the Divine Liturgy, the celebrant exhorts us to dedicate ouselves to Christ, so that He may dwell within us. He exhorts us to become like the Most Pure Virgin — 'the dwelling-place of Jesus, beautiful and lovely'.[77]

The Priest, in a low voice, reads the prayer: *Lord, our God, whose might is ineffable and whose glory is beyond understanding, whose mercy is without measure and whose love for mankind is beyond all telling, look down upon us and upon this holy house, Master, according to your loving kindness, and bestow on us and on those who pray with us your acts of abundant mercy and compassion.*

(aloud) *For to you belong all glory, honour and worship, to the Father, and to the Son, and to the Holy Spirit, now and for ever, and to the ages of ages.*

Choir: *Amen.*

God's love for mankind beyond all telling

In the first prayer of the Divine Liturgy, the priest addresses God Himself. 'Just as when you have boldness and a close friendship with some important person you are able to approach him and speak to him privately — that is how it is with a priest. Having

---

[77] Entry of the Mother of God into the Temple (21 November), *Doxastikon* at the *Lity** and the *Aposticha.**

boldness before Christ because of the grace and dignity of the priesthood, he approaches Him and tells Him all his secrets privately, that is, in a very careful, quiet and low voice. For that is how the priest says the prayers, and it demonstrates two things: first, the extreme majesty of the Person with whom he is speaking, and secondly the pure love and great boldness that [the priest] has towards Him.'[78]

* * *

As the priest says in the prayer, God's love for mankind and His mercy are beyond human measure and beyond human words. The measure that does reveal God's love for mankind is the event of the Incarnation: *On account of Your inexpressible and boundless love for mankind, You became man without change or alteration.* 'We human beings were the reason for the Incarnation of God the Word, and it was for our salvation that He showed such love for mankind as to be born and manifest Himself in a human body.'[79]

God's love is unbounded in magnitude and noble in character. From God we receive not merely a human sympathy, but the love of a king and leader. 'Just as His love for mankind is ineffable... so also the manner in which He approaches us and works for our good is wonderful, such as is fitting only to the God who does wondrous things.'[80]

God loves us in an exclusive manner, and wants us to love Him in the same way. 'From wherever we are He brings us back to Himself, and does not allow us to fix our intellect on anything else, nor to love any created thing... With a wondrous compul-

---

[78] Anonymous Hesychast, *Niptiki Theoria [Neptic Contemplation]*, (Thessaloniki: Orthodoxos Kypseli, 1979), pp. 199–200. The spiritual experience of this anonymous saint is an answer to concerns about the way in which the prayers at the Divine Liturgy are read.

[79] Divine Liturgy, Prayer of the Cherubic Hymn; St Athanasius the Great, *On the Incarnation*, 4, PG 25.104A.

[80] St Nicholas Cabasilas, *On the Life in Christ*, 1, PG 150.501CD.

sion and an authority full of love for mankind, He draws us towards Himself alone, and unites us to Himself alone. By this "force" he has gathered into the house and to the feast those He invited, saying to His servant: *Compel them to come in, that my house may be filled* [Luke 14: 23].'[81]

God prepares the Table of Life and invites man to seat himself at it. Yet His love for mankind has limitless room. The pastors of the Church, who invite the guests, tell Him: Lord, what You commanded has been done, and *still there is room* (Luke 14: 22). It is the 'room' of His noble love which remains empty as long as there are people who refuse to come into His house and sit down to His Supper. Until then, the mystery of love towards mankind will be at work: the Good Shepherd will be seeking the lost sheep; Love will be searching for the lost coin (cf. Luke 15: 4–10).

The first Antiphon is sung, with the refrain:*
Through the prayers of the Theotokos, O Saviour, save us.

The soul is a consummate musician

Psalmody or singing is one of the three ways in which we address God: we *sing* sacred hymns, we *read* prayers and we *intone* petitions and readings.

Psalmody is especially helpful when we are struggling to communicate with Christ: 'Nothing so exalts the soul...and aids it to live spiritually and not be concerned with everyday matters, as a harmonious melody and a rhythmical hymn to God... Great benefit and abundant sanctification are to be gained from spiritual

---

[81] St Nicholas Cabasilas, *On the Life in Christ*, 1, PG 150.500D–501A.

psalmody, and it can become the foundation for the whole of spiritual life. For the words of the hymns purify the soul, and the Holy Spirit enters immediately into the soul that sings them.' 'One who sings in a genuine manner [that is, attentively] renews his soul and becomes a temple of the Holy Spirit.'[82]

If the soul that sings is to draw to itself the grace of the Holy Spirit, it is not enough for the melody to accord with the rules of music; it must also be consonant with the praises sung by the angels. In church psalmody, 'if someone is aged, or very young, or has a poor voice, or is entirely ignorant of rhythm, he cannot be reproached, for what is required is a vigilant soul, a wakeful intellect, a heart filled with compunction, a healthy mind and a clear conscience.' *Sing praises to the Lord, O you His saints*, says the Prophet David (Ps. 29: 5). 'Those who are able to sing to God are those who send forth their psalmody with a pure heart and who are saintly and keep His commandments, for it is they who fittingly observe the spiritual rhythms.'[83]

It is possible to sing praises to the Lord without ceasing. 'The soul is a consummate musician, an instrumentalist. The instrument is the body, which serves as lute, harp and lyre... Desiring to teach you that you should sing praise to Him and glorify Him always, God joined together instrument and player [that is, the body and the soul] in a permanent union.'[84]

In the Orthodox Church, we do not use musical instruments in worship. Every believer is a musical instrument made by God, and at the same time a musician. If the musician (the soul) keeps the instrument (the body) pure and uses it properly, the two together raise to the Creator a hymn of praise that is pleasing to God. For the hymn that is sacred 'is born from the soul's piety,

---

[82] St John Chrysostom, *On Psalm 41*, 1, PG 55.156-7; *One Lawgiver*, 3, PG 56.402.

[83] Ibid. *On Psalm 41*, 2, PG 55.158; St Basil the Great, *On Psalm 29*, 3, PG 29.312C.

[84] St John Chrysostom, *Homily on Holy Week and on Psalm 145*, 3, PG 55.522.

nourished by a good conscience, and accepted in heaven by God.'[85]

In the worship of the Church, psalmody in usually antiphonal, meaning that the hymns are sung alternately by two choirs. St Ignatius the Godbearer first introduced antiphonal hymns into the Antiochian Church, when 'in a vision, he saw angels singing hymns to the Holy Trinity in antiphonal style'. Like the holy angels, man too is created to glorify God. He was created in order to sing antiphonally with the angels. According to St Gregory the Theologian, man is a 'creature antiphonal to the angels'.[86] The angels on the one side and humans on the other form two choirs so as to sing ceaseless praise to their Creator.

Behold the Lamb of God

The Divine Liturgy as an entity is the Mystery of the life of Christ. This means that each moment of it is the sacramental re-living of a particular period in Christ's life. The verses of the Antiphons, which are taken from the prophetic Psalter, 'signify the beginning of Christ's presence on earth...when He was in the world, and the world did not recognise Him. They signify the period before John the Baptist, before that Lamp [the Forerunner] was lit [cf. John 5: 35]. For at that time, there was a need for words of prophecy. Later, the One who was prophesied appeared in person, and then there was no need even for the prophets themselves, since John the Baptist simply pointed to the One who stood before him [cf. John 1: 29].'[87]

The Psalms 'are sung as a prelude to the sacred mystagogy', and prepare us spiritually: 'They are a preliminary cleansing and an initial preparation'[88] for the Divine Liturgy. The Psalms do the work

---

[85] St John Chrysostom, *Homily on being ordained Priest*, 1, *PG* 48.694.
[86] Bishop George of Alexandria, *Halkin*, p.156; *Dogmatic Poem 32*, *PG* 37.513.35.
[87] St Nicholas Cabasilas, *Comm. Liturgy*, 18, *PG* 150.408C.
[88] Ibid. 16, *PG* 150.404BC.

of the Baptist: they prepare the way of the Lord (cf. Matt. 3: 3) and summon us to receive Him. And when He comes into the eucharistic assembly, they point Him out to us: *Behold the Lamb of God* (John 1: 29). Therefore *come, let us rejoice in the Lord; let us make a joyful noise to God our Saviour* (Ps. 94: 1).

Deacon: *Again and again in peace, let us pray to the Lord. Help us, save us, have mercy on us...*
Commemorating our all-holy, pure, most blessed and glorious Lady...
Choir: [*All-holy Theotokos, save us.*] *To you, O Lord.*

Again and again let us pray to the Lord

The Divine Liturgy is the journey that enables man to encounter, see and commune with God. On this journey, every step is at the same time an end and a beginning.

Again and again... This is not a repetition of earlier supplications; it is a search for new experiences. Whatever good 'that is obtained each time is certainly greater than everything obtained previously. Yet that good does not limit the search; instead, for those who are progressing upwards, the end of that which has already been found becomes the starting point for obtaining higher things. So one who progresses upwards never stops, because every starting point gives rise to a new starting point... As the soul progresses upwards, it passes through ever higher states and makes its way towards that which has no limits.'[89]

Again and again... We never tire of saying the same words to the Lord and asking for the same things. And when His love gives

---

[89] St Gregory of Nyssa, *On the Song of Songs*, 8, PG 44.941C.

them to us, we see that they are not the same as those we already have. We discover that as long as we are in this world, there is always the possibility of coming closer to God's peace, to the love of the Mother of God, to the communion of the saints. For the more our bodies and souls are cleansed from sin, the more abundantly the grace of the Divine Liturgy is given to us.

The Priest, in a low voice, reads the prayer: *Lord, our God, save your people and bless your inheritance; protect the fullness of your Church, sanctify those who love the beauty of your house, glorify them in return by your divine power, and do not forsake us who hope in you.*

(aloud) *For yours is the might, and yours the kingdom, the power and the glory, of the Father, and of the Son, and of the Holy Spirit, now and for ever, and to the ages of ages.*

Choir: *Amen.* And the second Antiphon is sung, with the refrain: *At the prayers of your Saints, save us, O Lord.*[90]

To share in the inheritance of the saints

Through Baptism, we have become children of God. We have not simply been freed from sin; we have also gained boundless good things. Previously, we were prisoners of the Devil; now we are 'freemen and citizens of the Church. We who formerly lived in

---

[90] Having sought the intercession of the Mother of God in the first antiphon, we now supplicate 'all who have been well-pleasing to her Son' (St Germanus, *Contemplation*, PG 98.404D). This refrain appears in early manuscripts, and is used today on the Holy Mountain.

the shame of sin now enjoy boldness of approach and justification. For we are not only freemen but also saints; not only saints, but also righteous; not only righteous, but also sons; not only sons, but also heirs; not only heirs, but also brethren of Christ.'[91]

When the Divine Eucharist is celebrated, we are gathered together in the church 'where so many brethren are present, where the Holy Spirit is, where Jesus and His Father are in our midst'.[92] At the Divine Liturgy, we stand before the holy Altar, *with joy, giving thanks to the Father who has made us fit to share in the inheritance of the saints in light* (Col. 1: 11–12).

Through the Divine Liturgy, however, not only do we become Christ's inheritance. Christ Himself becomes the inheritance of all the faithful: 'He who is seated on high with the Father is at that moment held in the hands of all.' 'This is what God in His love for mankind accomplishes in the soul that longs for Him and draws near to Him... He Himself becomes the inheritance of the soul, and the soul becomes the inheritance of the Lord.'[93]

Choir: *Glory to God...both now...*
Only-begotten Son and Word of God, who, being immortal, accepted for our salvation to take flesh from the holy Theotokos and Ever-Virgin Mary, and without change became man; you were crucified, O Christ God, by death trampling on death, being one of the Holy Trinity, glorified with the Father and the Holy Spirit: save us![94]

---

[91] St John Chrysostom, *Baptismal Catecheses*, 3.5, *SC* 50, p. 153.

[92] Ibid. *To those who have deserted the Assembly*, 2, *PG* 51.70.

[93] Ibid. *On the Priesthood*, 3.4, *PG* 48.642; *Macarian Homilies*, 46.3–4, *PG* 34.793C–796A.

[94] The *troparion* 'Only-begotten Son...' 'was introduced by the Emperor Justinian' (Theodore of Andida, *Protheoria*, 12, *PG* 140.433C).

The God who is not proud

The *only-begotten Son and Word of God* is a God who meets us on our level, 'who is not proud'. 'He who transcends all understanding and overwhelms all thought...accepted to become man, to take flesh — the flesh He had fashioned out of soil and clay —, to enter into a virginal womb, to be carried in that womb for nine months, to be nourished with milk and to undergo everything proper to humans.'[95]

St John Chrysostom was particularly aware of the magnitude of the divine condescension: 'He who was in the bosom of God the Father accepted to take the form of a servant and to undergo all the states pertaining to the body...gradually growing up, being circumcised, offering sacrifice, being hungry, thirsty and tired, and finally enduring death itself... The Creator of all accepted all this for us and for our salvation... He who created all things out of nothing, He who makes the earth tremble when He so much as glances at it [cf. Ps. 103: 32], the radiance of whose glory even the Cherubim cannot look upon... This is He who for us and for our salvation accepted to become man!'[96]

For our salvation Jesus Christ accepted to become man from the Most Holy Mother of God and to combat the Devil who slays humans. As man, He fought the battle that we ourselves should have fought, but were unable to; and as God, He won a great victory: 'God takes up the struggle on behalf of mankind because He was also human. And again, man [the man Jesus Christ] conquers sin as He is pure of any sin, because He is also God. In this way our nature is freed from reproach and crowned with the wreath of victory, because sin has been defeated.'[97]

Christ has triumphed over the Devil, sin and death. And that

---

[95] St Symeon the New Theologian, *Thanksgiving 2, SC* 113, p. 340; St John Chrysostom, *On 'Father, if it be possible...'*, 3, *PG* 51.37.

[96] *On Genesis*, 23.6, *PG* 53.205.

[97] St Nicholas Cabasilas, *On the Life in Christ*, 1, *PG* 150.513B.

is why the paean of victory is sung with gratitude in the assembly of the faithful.

Deacon: *Again and again...*

Help us, save us...

Commemorating our all-holy, pure, most blessed and glorious Lady...

Choir: *[All-holy Theotokos, save us.] To you, O Lord.*

The Priest, in a low voice, reads the prayer: *You have given us grace to make these common and united prayers, and have promised that when two or three agree in your name you will grant their requests; fulfil now the petitions of your servants as is expedient, granting us in this present age the knowledge of your truth and in the age to come eternal life.*

(aloud) *For you, O God, are good and love mankind, and to you we give glory, to the Father, and to the Son, and to the Holy Spirit, now and for ever, and to the ages of ages.*

Choir: *Amen.* And the third Antiphon is sung, with the refrain: *Son of God, wonderful in the Saints, save us who sing to you: Alleluia!**

Common and united prayers

The Church is a communion of love, and this is made clear in the common and united liturgical prayers given to us by the Lord. The church building too, as the place where the assembly of the faithful takes place, expresses this communion of love. 'Churches came into being, not so that we who come together should be di-

vided, but so that we who are divided should be united. And this is shown by the eucharistic assembly [that takes place in the church].'[98]

This loving unity of the faithful is evident in the descriptions of the eucharistic assemblies of the first Christians. On the Lord's Day 'there is a gathering of all the faithful in the same place and the memoirs of the Apostles are read', records St Justin Martyr, writing in the second century. 'Then we all stand and pray... After that, bread and wine and water are offered, the celebrant again offers up prayers and thanksgiving to the Lord according to his ability, and the people show their affirmation by saying *Amen*.'[99]

* * *

The gathering for the Liturgy is also called a *syn-odos* (literally, a 'way together'), which signifies that we are all journeying together and travelling along the same way, that Way being Christ (cf. John 14: 6). Even if they are only two or three in number, the faithful who offer the bloodless Sacrifice together with the celebrant form 'the whole body of the Church, which with one soul and one voice offers up its prayer to God'.[100]

Christ gave His promise that wherever two or three believers are gathered in His name, He will be in their midst; He will hear their common prayers and fulfil their petitions (cf. Matt. 18: 19–20). Even so, it often happens that we come together in Christ's name and ask something of His love, but our petition is not answered. St John Chrysostom explains why this happens. When Christ speaks of a gathering of the faithful in His name, He does not only mean their coming together, but principally He is looking for love in Christ between them as well as for virtue in general. The saint says: 'If you ask for that which is for your good, if you contribute all that is required of you, if you live in an apos-

---

[98] St John Chrysostom, *On 1 Corinthians*, 27.3, PG 61.228.

[99] *First Apology*, 67, PG 6.429B.

[100] St John Chrysostom, *On the Obscurity of the Old Testament*, 2.4, PG 56.182.

tolic manner and in concord and with love for your neighbour, then your prayers will be heard; for the Lord loves mankind.' Our effort to express love in the way we live bears fruit if it is undertaken for the Lord's sake. Whatever we do should be for love of Him. 'For the love that has Christ as its foundation is constant, strong and inexhaustible.'[101]

It is this love, grounded in Christ, that nourishes the united prayers offered by the faithful. St John underlines this: 'It is possible, of course, to pray at home; but it is impossible to pray at home as you would in church, where there is such a throng of Fathers, and where powerful prayer is offered up to God with one mind. When you petition the Lord on your own, you are not heard as when you petition Him together with your brethren. For here in the church there is something in addition: the concord and agreement of the faithful, the bond of love and the prayers of the priests.'[102]

The Lord who gave us common and united prayers is Himself the 'song' of the faithful. St Ignatius writes: 'It is through your harmonious love that Jesus Christ is the hymn sung. May you all become one choir, so that you have agreement and concord, and become deiform by grace [imitators of God], and in unity and with one voice sing to God the Father through Jesus Christ. Thus He will hear you and will recognise you by your good works as members of His Son...and you will be for ever participants in God.'[103]

From the assembly of the faithful 'one prayer, one supplication, one mind, one hope in love' is offered up with one voice 'in blameless joy'.[104]

---

[101] *On Matthew*, 60.2-3, PG 58.587-8.

[102] *On the Incomprehensible*, 3.6, PG 48.725.

[103] *On Ephesians*, 4, PG 5.648B.

[104] St Ignatius of Antioch, *Magnesians*, 7, PG 5.668B.

2. THE ENTRANCE WITH THE GOSPEL BOOK AND THE SACRED READINGS

While the third Antiphon is being sung, the Priest takes the Gospel Book from the Altar, gives it to the Deacon, and circling the Altar anti-clockwise they process out of the sanctuary through the north door, preceded by servers carrying lighted candles and liturgical fans, to the middle of the church, where they bow their heads reverently.

Deacon: *Let us pray to the Lord. Lord, have mercy.*

The Priest, in a low voice, says the Prayer of the Entrance:

Master, Lord our God, who has established orders and armies of Angels and Archangels in heaven to minister to your glory; grant that with us the holy Angels may enter, concelebrating, and glorifying with us your goodness. For to you belong all glory, honour and worship, to the Father, the Son and the Holy Spirit, now and for ever, and to the ages of ages. Amen.

The Deacon says to the Priest: *Master, bless the holy entrance.*

And the Priest, blessing the entrance, says: *Blessed is the entrance of your holy ones, now and for ever, and to the ages of ages. Amen.*

The Deacon, lifting up the Gospel Book, says aloud: *Wisdom. Stand upright.*

The Choir sings: *Come, let us worship and fall down before Christ. Son of God, wonderful in the Saints, save us who sing to you: Alleluia!*

Angels and humans intermingle

Until the seventh century, the Divine Liturgy began with the entrance with the Gospel Book. The celebrant vested in the sacristy,* took the Gospel Book from there and entered into the church accompanied by the faithful.[1] If a bishop was celebrating, he would also enter the church at this point and put on his episcopal vestments in front of the faithful.

The entrance with the Gospel Book is called the Little Entrance, and signifies 'the coming of the Son of God and His entry into this world'. Likewise, the bishop's entry into the church 'is an image and type of the Son of God's first coming into the world in the flesh... Through this coming, Christ brought the human race back to the original Grace of the Kingdom.'[2] Now, through the Divine Liturgy, Christ invites us to sit at table with Him in His Kingdom.

The entry of the faithful into the church, which in earlier centuries took place at this time, immediately before the entrance of the bishop, signifies 'that they are transported from wickedness and ignorance to virtue and knowledge'.[3] Man changes his orientation: the centre of his life becomes the Divine Liturgy. So the entry of the Christian believer into the church for the sacred assembly is not only a symbol, but an act: it is the believer's entry into the life of Christ. It is man's participation in the life of the *Theanthropos*.

According to the present-day order of the Divine Liturgy, the priest takes the Gospel Book, which is an image of Christ, from

---

[1] A clear indication that the faithful used to enter the church at this point with the celebrant is to be found in the Prayer of the Entrance in the oldest *Euchologion** [Prayer Book] (8th century): 'Benefactor and Maker of all creation, accept the Church as she draws near...'. This prayer was read in front of the church door, after which the celebrant would bless the door, saying, 'Blessed is the entrance of Your holy [ones]' (Trembelas, *Leitourgiai*, p. 38).

[2] St Germanus, *Contemplation*, *PG* 98.405C; St Maximus the Confessor, *Mystagogy*, 8, *PG* 91.688C.

[3] Ibid. *Mystagogy*, 9, *PG* 91.689A.

the Altar, and holding it at head height, so that his face is covered by Him who comes — Christ — he enters the nave. The lighted candle that precedes the Gospel Book is the symbol of the Forerunner, who is *the burning and shining lamp* (John 5: 35).

The deacon proclaims: *Wisdom. Stand upright.* It is as if to say: *Behold, I bring you good news of a great joy, which will be to all people* (Luke 2: 10). The faithful experience the miraculous appearance of angels that took place in Bethlehem: *And suddenly there was with the angel a multitude of the heavenly host, praising God* (Luke 2: 13). What happened in Bethlehem happens also in the Divine Liturgy: 'Angels and humans intermingle; for where the King is present, there His retinue appears as well.'[4]

In the Prayer of the Entrance, the priest asks that we may experience the mystery of the presence of the angels and their concelebration in the Divine Liturgy; to live this as did our God-bearing Fathers. It is recounted in the life of St Spyridon that 'when he celebrated, angels were in attendance and concelebrated with him. When he said *Peace be to all*, they would answer melodiously from outside the sanctuary, *And with your spirit*. They would respond similarly to the other proclamations.' St John Chrysostom also tells of a virtuous Elder who 'during the Divine Liturgy was accounted worthy to see a host of angels with shining garments surrounding the holy Altar, with their heads inclined downwards as soldiers stand in the presence of the King'.[5]

The Choir sings the *Apolytikia* and *Kontakion* for the day.

Deacon: *Let us pray to the Lord.*

Choir: *Lord, have mercy.*

---

[4] Theophany, *Lity.*

[5] St Nikodimus of the Holy Mountain, *Synaxarion*, 12 December; *On the Priesthood*, 6.4, PG 48.681.

Priest: *For you, our God, are holy, and to you we give glory, to the Father, and to the Son, and to the Holy Spirit, now and for ever,*

Deacon: *and to the ages of ages.*

Choir: *Amen.* Then the Choir sings the Trisagion Hymn: *Holy God, Holy Mighty, Holy Immortal, have mercy on us* (three times).[6]

While the hymn is being sung, the Priest, in a low voice, says the Prayer of the Trisagion:

O holy God, who rest among the holy, are hymned with the thrice-holy acclamation by the Seraphim, glorified by the Cherubim and worshipped by every heavenly Power, who brought all things out of non-being into being and created man according to your image and likeness and adorned him with every gift of your grace, who give wisdom and understanding to those who ask, and do not reject the sinner, but for our salvation have established repentance; you have counted us, your humble and unworthy servants, worthy to stand at this time before the glory of your holy Altar, and to offer you due worship and praise. Accept, Master, the Thrice-holy Hymn even from the mouth of us sinners, and visit us in your goodness. Pardon us every offence, voluntary and involuntary; sanctify our souls and bodies, and grant that we may worship you in holiness all the days of our life; at the prayers of the holy Theotokos and of all the Saints who have been well-pleasing to you in every age. For you, our God, are holy, and to you we give glory, to the Father, and to the Son, and to the Holy Spirit, now and for ever, and to the ages of ages. Amen.

---

[6] Cf. Isa. 6: 3, Ps. 41: 3.

The Priest and the Deacon also say the Trisagion alternatively, making three bows before the Holy Table.

Then the Deacon says to the Priest: *Master, command.* The Priest goes to the holy Prothesis, saying, *Blessed is he who comes in the name of the Lord.*[7] And on returning, as the Priest turns to the throne on high* the Deacon says: *Master, bless the throne on high.*

Priest: *Blessed are you on the throne of glory of your Kingdom, who are seated upon the Cherubim,*[8] *always, now and for ever, and to the ages of ages. Amen.*

A festival shared by heaven and earth

At the holy entrance, the angels enter together with Christ. After the entrance, angels and humans together sing the Thrice-holy Hymn: '*Holy God* — meaning God the Father; *Holy Mighty* — the Son and Word, for He bound the Devil who had power over us, and through the Cross He rendered powerless him who had the power of death, and gave us life and the power and authority to trample the Devil underfoot; *Holy Immortal* — that is, the Holy Spirit, the Giver of life, through whom the entire creation is quickened and preserved, and cries out *Have mercy on us…* The Thrice-holy Hymn is sung three times, because the three-fold appellation of *Holy* applies to each of the three Persons of the one Godhead: each of Them is holy, and mighty, and immortal.'[9]

The Thrice-holy Hymn 'has been taken in part from the angels, and in part from the Book of Psalms by the Prophet David; it was made into one hymn by the Church of Christ and dedicated to the Holy Trinity. The *holy*, which is sung three times, belongs to the

---

[7] Ps. 117: 26.

[8] Dan. 3: 54–5 [Hymn of the Three Young Men]; Ps. 98: 1.

[9] St Germanus, *Contemplation*, PG 98.408C–409A.

angels [cf. Isa. 6: 3], while *God, mighty* and *immortal* come from
the blessed David, who says: *My soul thirsts for God, the mighty,
the living* [Ps. 41: 3]. Our holy Church received all this and joined
the psalm with the angelic hymn and added the petition, *Have
mercy on us...*, in order to show both the harmony of the Old Testament with the New, and that angels and men form one Church
and one choir.'[10]

During the Divine Liturgy we participate in the choir of the angels, we sing with the Seraphim. That is why St John Chrysostom
urges us: 'Consider who they are who sing with you, and that should
be enough to move you to vigilance. It should be sufficient when
you remember that, while being clothed in a body and bound up
with the flesh, you have been accounted worthy to hymn the
Lord, who is common to all, together with the bodiless powers.'[11]

Together with the angelic powers, we sinful and feeble humans offer up the Thrice-holy Hymn. 'How marvellous are the
gifts of Christ! In heaven above, the companies of angels praise
Him. In the holy Churches below, men sing and imitate the angelic doxology. Above, the Seraphim chant the Thrice-holy Hymn
with vigour. Below, the host of believers raises the same hymn.
This is a festival shared by heaven and earth: one thanksgiving,
one rejoicing, one joyful shared psalmody. For this festival has
been established by the indescribable condescension of the Lord,
brought into unity by the Holy Spirit, and the harmony of its music has been accomplished by the will of the Father. The harmonious rhythm of its songs comes from heaven; and as it is moved
by the Holy Trinity, as by a plectrum, it produces a pleasing and
blessed melody, the angelic song, the unceasing harmony.'[12]

Heaven and earth together move forward towards the Altar.
All creation, both visible and invisible, is gathered together in
one place and keeps festival, praising the Lord.

---

[10] St Nicholas Cabasilas, *Comm. Liturgy*, 20, *PG* 150.412D.

[11] Cf. *On Matthew*, 19.3, *PG* 57.277; *On the Incomprehensible*, 4.5, *PG* 48.734.

[12] St John Chrysostom, *Homily on Isaiah 1*, 1, *PG* 56.97–8

The throne on high

In the singing of the Thrice-holy Hymn, the celebrant and faithful have identified themselves with the angelic hosts in the task of glorifying God. Now the priest, as he moves between the holy Prothesis and the throne on high, imitates the angelic hosts 'which fly on two wings' around the throne of God, 'praising Him with never-silent hymns of praise'.[13] So not only through the angelic Thrice-holy Hymn, but also through angelic movements do we experience the reality of heaven and earth concelebrating together.

As he goes to the holy Prothesis, the celebrant glorifies the Lord who is coming into our world: *Blessed is He who comes in the name of the Lord*. The Lord is *blessed* and *Son of the Blessed One* (Mark 14: 61). We bless and glorify Him, and that does not mean 'that we add anything to Him, but rather that we ourselves gain something of great magnitude.'[14] We bless (*eulogo* in Greek) Christ meaning, literally, that we offer Him *a good word* (Ps. 44: 2). And He reciprocates by offering Himself, who is the Word and the Good: the 'good Word' who was born of the Father.[15]

* * *

From the holy Prothesis, the celebrant goes to the *throne on high*, that is, to the bishop's throne, traditionally situated on the east side of the Holy Table, which symbolises the throne of God. 'The throne on high signifies that Jesus is seated above the heavens.'[16] This symbolism is underlined also by the doxology pronounced by the celebrant: *Blessed are You on the throne of glory of Your Kingdom*. At the same time, the celebrant is imitating the Cherubim who bless God: *Blessed is the glory of the Lord from His place* (Ezek. 3: 12).

---

[13] Liturgy of St Basil, Prayer of the Anaphora.
[14] St John Chrysostom, *On Psalm 134*, 7, PG 55.399.
[15] St Athanasius the Great, *Homily III against the Arians*, 67, PG 26.464C.
[16] St Symeon of Thessaloniki, *Consecration*, 135, PG 155.345B.

The earthly Divine Liturgy is a living image of the heavenly Liturgy: *After this I looked, and behold, a great multitude which no man could number, from every nation, from all tribes and peoples and tongues, standing before the throne and before the Lamb, clothed in white robes, with palm branches in their hands, and crying with a loud voice, 'Salvation belongs to our God who sits upon the throne, and to the Lamb!' And all the angels...worshipped God, saying, 'Amen! Blessing and glory and wisdom and thanksgiving and honour and power and might be to our God for ever and ever! Amen* (Rev. 7: 9–12).

Reader: *Prokeimenon* of the Apostle.*
Deacon: *Let us attend.*
The Reader proclaims the *prokeimenon's* verse.
Deacon: *Wisdom.*
The Reader proclaims the title of the apostolic reading.
Deacon: *Let us attend.*
The Reader intones the proscribed passage from the Apostle, and the Deacon censes the sanctuary, the principal icons and the people.
When the Reader has finished, the Priest says: *Peace to you, the reader.* And the *Alleluia* is sung with its verses.

The foretelling of Christ's coming

The reader proclaims the *prokeimenon* before the reading from the Apostle because this introduces us to the mystery of the Word.

The *prokeimenon* symbolises 'the revelation of divine mysteries by the prophets, and the foretelling of the coming of Christ

the King'.[17] Verses from the Psalms are used as *prokeimena* because these above all recount the wonders of the divine economy.

In earlier times, the *prokeimenon* was an entire psalm, sung by the faithful divided into two choirs. The delightfulness of the songs of the *prokeimenon*, as of all the hymns, reveal 'the sweetness of divine good things; that sweetness that stirs our souls to perfect and blessed desire for God'. Fortified by divine pleasure, our souls 'forget their previous labouring for virtue and, renewed, they ardently pursue the divine and incorruptible good things which they have not yet obtained'.[18]

Psalmody purifies the heart and illumines the intellect so as to receive the message of salvation. Through its sacred content, 'hymnody brings the disposition of our souls into harmony with that which will shortly be celebrated; and the accord of the divine songs teaches oneness of mind with things divine, with ourselves and with others... Then whatever in the sacred Psalms is abbreviated and obscure is expounded in more numerous and clearer images by the readings from the sacred texts of the holy Apostles.'[19]

Through the fire of their poetry and the ardour of their words, the verses of the *prokeimenon* prepare us to hear the Word of God. And the word of the New Testament illuminates the prophetic word of the Old.

We beheld His glory

The entire first part of the Divine Liturgy is summarised in the words of St John the Evangelist: *The Word became flesh and dwelt among us, and we beheld His glory, glory as of the only-begotten of the Father, full of grace and truth* (John 1: 14).

The readings from Scripture 'signify the manifestation of the Lord, as it came about gradually after He entered into public life.

---

[17] St Germanus, *Contemplation*, PG 98.412A.
[18] St Maximus the Confessor, *Mystagogy*, 11, 24; PG 91.689C, 708A.
[19] St Dionysius the Areopagite, *Church Hierarchy*, 3.3.5, PG 3.432AB.

For at first [at the Little Entrance] the Gospel Book is presented closed. This signifies the Lord's epiphany [in the River Jordan], at which He Himself was silent while the Father showed Him forth… The readings, however, signify His fuller manifestation, when Christ mingled with everyone publicly and made Himself known, not only through His own words but also by what He taught the disciples to say when He sent them to *the lost sheep of the house of Israel* [Matt. 10: 6]. That is why the apostolic writings and the Holy Gospel itself are read.'[20]

By means of the readings, we experience the mystery of the Incarnation of the Word. Through the Holy Anaphora, the offering of the Word and communion in that Word are celebrated. The readings are the word of God: *theo-logia* (theology). The Holy Anaphora is God's work of love: *theo-ergia* (divine action — theurgy). And '*theoergia* is the consummation of *theologia*.'[21] Through the divine word and divine action, in the Divine Liturgy as a whole, we hear, see and commune in Christ.

Praise God

The hymn *Alleluia*, which means 'Praise God', expresses the joy of the faithful at the manifestation of the Word of God which takes place when the Gospel is read. The very word, and the way it is sung, show that it is an exclamation of praise and joy. It is a joyful greeting to the Lord as He comes to the assembly of His children.

True joy has been brought into the world by Christ. 'Before the coming of the Lord, is was not possible for man to be joyful, because Christ alone brought us joy. If anyone was joyful before He came to earth, they were joyful because they had been admitted to the mysteries concerning Him, as Christ said of the Patriarch Abraham: *Abraham rejoiced that he was to see my day; he saw it*

---

[20] St Nicholas Cabasilas, *Comm. Liturgy*, 22, *PG* 150.416CD.
[21] St Dionysius the Areopagite, *Church Hierarchy*, *PG* 3.432B.

and was glad [John. 8: 56].' Christ is the exultation that arises in our souls when we gather together to worship Him.[22]

Before the holy Altar, the faithful experience the presence of Christ and rejoice, just like the angelic hosts. 'Because [the angelic hosts] ceaselessly serve around the royal throne of God, they are in a state of constant joy, everlasting gladness, rejoicing without end. They are filled with delight, and dance and glorify without ceasing. For to stand before that divine glory and be illumined by the brightness which it radiates is their joy and cause of rejoicing, their gladness and glory.'[23]

Like the holy angels, so we too delight in the coming of Christ who is the 'joy of all', and spontaneously sing: *Alleluia, Alleluia, Alleluia.*[24]

Deacon: *Let us pray to the Lord. Lord, have mercy.*
The Priest reads the Prayer of the Gospel:
Master, Lover of mankind, make the pure light of your divine knowledge shine in our hearts and open the eyes of our mind to understand the message of your Gospel. Instil in us the fear of your blessed commandments, so that, having trampled down all carnal desires, we may seek after a spiritual way of life, thinking and doing all things that are pleasing to you.

---

[22] St Nicholas Cabasilas, *Comm. Liturgy*, 19, *PG* 150.409D; cf. St Basil the Great, *Letter 243*, 2, *PG* 32.905B.

[23] St John Chrysostom, *Homily on Isaiah 1*, 2, *PG* 56.100.

[24] *Kontakion* for Lazarus Saturday; This triple *Alleluia* is called the *Alleluiarion* in Greek, and is usually sung as the refrain to certain verses from the Psalms. In earlier times, the *Alleluiarion* consisted of an entire Psalm, with *Alleluia* as the refrain for each verse (as we now sing, for example, Ps. 135: *O give thanks to the Lord*). In the present-day order of the Liturgy, the deacon censes during the singing of the *Alleluiarion*. The offering of incense is made 'because of the grace of the Spirit, given by the Gospel to the whole world' (St Symeon of Thessaloniki, *Church Building*, 68, *PG* 155.724C).

For you are the illumination of our souls and bodies, Christ God, and to you we give glory, together with your Father who is without beginning, and your All-holy, good and life-giving Spirit, now and for ever, and to the ages of ages. Amen.

The light of divine knowledge

When the Lord became incarnate, the spiritual darkness which had reigned over the earth was dispelled and the true Light shone forth. 'Scripture customarily gives the name *night* to the period before the coming of Christ, when...the darkness of ignorance reigned upon earth. But it uses the name *day* for the time of our Saviour's coming, when we were enlightened, for we gave assent to the light of the true divine knowledge in our minds and now see the Sun of righteousness with the eyes of our soul.'[25]

Before the reading of the Gospel begins, we ask the Lord for the light of divine knowledge because He is the Sun of righteousness who bestows it on our souls. 'Knowledge is called light because it is provided, as the great Paul says, by that light [of divine Grace]: *The God who said "Let light shine out of darkness" has shone in our hearts to give the light of the knowledge of the glory of God* [2 Cor. 4: 6]... Do you see that the light of knowledge is provided by the presence of the light of Grace?'[26]

Divine knowledge is conveyed in two ways. First, it is inherent in the fact that God knows us as His own and as partakers in His grace; as the Apostle's words affirm: *you have known God, or rather you are known by God* (Gal. 4: 9). Secondly, it is imparted by whatever God reveals to us. Through revelation, Christ enlightens our hearts and gives us true life, for it is divine knowledge

---

[25] St Cyril of Alexandria, *On Worship in Spirit and Truth*, 3, PG 68.268D.
[26] St Gregory Palamas, *In Defence of the holy Hesychasts*, 1.3.3, *Chrestou*, I, p. 411.

that engenders life: 'The beginning of the blessed life is true knowledge about God. The wise Solomon says, "To know You is the root of immortality" [cf. Wisd. Sol. 15: 3]. And also the converse: it was ignorance of God in the beginning [on the part of the first-formed man] that brought in death.' Abba Isaac asks, 'What is knowledge?' And he answers: 'The perception of immortal life.'[27]

Divine knowledge is the power than enables us to obtain life incorruptible, and in accordance with the Lord's words, eternal life is knowledge of God: *This is eternal life: to know You who alone are the only true God, and Jesus Christ whom You have sent* (John 17: 3). We look for both of these — divine knowledge and life — in the Divine Liturgy, because they are offered there as food and drink. One of the most ancient texts of the Liturgy says: *We thank You, our Father, for life and knowledge, which You have made known to us through Jesus Your child: to You be glory unto the ages.*[28] We give thanks for the life and knowledge which Christ bestows on us.

From the height of the life-bearing Cross, the tree of life, Christ has opened the door of Paradise and brought us into it — He has brought us into the Divine Liturgy, where the tree of knowledge and the tree of life are planted and flourish and offer their fruit (cf. Gen. 2: 9).

* * *

In order to enter into the joy of the Lord, into the Divine Liturgy, we need to trample down our carnal desires. This is precisely what the celebrant asks: *Instil in us the fear of your blessed commandments, so that, having trampled down all carnal desires, we may seek after a spiritual way of life.* The person who is devoted to sensual pleasures refuses Christ's invitation to participate in the Supper of His love. For 'when the human mind inclines to-

---

[27] St Nicholas Cabasilas, *On the Life in Christ*, 2, PG 150.529A; *Asc. Hom.*, 62, p. 298.

[28] Cf. St Cyril of Alexandria, *On John*, 11.5, PG 74.484D; *Didache*, 9.3, ANF 7, p. 380.

wards the sensuality of this world, it is weak and sluggish in the works of God. And it will have no share in the divine and heavenly festival.' Furthermore, 'God the Father does not give the impure [the blessing] of knowing Christ, nor does He offer the most beneficial grace of the Holy Spirit to those who have considered deviating into unseemly transgressions; the precious oil of myrrh should not be spilt into the mud.'[29]

When by the grace of Christ we have overcome our carnal desires, the Lord transfigures our whole being. Body and soul become sources of spiritual powers. 'Once the body has been fired in the furnace of ascetic practice and tempered by the water of tears,...immersed in the silence and serenity of inward peace, it becomes full of a new power,...that of the Holy Spirit. When the soul works hand in hand with such a body,...it changes its physical labours into spiritual warfare,...[it] goes out of the body and enters into the darkness of mystical theology.'[30]

Once our carnal desires have been obliterated, we are able to enjoy a spiritual way of life and come to know the Lord who loves mankind. St Gregory the Theologian summons us to the heights of theology: 'Do you want to become a theologian and worthy of the Deity? — Keep the commandments, go through life observing God's ordinances; for action is the foundation for the contemplation [of spiritual mysteries].'[31]

Let us approach the Bridegroom bearing lamps

We asked Christ to enlighten us with the light of divine knowledge because He is the illumination of our souls and bodies. This Light of Christ is symbolised by the light of the candles and lamps which we light at the Divine Liturgy and other services.

---

[29] St Cyril of Alexandria, *On Worship in Spirit and Truth*, 4, PG 68.313C; *On John*, 4.3, PG 73.605D.

[30] St Nikitas Stithatos, *One Hundred Texts on Spiritual Knowledge*, 39, *Philokalia*, vol. 4, p. 150.

[31] *Homily 20*, 12, PG 35.1080B.

The use of lighting in worship — particularly with lamps that burn pure olive oil — was a law given by God to Moses: *Command the people of Israel to bring you pure oil from beaten olives for the lamp, that a light* [in the tent of testimony] *may be kept burning continually...* [They will burn it] *from evening to morning before the Lord continually; it shall be a statute forever throughout your generations* (Lev. 24: 2–3).

The use of lamps and candles in the Divine Liturgy dates from apostolic times. It is recorded in the Acts of the Apostles that when St Paul celebrated the Eucharist in Troas there were many lamps alight in the room where the assembly took place (cf. Acts 20: 7–8). St Nikodimus of the Holy Mountain explains why we have lights in church: 'Firstly, to the glory of God, the true Light who enlightens every man [cf. John 1: 9]. Secondly, to banish the darkness of night and give consolation... Thirdly, as a sign of joy and delight... Fourthly, in honour of the martyrs and saints... Fifthly, to suggest the light of our good works. And sixthly, for the forgiveness of our sins.'[32]

St Symeon the New Theologian writes in this connection: 'The candles which you light reveal to you the intelligible light. Just as the church, that house of great beauty, is full of light from many candles, so the house of your soul, which is more precious than that church, should be illumined and full of light in a noetic sense — that is to say, that within you all the spiritual virtues should burn with divine fire... The multitude of burning lamps signify the illumined thoughts which should shine within you like lamps, so that there should be no dark thought in the house of your soul, but that all should be aflame and shining with the light of the Holy Spirit.'[33]

In the eucharistic assembly, the Lord comes like a Bridegroom 'in the middle of the night' of this life. He Himself commanded

---

[32] *Eortodromion* (Thessaloniki: Orthodoxos Kypseli, 1995), on the Easter Canon, ode 5, vol. II, pp. 303–4, n. 106.

[33] *Ethical Discourse 14*, 3, *SC* 129, p. 428.

us to await Him with the lamps of our souls burning: *Let your lamps be burning* (Luke 12: 35). And the Church exhorts us to go out to meet the Bridegroom carrying lamps, so that together with the angelic hosts we may celebrate the eucharistic Passover:

> Bearing lamps, let us come unto Christ
> who comes forth from the tomb like a Bridegroom;
> and with the hosts who love festivals
> let us celebrate the saving Passover of God.[34]

The Deacon says to the Priest: *Master, bless the herald of the Good Tidings of the Holy Apostle and Evangelist* [name].

The Priest blesses him, saying: *May God, through the prayers of the holy, glorious Apostle and Evangelist* [name]*, grant you the herald to proclaim the word with much power,*[35] *for the fulfilling of the Gospel of his Beloved Son, our Lord Jesus Christ.*

Deacon: *Amen. Amen. Amen. Be it unto me according to your word.*[36]

We see and hear Christ

At the Little Entrance, the celebrant held the Gospel Book before his face so that the face symbolically shown to the faithful was that of Christ. Now, when the Gospel is read, the celebrant lends his mouth to the Word of God so that the faithful may hear His voice. In the person of the celebrant we *see* Christ, and from his mouth we *hear* Him.

---

[34] Holy Monday Matins, *apolytikion*; Easter Matins, Canon, ode 5.2.
[35] Ps. 67: 12.
[36] Luke 1: 38.

Because 'the Gospel is the presence of the Son of God',[37] when the lesson is read we both see and hear Christ calling us to repent and enter into His Kingdom. We see and hear Him with our spiritual senses. When the eyes of faith are open, we see Him more clearly than those who saw Him in the flesh, but without faith. For 'the eyes of faith see things that are not visible'.[38]

St John Chrysostom, who, like all the Spirit-bearing Fathers, saw things invisible and heard things ineffable, assures us that the only true senses are the spiritual senses of faith. Interpreting Christ's words, *Blessed are your eyes, for they see, and your ears, for they hear* (Matt. 13: 16), he writes: 'Christ does not bless the outward [that is, physical] sight, because that of itself does not see miracles, but rather the inward sight. The Jews saw a blind man [who had been healed], and they said: "It is he — it is not he." (cf. John 9: 8ff.) Do you hear how they are in doubt?... While we, who were not present, do not say, "It is he — it is not he", but rather: "It is he." Do you see that being absent does one no harm when one has the eyes of faith, and being present does one no good when the eyes of faith are lacking? For what good did it do the Jews that they saw Christ? None at all. We, therefore, have seen more clearly than they did.'[39]

When the Lord taught the Jews, He spoke in parables because, as He said, 'While they see my miracles, they do not want to see, and while they hear my teaching they do not want to listen' (cf. Matt. 13: 13). The faithful see and hear Christ and follow Him because they know His voice (cf. John 10: 4), even though centuries have passed since His coming in the flesh. Through the senses of faith, the faithful experience the mystery of the new age: *Even though we once regarded Christ according to the flesh, we regard Him so no longer. Therefore, if anyone is in Christ, he is a new*

---

[37] St Germanus, *Contemplation*, PG 98.412D.
[38] St John Chrysostom, *Homily on 'In the last days'*, 2, PG 56.272.
[39] Ibid. PG 56.273.

creation; the old has passed away, behold, all things have become new (2 Cor. 5: 16–17).

Then the Priest standing at the Royal Doors, facing the people, says: *Wisdom. Let us stand up to listen to the Holy Gospel. Peace to all.*
Choir: *And to your spirit.*

Let us raise our minds above earthly things

The celebrant's exhortation to listen to the Lord standing up means 'that we should show zeal and great reverence in our communication with God, whether we need to look, or to pray, or listen to something from the divine service. And as a primary sign of our zeal and reverence, we should be upright in our bodily posture,...for this is the posture of suppliants. This is the posture of servants whose whole mind is focussed on the beck of their master, so as to be ready to run to serve him... And we stand before God as suppliants, asking the greatest of good things.'[40]

The words *Let us stand up to listen to the Holy Gospel* also have a more spiritual meaning: 'Let us raise our minds and our works above earthly things, and we shall understand the manifestation of divine good things.'[41]

The greatest opportunity for the Devil to steal the good things offered us by the holy reading is afforded by our slothfulness: 'This spiritual treasure [of the Holy Gospel] is unassailable; and once it is placed in the treasury of our minds, it becomes immune to any attempt upon it. Unless, that is, we give occasion through

---

[40] St Nicholas Cabasilas, *Comm. Liturgy*, 21, *PG* 150.413D–416A.
[41] St Germanus, *Contemplation*, *PG* 98.412D.

our own slothfulness to him who wants to take it from us. For when our enemy, the crafty Devil, sees spiritual treasure amassed, he flies into a fury and gnashes his teeth. He is constantly on the alert to find his chance to take away some of what is stored within us. But there is no opportunity for him other than our own slothfulness. That is why we need to be constantly on the alert, and to repel his assaults.'[42]

The reading of the Holy Gospel takes us to the city of the heavenly Kingdom. The Evangelist whom we hear is our guide to this city. Let us enter it with sobriety and vigilance. For 'this city is royal and most glorious...let us therefore open wide the doors of our intellect, let us open our ears, and with great fear, as we prepare to set foot on the threshold, let us worship its King... Let us not enter into this city with noise and commotion, but in mystical silence... For a letter is going to be read, not from some earthly king but from the Lord of the angels.'[43]

My peace I give to you

Through the mouth and the hand of the celebrant, Christ gives His peace to the struggling Christian: *My peace I give to you* (John 14: 27). 'I will be with you again, even though I am absent in the body,...and I will lift you above every disturbance... A divine power will rise within you; while your minds will be free from care and your hearts at peace, it will guide you to the revelation of things more exalted than the human mind.'[44] This divine power which rises in our souls is the peace of God, which in the Divine Liturgy becomes our guide to the understanding of the mystery of divine Love.

When the celebrant offers peace, this signifies 'the grace of dispassion which God offers to the saints, in return for their

---

[42] St John Chrysostom, *On Genesis*, 5.1, PG 53.48.
[43] Ibid. *On Matthew*, 1.8, PG 57.23–4.
[44] St Cyril of Alexandria, *On John*, 10, PG 74.304D.

labours in virtue. So that they are freed from war [with the forces of the Devil], and can direct the powers of their souls towards spiritual growth.'[45]

* * *

The people reply to the celebrant, *And to your spirit*; and with these words, they wish the peace of God also to him, their shepherd and father.

Man's mind is in need of the peace of God. The turmoil we feel is caused 'by the sickness of our mind. If it were not so, then everyone would be perturbed by things that happen, since we all sail the same sea [of life].' 'So if we prepare our mind in such a way that it can endure all sorrows with ease, then for us there will be no hard winters or stormy seas, but always undisturbed tranquillity.' This is the tranquillity that St John Chrysostom asks of those who listen to the Holy Gospel: 'I ask of you that stillness which is to be found in the mind and in the soul.'[46]

Deacon: *The reading is from the Holy Gospel according to* [name].
Priest: *Let us attend.*
Choir: *Glory to you, O Lord, glory to you.*
The Deacon intones the Gospel for the day. When it is finished the Priest blesses the Deacon saying: *Peace to you, who has proclaimed the Gospel.*
Choir: *Glory to you, O Lord, glory to you.*
The Priest takes the Gospel Book from the Deacon, kisses it and blesses the people with it. He then replaces it on the Holy Table.

---

[45] St Maximus the Confessor, *Mystagogy*, 12, *PG* 91.692A.
[46] St John Chrysostom, *On John*, 3.2, *PG* 59.38; *On John*, 1.2, *PG* 59.27.

The good news of the Kingdom

The word that reveals the mystery of the divine economy to human beings is called the Gospel (from the old English, godspel, meaning 'good news', *Evangelion* in Greek, also meaning, literally, 'good news'), because it is the joyful news that God has come down to earth to save man: *Behold, I bring you good news of great joy...for to you is born this day...a Saviour, who is Christ the Lord* (Luke 2: 10–11). Jesus Christ is the joyful news of the Gospel: 'He is the Gospel of [our] salvation.'[47]

Gospel, then, means words about the Word of God. Reflecting on the mystery of the Lord's Incarnation and all the gifts arising from it, St John Chrysostom explains why the account of it was called 'Good News': 'What could ever be compared to these joyful tidings? God on earth, man in heaven. All became one: angels joined in singing with humans, humans communicated with the angels and the other heavenly powers. You could truly see the end of the protracted war, reconciliation made between God and our nature, the Devil put to shame, demons in headlong flight, death abolished. You could see Paradise being opened, the curse wiped out, sin banished, delusion being hunted down. Still more, you saw truth returning, the word of Christian faith sown everywhere bringing forth abundant fruit, the life of heaven planted on earth.' That is why the evangelist called the account of Christ's life 'good news'. For 'everything else — everything that humans think of as happiness — is mere words, devoid of real substance... The enunciations of the fishermen disciples of Christ, however, can truly and literally be called Gospels, good news, not only because they are immutable and unshakeable good things surpassing what we are worthy of, but also because they were given to us with the greatest of ease. For not by labouring and sweating...,

---

[47] St Cyril of Alexandria, *Address to the most pious Empresses*, PG 76.1328B.

but merely as being beloved of God, we received what we have received.'[48]

On account of all these good things, the faithful glorify God in thankfulness even before the Gospel reading begins: *Glory to You, O Lord, glory to You.* The same doxology also marks the end of the reading.

* * *

St Maximus the Confessor gives an eschatological interpretation of the reading of the Holy Gospel, saying that it 'signifies the end of the world. For after the reading of the Holy Gospel, the bishop descends from the throne, and the celebrants dismiss and send away the catechumens and those unworthy of divine contemplation of the Mysteries which are about to be presented.' The reading, then, manifests 'that which is written: that the *Gospel of the Kingdom will be preached throughout the world...and then the end will come* [Matt. 24: 14]'.[49]

During the eucharistic assembly, Christ descends in glory, 'as is shown by the descent of the bishop from the high priestly throne'.[50] With the dismissal of the catechumens and those who are not worthy to participate in the Mystery, we have already a prefiguration of the dreadful Judgement. The eucharistic Mystery performed thereafter is the foretaste of the Kingdom and the eternal rejoicing of the faithful, who in full reality will partake of the Supper of the Kingdom.

---

[48] *On Matthew*, 1.2, PG 57.15–6.
[49] *Mystagogy*, 14, PG 91.692D–693A.
[50] Ibid. 23, PG 91.700B.

3. THE LITANY AND THE GREAT ENTRANCE

Then the Deacon, standing before the Royal Doors and facing the sanctuary, intones the Litany* of Fervent Supplication:

Let us all say, with all our soul and with all our mind, let us say.

Choir, after each petition: *Lord, have mercy* (three times).

Deacon: *Lord almighty, the God of our fathers, we pray you, hear and have mercy.*

Have mercy on us, O God, according to your great mercy, we pray you, hear and have mercy.

Also, we pray for devout and Orthodox Christians.

Also, we pray for our Archbishop [name].

Also, we pray for our brothers the priests, hieromonks, hierodeacons and monks, and all our brotherhood in Christ.

Also, we pray for mercy, life, peace, health, salvation, visitation, pardon and forgiveness of sins for the servants of God, all devout and Orthodox Christians, those who dwell in or are visiting this city and parish, the wardens and members of this holy church.

Also, we pray for the blessed and ever-remembered founders of this holy church [or monastery], *and for all our fathers and brothers who have gone to their rest before us, and who lie asleep here in the true faith; and for the Orthodox everywhere.*

Also, we pray for those who bring offerings, those who care for the beauty of this holy and venerable

house, for those who labour in its service, for those who sing, and for the people here present, who await your great and rich mercy.

While the Deacon is reciting these petitions, the Priest, in a low voice, says the following Prayer of Fervent Supplication:

Accept, O Lord our God, this fervent supplication from your servants, and have mercy on us according to the fullness of your mercy; and send down your pity upon us and upon all your people, who await your abundant mercy.

(aloud) *For you, O God, are merciful and love mankind, and to you we give glory, to the Father, and to the Son, and to the Holy Spirit, now and for ever, and to the ages of ages.*

Choir: *Amen.*

Christ is the abyss of mercy

This series of petitions is called *ektenis ikesia*, or 'long supplication' (usually known as 'fervent supplication').[1]

Like the Canaanite woman (cf. Matt. 15: 21–8), we run to Christ and ceaselessly implore His mercy: '*Have mercy on me.* My way of life does not permit me to speak to You. I seek refuge in mercy, in the haven which accepts all sinners. I seek refuge in mercy, where there is no court of judgement, where salvation is offered without examination.' 'Observe the woman's prudence', says St John Chrysostom. 'She does not beseech James, she does not petition

---

[1] In early times, this 'long supplication' was longer than it is today. The faithful would petition the Lord for the local Churches and for all orders of the faithful: the living, the departed, the sick, penitents, etc. There is a litany of this sort in the Liturgy of St James.

John, she does not approach Peter... She thinks: "I have no need of an intermediary. I am taking repentance as my advocate and going to the very source. This is why Christ descended to earth, this is why He took flesh, so that even I might be able to speak with Him"... *Have mercy on me.* It is a simple phrase, but it elicits a boundless ocean of salvation. *Have mercy on me.* "That is why You came to us, that is why You took flesh just like ours, that is why You became as I am." In heaven above [among the holy angels], fear; on earth below [in a woman], boldness of approach!'[2]

Even though we do not hear Christ's response to our petitions, even though we are not worthy of His mercy, yet we too, like the Canaanite woman, kneel before Him and implore Him: *Lord, have mercy.*

Christ came to earth out of His mercy for us, and to the mystery of His coming to earth is given the names of 'mercy' and 'truth': ' "Mercy", because while we were all in an utterly wretched state and were enemies at war with Him, in His great kindness and love for mankind He did not despise us. And not only did He have compassion for our plight...but He even accounted us worthy of His Kingdom... For these reasons, the Psalmist calls the divine economy *mercy*. And he calls it *truth* [Ps. 91: 3] because during the period of the Old Testament, everything looked towards it as shadows and figures towards reality.'[3]

Christ is the 'abyss of mercy'. So we take refuge in that abyss, certain that we shall find mercy, because *with the Lord there is mercy* (Ps. 129: 7). Christ is a 'fount and treasury of love for mankind, welling up inexhaustibly'. He is 'the boundless ocean of love for mankind'.[4]

This boundless ocean of love for mankind, which is Christ, has appointed the Mystery of the Divine Eucharist as the means of en-

---

[2] St John Chrysostom, *On the Canaanite Woman*, 4, PG 52.452.

[3] St Nicholas Cabasilas, *Comm. Liturgy*, 17, PG 150.405CD.

[4] Vespers for 25 January, *Theotokion** at the *Aposticha*; St John Chrysostom, *On Psalm 129*, 3, PG 55.376.

try into the Kingdom of heaven. When the Divine Eucharist is celebrated, the entrance into the Kingdom is open. And 'in His great
love for mankind the Lord has compassion upon us, awaiting the
total return of all of us to Him.' He who is 'mighty in mercy and
gracious in strength' awaits us at His assembly; he waits for us to
encounter Him and ask for His mercy. And He has mercy on us
and offers Himself to each of us, since by His Incarnation 'He
united Himself completely with man in his totality, that He
might give salvation to the whole human being'.[5]

Lord, have mercy

After each of the petitions addressed to God by the celebrant, the
faithful sing three times: Lord, have mercy. 'To ask mercy from
God is to ask for His Kingdom, that Kingdom Christ promised to
give to all who seek it, assuring them that all other things of which
they have need will be added unto them [cf. Matt. 6: 33]. That is
why this prayer, which achieves all this, suffices for the faithful.'[6]

Lord, have mercy: 'This is the plea of the condemned who have
no defence and no justification to put forward and make this last
appeal to the judge. And they count on obtaining what they ask,
not because it is just, but because of the judge's benevolence. This
behaviour of people bears witness to the great kindness of the
judge and to the wickedness of themselves; the first is an act of
thanksgiving, and the second an act of confession.'[7] By asking for
divine mercy, we also show that we put no trust in our own works:

> You know, O Master, that I have never entrusted
> the salvation of my soul to acts or deeds,
> but I have fled, O Lover of mankind, to Your mercy

---

[5] *Macarian Homilies*, 4.16, *PG* 34.484D; First prayer of Vespers; St John of
Damascus, *On the Orthodox Faith*, 3.50, *PG* 94.1005B.

[6] St Nicholas Cabasilas, *Comm. Liturgy*, 13, *PG* 150.396D–397A.

[7] Ibid. 12, *PG* 150.393B.

boldly supposing that You will save me as a favour,
    O most-compassionate,
and as God You will have mercy on me, as once upon the harlot
and upon the prodigal son who cried, 'I have sinned!'
Believing this I have run to You;
with this audacity I have come to You.[8]

* * *

The Lord has revealed one way in which we can be sure of receiving His great mercy: by forgiving our fellow man. 'Let us love one another, and we shall be loved by God. Let us show longsuffering to each other, and God will show longsuffering towards our sins. Let us not return evil for the evil done to us [cf. Rom. 12: 17], and we shall not be punished according to our sins. For the forgiveness of our transgressions is to be found in our forgiveness of our brethren. And the mercy of God is to be found hidden in our compassion towards our neighbour…. So you see, the Lord has given us a way in which we can be saved, and has endowed us eternally with the capacity to become children of God [cf. John 1: 12]; thus it is on what we ourselves desire that our salvation depends.'[9]

Deacon: *Catechumens, pray to the Lord.*
To each petition the Choir answers: *Lord, have mercy.*
Deacon: *Believers, let us pray for the catechumens;*
That the Lord will have mercy on them;
Instruct them in the word of truth;
Reveal to them the Gospel of righteousness;

---

[8] St Symeon the New Theologian, *Hymn 42*, 48–54, SC 196, p. 40.
[9] St Maximus the Confessor, *Ascetic Discourse*, 42, PG 90.953AB.

Unite them to his holy, catholic and apostolic Church.

Save them, have mercy on them, help them and keep them, O God, by your grace.

Catechumens, bow down your heads to the Lord.

Choir: *To you, O Lord.*

Meanwhile the Priest, in a low voice, says the Prayer for the Catechumens: *Lord, our God, dwelling on high and beholding things below, who for the salvation of mankind sent forth your only-begotten Son, our Lord and God, Jesus Christ, look down upon your servants the catechumens, who have bowed their necks to you; and count them worthy in due time of the waters of regeneration, the forgiveness of sins and the garment of incorruption; unite them to your holy, catholic and apostolic Church, and number them among your chosen flock.*

(aloud) *That they also with us may glorify your all-honoured and majestic name, of the Father, and of the Son, and of the Holy Spirit, now and for ever, and to the ages of ages.*

Choir: *Amen.*

The catechumens

Catechumen is the name given to a person who has heard about Christ and expressed the desire to be baptised. In the period preceding Baptism, the Church prepares the catechumens to become her members through appropriate instruction. This instruction is called *catechesis* (catechism*), and the person administering it is called a catechist.

In apostolic times, the catechism of the catechumens was very

brief. Usually it was just one address, such as St Peter's homily on the day of Pentecost (cf. Acts 2: 14–40), and the systematic catechising of the newly-enlightened took place after their Baptism.

In the post-apostolic period however, catechism took considerably longer. The *Apostolic Constitutions* speak of a three-year period of catechism: 'Let him who is going to be catechised, be catechised for three years. If, though, he has zeal and a great desire for Holy Baptism, let him be received [earlier]. For what matters is not the time, but the manner [in which the catechumen comes to Baptism].' The *Apostolic Tradition* of St Hippolytus also refers to a three-year catechumenate.[10]

∗ ∗ ∗

Catechumens do not yet have boldness before God. They require the support and intercession of the faithful, and that is why the celebrant asks us to pray for them. Like a loving mother, the Church 'urges the entire assembly of the faithful to pray for the catechumens, even though they are still strangers. Indeed, they do not yet belong to the Body of Christ, they have not partaken of the Holy Mysteries; they are still apart from the spiritual flock… They stand outside the royal court, far from the sacred forecourts. That is why they are sent away before those fearful prayers [of the Anaphora] are said. So she asks you to pray for them, that they may become fellow members with you and no longer be strangers and cut off.'[11]

We ask Christ to have mercy on His servants the catechumens. We ask that He Himself, through the mouth of the catechist, will teach them *the word of truth*, that He will *reveal to them the Gospel of righteousness*, that is, Himself, and make them members of His holy Church. This should happen when the right time

---

[10] *Apostolic Constitutions*, 8.32, PG 1.1132B; *Apostolic Tradition*, 17, SC 11bis, p. 75. Nowadays, the common practice is infant baptism, and the catechism of the 'newly-enlightened' is the responsibility of the child's godparent and parents.

[11] St John Chrysostom, *On 2 Corinthians*, 2.5, PG 61.399.

comes for their spiritual regeneration; in the words of the Liturgy, *in due time.*

The catechumens should not, however, delay Baptism out of indifference. With abundant love, the Church invites them: 'You are outside Paradise, catechumens; you participate in the exile of our ancestor Adam. But now that the door is gradually opening to you, enter into the Paradise which you left. Do not delay, lest death should intervene and bar your entry... Put off the old man like a dirty garment, full of shame from multitudinous sins... Accept the garment of incorruption which Christ has unfolded and offers to you. Do not refuse the gift, so as not to insult the Giver.'[12]

The catechumens need to be illumined and regenerated through Holy Baptism. Our holy Church prays for them, and invites them to participate in the true Life.

Deacon: *As many as are catechumens, depart; catechumens, depart; as many as are catechumens, depart. Let not any of the catechumens remain. As many as are believers, again and again in peace, let us pray to the Lord.*

Choir: *Lord, have mercy.*

Deacon: *Help us, save us, have mercy on us, and keep us, O God, by your grace.*

Choir: *Lord, have mercy.*

Deacon: *Wisdom.*

The dismissal of the catechumens

The dismissal of the catechumens is an act of love on the part of the Church so as to protect those who have not yet been born in

---

[12] St Gregory of Nyssa, *To those who delay Baptism*, PG 46.417CD–420C.

Christ. The catechumens are embryos carried in the womb of the Mother Church. Through catechism they are fashioned and take shape and progress towards 'divine birth'[13] — towards Baptism.

Knowing that the word of God concerning the Mysteries may harm the weak rather than being of benefit to them, St Paul wrote to the Christians of Corinth: *I have fed you with milk, not with solid food* (1 Cor. 3: 2). How much more so, then, should the catechumens be nourished with easily digestible food? The Church 'allows the catechumens to hear the sacred words of the Psalms and the divine reading of the Holy Scriptures, but she does not invite them to the sacred rites and contemplation [of the Holy Mysteries] that follow.'[14]

*   *   *

The faithful are the *living stones* which build up the *spiritual house* of the Church (1 Pet. 2: 5). 'They are raised to the heights by Jesus Christ's "crane", which is the precious Cross, using the All-holy Spirit as the rope. Faith is the strap that holds them, and love is the road that leads them up to God.'[15] The catechumens, however, have not yet received the gift of the Holy Spirit — the rope whereby man climbs up to the peak of Mount Tabor — nor have they yet acquired faith, the bond that connects man with the Holy Spirit. So the door of love — the road leading to God — is still closed to them.[16]

The holy Offering is the Supper of the Kingdom. Any who have not put on the wedding garment which is given at Baptism are sent away from the place where the Divine Eucharist is celebrated (cf. Matt. 22: 2–14). Those who remain to greet Christ are the

---

[13] St Dionysius the Areopagite, *Church Hierarchy*, 3.3.6, PG 3.433B.

[14] Ibid. PG 3.432C.

[15] St Ignatius of Antioch, *Ephesians*, 9, PG 5.652B.

[16] Perfect love for God is a gift of the Holy Spirit and until the catechumens have received that gift through Holy Baptism they cannot attain that perfect love. Similarly, until they are properly instructed in the tenets of the Church they are unable to fully participate in and acquire faith.

ones who have received the seal of the gift of the Holy Spirit, and they will sit down at the wedding feast of the Kingdom, to delight in the contemplation of God and the communion of the Holy Mysteries.

The Priest then unfolds the *eileton** (corporal) on the Altar and, in a low voice, says the First Prayer of the Faithful:

We thank you, Lord, God of the powers of heaven, for counting us worthy to stand even now before your holy Altar and implore your compassion for our sins and for those committed in ignorance by the people. Receive our supplication, O God; make us worthy to offer you prayers and entreaties and bloodless sacrifices for all your people. And enable us, whom you have placed in this your ministry by the power of your Holy Spirit, to invoke you at every time and place without blame and without offence, with the witness of a pure conscience, so that you may hear us and be merciful to us in the abundance of your goodness.

(aloud) *For to you belong all glory, honour and worship, to the Father, and to the Son, and to the Holy Spirit, now and for ever, and to the ages of ages.*

Choir: *Amen.*

Make us worthy

Temperance and purity of soul on the part of the priest are a precondition for him to celebrate the Holy Mysteries without condemnation. Otherwise, 'if he mingles darkness with light and a foul stench with myrrh, he will undoubtedly inherit calamity

and destruction because of his sacrilege...'. St John Chrysostom says that the priest's soul must be purer than the rays of the sun: 'Consider what those hands which minister at the Holy Mysteries should be like, what that tongue should be like that utters the words that invoke the Holy Spirit! And the soul that has received so much of the grace of the Holy Spirit — how much holier and purer must it be than anything else!'[17]

But this purity which is demanded of the celebrant of the Mysteries is essentially a gift of the Holy Spirit and of Christ's love. This truth is expressed in the corresponding prayer in the Liturgy of St Basil: 'By the power of Your Holy Spirit, make us adequate to this ministry.' So the priest thanks the Lord for accounting him worthy to flee to the bowels of His mercy, and beseeches Him to make him worthy of offering the eucharistic Sacrifice. The Lord, who is the abyss of mercy, has compassion on His celebrant when he in turn is distinguished by the 'abyss of humility'. It is this humility which makes the celebrant worthy to perform the Holy Anaphora. That is why St Theognostus advises the celebrant: 'Humble yourself as if you were a sheep for slaughter, truly regarding all men as superior to yourself', and 'consider yourself dust and ashes [cf. Gen. 18: 27]'.[18]

Through humility, the priest comes to realise that he stands before the Altar in the place of Christ. Just as at the Last Supper the Lord was the celebrant of the Mystery that is the salvation of the world, so too in the Divine Liturgy 'it is He that performs all things, and imparts' the Holy Mysteries to the faithful.[19]

The *Amen* sung by the choir (who represent the people) at the end of the First Prayer of the Faithful signifies that the people too, like the celebrant, sense the loftiness of the priestly ministry.

---

[17] St Theognostus, *On the Practice of the Virtues, Contemplation and the Priesthood*, 49, *Philokalia*, vol. 2, p. 370; *On the Priesthood*, 6.2, 4, *PG* 48.679, 681.

[18] *On the Practice of the Virtues*, 62, 70, 16 (*Philokalia*, vol. 2, pp. 373, 376, 362).

[19] St John Chrysostom, *On 1 Corinthians*, 27.4, *PG* 61.229.

'That is why the whole people, who are present outside the sanctuary, empathise and pray together with the priest.'[20] This *Amen* affirms the solidarity of the faithful with the struggle and anguish of the celebrant.

Deacon: *Again and again in peace, let us pray to the Lord. Help us, save us, have mercy on us, and keep us, O God, by your grace. Wisdom!*

The Priest meanwhile says in a low voice the Second Prayer of the Faithful:

Again and many times we fall down before you and beseech you, who are good and the lover of mankind, that heeding our prayer you will cleanse our souls and bodies from every defilement of flesh and spirit, and will grant us to stand without guilt or condemnation before your holy Altar. Give also to those who pray with us advancement in right living, in faith and spiritual understanding. Grant that they may always worship you with fear and love, may partake of your Holy Mysteries without guilt or condemnation, and be counted worthy of your heavenly Kingdom.

(aloud) *That being always protected by your might, we may give glory to you, to the Father, and to the Son, and to the Holy Spirit, now and for ever, and to the ages of ages.*

Choir: *Amen.*

---

[20] Samonas, Bishop of Gaza, *Discourse*, PG 120.825C.

Make radiant the garment of my soul

Whenever we fall at the Lord's feet in contrition, we have the sense of standing firm, for we are not supported by our own sickly legs (those of self-confidence and pride) but by His grace, which is where humility leads.

When *again and many times* we fall down before the Lord, we are standing uncondemned before the terrible Altar. So we fall at Christ's feet in order to cleanse our souls, to be able to stand *without guilt or condemnation* at the Holy Table. We humbly fall down before Christ, asking Him that we may advance *in right living, in faith and spiritual understanding*, so that we may come to understand that one who truly lives in humility lives in the grace of His constant presence.

* * *

As the moment of Consecration and of Holy Communion approaches, we become conscious that we need to be totally pure in order to receive Christ, for it is not possible to serve Christ and the Devil with the same body. St John Chrysostom asks: 'Are you not afraid to look at lewd scenes of adultery being played out on a bed on stage in the theatre with the same eyes that look on the Holy Table upon which these terrible Mysteries are performed? Or to listen with the same ears to a prostitute using foul language and to the Prophet and the Apostle guiding you into the Mysteries? Or to receive into the same heart both spiritual poisons and the terrible and holy Sacrifice?'[21]

We must strive to keep both body and soul pure: 'Having taken account of the magnitude of the Sacrifice, make your body beautiful. Understand what your hand receives, and never raise that hand to strike someone... Bear in mind that you do not receive Christ in your hand only but also put Him into your mouth, and keep your tongue pure of foul and abusive language, free from

---

[21] *On David and Saul*, 3.2, PG 54.696-7.

blasphemies and perjury... When you recall that your heart receives that terrible Mystery, never scheme against your neighbour but keep your heart pure of any wickedness. In this way you will also be able to guard your eyes and your hearing... You are invited to a wedding, my beloved; do not go in wearing dirty clothes, but provide yourself with the appropriate garment [cf. Matt. 22: 2–14].'[22]

The wedding garment — the brightness of our souls — is a gift from the Bridegroom who invites us to His Supper. We ask for this brightness from Christ when we say: 'Make the garment of my soul to shine.'[23] And once we receive it, we ask Him to preserve it pure *from every defilement of flesh and spirit.*

The Choir begins the Cherubic Hymn:
We, who mystically represent the Cherubim and sing the Thrice-holy Hymn to the life-giving Trinity, let us now lay aside all worldly cares. For we are about to receive the King of all, invisibly escorted by the angelic hosts. Alleluia, alleluia, alleluia.[24]

---

[22] St John Chrysostom, *To those who are about to be illumined*, 2.2, PG 49.233–4. Laypeople used to receive Communion as the clergy do now, receiving first the Holy Body of Christ in their hands then drinking His Holy Blood from the Chalice.

[23] Matins of Holy Monday, *exapostilarion.**

[24] According to the Byzantine historian Georgios Kendrinos, from the reign of Emperor Justin II, circa the year 574 '...it was decreed that the Cherubic Hymn should also be sung [PG 121.748B]'. The phrase *pasan nyn biotikin*, 'let us now lay aside...' (as opposed to contemporary Greek usage *pasan tin biotikin*, which omits the 'now') is attested in all the early manuscripts of the Divine Liturgy, and in early translations. Other hymns sung in place of the Cherubic Hymn likewise stress the sacredness of this moment: '*Now* the powers of heaven...' (Liturgy of the Presanctified Gifts); 'Of Your mystical supper, *today*...' (Holy Thursday). (See I. Foundoulis, *Apanteseis eis leitourgikas aporias* [*Answers to liturgical queries*] II, 5th ed. [Athens: Apostoliki Diakonia, 2006], answer 199, pp. 136–8.)

The Cherubic Hymn

The Great Entrance is the name given to a series of hymns, prayers and actions carried out by the celebrant and the people, which begins with the Cherubic Hymn and the reading of the Prayer of the Cherubic Hymn. The Church summons us to make ourselves ready to receive the King of glory, who is entering the Holy City to be crucified for the sake of the world. She summons us to journey with Christ on His road to martyrdom and to stand beside Him at the Cross with His most holy Mother and the beloved Disciple.

At this moment (*now*), says the hymn, let us put aside every care concerned with daily life because we are going to receive the King of all. Let us try to make an exit from the world of everyday matters so that we may attain entry into the realm of Christ's of- fering. St John exhorts us: 'The Magi came out of Persia in order to go to worship Christ [cf. Matt. 2: 1–2]; so you likewise should withdraw from the concerns of everyday life and make your way towards Jesus.'[25]

Love for God is the spiritual power which will help us rise above the things of this world: 'When someone is aflame with love for God, he can no longer bear to see those things visible to our sensible eyes. For now that he has received other eyes, the eyes of faith, at all times he intellectually perceives the things of heav- en, and it is upon them that he fixes his intellect. While he walks upon earth, it is as if he lives in heaven… Whoever is concerned to pursue the path of virtue and wants to ascend from earth to heaven abandons all that is materially visible, and with all his powers devotes himself to the struggle that this path involves. Until he manages to ascend to the very height of heaven, he nei- ther pauses nor is he seduced by anything he sees [on his way].'[26]

We are impatient to reach the peak of Golgotha, and so as to be able to celebrate Christ's feast we leave all earthly cares be-

---

[25] *On the Incomprehensible*, 6.4, *PG* 48.754.
[26] St John Chrysostom, *On Genesis*, 28.6, *PG* 53.259.

hind. 'For the true festival is where there is salvation of souls, peace and concord, where no worldly activity remains... The true festival is there where absolute calm, tranquillity, love, joy, peace and meekness reign.' We put every care of this life into Christ's hands; or, rather, we surrender our whole life to Him. And He shoulders our burden and climbs up to Golgotha. He takes care of the needs of our life, as He tells us through the mouth of Abba Isaac: 'If you make your every concern to be for the Kingdom of heaven, I will not deprive you of what is needed by your material nature. *All these things shall be added unto you* [Matt. 6: 33]. I will not let you take thought for them.'[27]

St John Chrysostom assures us that 'the soul that has not learnt to despise the petty concerns of everyday life will not be able to marvel at the things of heaven'. And because he himself had tasted the grace of heavenly things, he exhorts us: Brethren, 'let no one enter into the church bringing with him the cares, distractions or fears of everyday life. Let us all enter having first left all these things outside, at the outer door of the church. For we are entering a heavenly palace; we are walking in places that radiate light.'[28]

It was to these radiant places that *Papa*-Tychon, of blessed memory, was transported by his guardian angel during the singing of the Cherubic Hymn. In the little Greek he knew, the Russian priest recounted: 'During Cherubic Hymn, guardian angel take me up. After half hour, guardian angel bring me down.' At the end of this ecstatic experience, the holy one of God realised that he was still in the middle of the Divine Liturgy and had to continue. When they asked him, 'Elder, what did you see and hear during that half hour?', he replied: 'Cherubim – Seraphim glorifying God!'[29]

---

[27] Ibid. 1.1, *PG* 53.21; *Asc. Hom.*, 59, p. 288.

[28] *On Compunction*, 2.2, PG 47.414; *Homily on Isaiah* 2, 1, PG 56.108–9.

[29] The righteous hieromonk Tychon († 23.9.1968) lived for many years on Mount Athos at the Cell of the Holy Cross, Stavronikita Monastery. The author had the blessing of knowing him personally.

Escorted by the angelic hosts, the Lord enters the Holy City to be sacrificed. The Church exhorts us to experience this mystery of Christ's utter love in total silence: 'Let all mortal flesh keep silence, and stand with fear and trembling; and let it take no thought for any earthly thing. For the King of Kings and Lord of Lords draws near to be sacrificed and given as food for the faithful. Before Him go the choirs of angels with all the principalities and powers, the many-eyed Cherubim and six-winged Seraphim, which cover their faces as they sing this hymn: *Alleluia, alleluia, alleluia.*'[30]

While the Choir is chanting the Cherubic Hymn, the Priest says in a low voice the Prayer of the Cherubic Hymn:

None of those who are entangled in carnal desires and pleasures is worthy to approach or draw near or minister to you, O King of glory; for to serve you is great and awesome even for the heavenly powers. Yet on account of your ineffable and boundless love for mankind you became man without change or alteration and were named our High Priest; and as Master of all you have committed to us the sacred ministry of this liturgical and bloodless Sacrifice. For you alone, Lord our God, are ruler over all things in heaven and on earth, sitting on the throne of the Cherubim, Lord of the Seraphim and King of Israel, the only Holy One, at rest among the holy. Therefore I entreat you, who alone are good and ready to hear: Look upon me, your sinful and unprofitable servant, and purify my soul and heart from an evil conscience; and by the

---

[30] Cherubic Hymn for Holy Saturday; *The Lenten Triodion*, tr. Mother Mary and Kallistos Ware (London: Faber and Faber, 1978), p. 659.

power of your Holy Spirit enable me, clothed with the grace of the priesthood, to stand before this your Holy Table and celebrate the Mystery of your holy and most pure Body and your precious Blood. For to you I come, bending down my neck, and beseech you: Do not turn away your face from me, nor reject me from among your children, but count me, your sinful and unworthy servant, worthy to offer these Gifts to you. For you are the One who offers and is offered, who receives and is distributed, Christ our God, and to you we give glory, together with your Father, who is without beginning, and your All-holy, good and life-giving Spirit, now and for ever, and to the ages of ages. Amen.

Lord, You offer and are offered

In parallel with the faithful who prepare themselves for the offering of Christ, the celebrants also prepare themselves with a series of prayers and actions.

The first of these is the Prayer of the Cherubic Hymn. In this prayer, the celebrant acknowledges and confesses his unworthiness, and the divine grandeur of the Mystery at which he is called to serve. He approaches the holy Altar however, despite his unworthiness, because he does not rely on his own purity and holiness but on the mercy of God. He relies on the ocean of God's love for mankind, for out of inexpressible love for mankind Christ became man, was crucified, and gave us the Mystery of the bloodless Sacrifice. Christ came to Golgotha and was offered once at a certain point in time, but He also comes and is offered always at every Divine Liturgy. He is the *One who offers and is offered, who receives* [the offering] *and is distributed* to the faithful as lifegiving nourishment.

Jesus Christ is the author of the mystery of our salvation. This fact is the foundation on which the mystery of the Liturgy rests. Christ 'is both the one who nourishes and the nourishment. He gives the Bread of life, and He Himself is what He gives. He is life for all who live, myrrh for all who breathe, clothing for all who want to be clothed. Furthermore, He gives us the possibility of making our way forward, but He Himself is the Way as well as the inn by the wayside and the final destination [cf. John 14: 6].'[31]

In the Mystery of the bloodless Sacrifice, 'Christ is the victim; He is the priest; He is the Altar; He is God; He is man; He is King; He is High Priest; He is the sheep; He is the lamb. For our sake He becomes everything for each of us, so that in every way He may become our life [cf. 1 Cor. 12: 6].'[32] The flood of divine Love brought into the world the flood of divine Life.

Christ becomes all things for every person: He is the Priest who offers the Sacrifice, the Lamb who is offered, the God who receives the offering and the *Theanthropos* who is distributed to the communicants for life eternal. We receive the Gift and offer thanks to the Lord who gives it: 'We give thanks to You, O Lord, God of our salvation, that You do all things for the benefit of our life, that we may ever look to You, the Saviour and benefactor of our souls.'[33]

After the prayer the Priest and the Deacon themselves say the Cherubic Hymn three times, as follows:
Priest: *We, who mystically represent the Cherubim and sing the Thrice-holy Hymn to the life-giving Trinity, let us now lay aside all worldly cares.*
Deacon: *For we are about to receive the King of all,*

---

[31] St Nicholas Cabasilas, *On the Life in Christ*, 1, PG 150.500D.
[32] St Epiphanius, *Against Heresies*, 2.1, Heresy 55, PG 41.980C.
[33] Sixth prayer at Matins.

invisibly escorted by the angelic hosts. Alleluia, alleluia, alleluia.

Then the Priest takes the censer and censes the Altar all round, the sanctuary and, going a little way beyond the Royal Doors, the principal icons and the people. In a low voice he says, *Let us who have beheld the Resurrection of Christ worship...* (if it is Sunday), *Come, let us worship...* (three times), and Psalm 50 up to the verse which begins *Then you will be pleased...* The celebrants then make three bows in front of the Holy Table and kiss the *Antimension*, quietly saying these *troparia* of compunction:

I have sinned before you, O Saviour, like the prodigal son. Receive me in repentance, Father, and have mercy on me, O God.

I cry to you, Christ my Saviour, in the words of the publican: have compassion for me, as you did for him, and have mercy on me, O God.[34]

Each then bows to his concelebrants and says: *Forgive me, brothers and concelebrants.* And they also bow to the people, asking forgiveness. They then go to the holy Prothesis, and having made three bows before it they kiss the covered Holy Gifts, saying: *God, have compassion for me, a sinner, and have mercy on me.*[35]

For we are about to receive the King of all

In order to hold the Holy Gifts in his hands, the celebrant must feel repentance deep within him and must approach the Altar *like the prodigal son* (cf. Luke 15: 21).

---

[34] See p. 288 below; *Octoechos*, Tone 2, Monday evening.
[35] Luke 18: 13.

The psalm of repentance which the celebrant recites as he censes, the *troparia* of compunction, the act of venerating the Altar and the holy Prothesis, the act of asking for forgiveness from God, his concelebrants and the people — all these things are manifestations of a *contrite heart* (Ps. 50: 19). By his own example, the celebrant shows the faithful the road to repentance and 'images the Forerunner and Baptist John, who first began to preach saying, *Repent, for the Kingdom of heaven is at hand* [Matt. 3: 2].'[36] The celebrant urges us to *prepare the way of the Lord* (Matt. 3: 3), meaning the road that will lead Christ the King to our souls. And this road is repentance. So, people and celebrant alike in repentance receive Christ who comes.

Through repentance we are sanctified; and then, when Christ enters our assembly, we are accounted worthy of the Holy Mysteries: 'If any is holy, let him approach; if any is not, let him become so through repentance', says the celebrant as he invites the faithful to receive Communion. Christ offers us His life. He 'who is wholly fire, whom the angels cannot approach nor bear', is offered as food for the faithful. And every believer, 'at once rejoicing and trembling, partakes of fire, and is cooled in a manner beyond expressing'.[37]

Sin engendered death, but repentance opens the way to Life: 'Sin is death. And is there anyone that dies as a result of it who then on his own account is raised up? Absolutely no one.' Through repentance then, we flee to Christ, who is without sin, who is the Resurrection and the Life. Repentance is the way out of sin and the way into the Divine Liturgy, where Life is offered: 'Leave the land of Haran which is sin, O my soul, and come into a land flowing with ever-living incorruption.'[38]

---

[36] St Germanus, *Contemplation*, PG 98.401A.

[37] *Apostolic Constitutions*, 7.26, PG 1.1020A; St Symeon the New Theologian, *Hymn 22*, 36, SC 174.172; Ibid., Service of Preparation for Holy Communion, prayer 7.

[38] St Symeon the New Theologian, *Catechesis 23*, 2, SC 113.18; Great Canon of St Andrew of Crete, ode 3.

According to the most ancient text that we have of the Liturgy, after the people have communicated, the celebrant says: 'Let grace come and let the world pass away.' It is into this realm of Grace that the Divine Liturgy leads us. St Maximus the Confessor also wants us to attain that realm. This great initiate of heavenly things and mystagogue of the faithful sees the Great Entrance as 'the beginning of and prologue to the new teaching which will be given in heaven concerning God's divine economy in relation to man, and the revelation of the mystery of our salvation which is concealed in the secret recesses of the divine'[39] — a teaching which has to do with the Teacher's act of sacrifice.

Then the Deacon says to the Priest: *Master, lift up.*

The Priest takes the *Aer* and places it on the shoulders of the Deacon, saying: *In peace, lift up your hands to the Holy Gifts and bless the Lord.*[40]

Then he takes the veiled Paten and gives it with every care and reverence to the Deacon, while he himself takes the holy Chalice, likewise veiled, saying: *God has gone up with a shout, the Lord with the voice of the trumpet.*[41]

When the Choir reaches the end of the phrase *For we are about to receive the King of all*, the Deacon and the Priest come out from the north door of the sanctuary and make the Great Entrance, processing down the left isle then up the middle of the church towards the

---

[39] *Didache*, 10.6, *ANF* 7, p. 380; *Mystagogy*, 16, *PG* 91.693C.
[40] Cf. Ps. 133: 2.
[41] Ps. 46: 6.

Royal Doors, preceded by attendants with a censor and candles. As they process, the Deacon proclaims: *May the Lord God remember you all in his Kingdom always, now and for ever, and to the ages of ages.*

Choir: *Amen.* And when the Priest and the Deacon enter the sanctuary through the Royal Doors the Choir completes the Cherubic Hymn.

The Priest then places the Chalice on the *Antimension*, and taking the Paten from the Deacon he places it to the left of the Chalice, saying: *The noble Joseph, taking your most pure Body from the Tree, wrapped it in clean linen with sweet spices and laid it for burial in a new tomb.*[42]

Deacon: *Do good, Master.*

The Priest censes the Gifts and says three times the last verse of Psalm 50, *Then they will offer calves upon your altar,* followed by, *and have mercy on me, O God.*

The transfer of the precious Gifts

At the Little Entrance, the celebrant covered his face with the Gospel Book to symbolise Christ who came and preached to the people. At the Great Entrance, the celebrant covers his face with the Gifts which are being offered, indicating Christ who goes up to Golgotha in order to be sacrificed.

The priest goes to the holy Prothesis, venerates the precious Gifts and raises them up 'level with his head, with great reverence, and goes out of the sanctuary. Holding them in this fashion, he transfers them to the Altar, going around the church in the proper manner, walking among the people at a slow pace. The

---

[42] *Apolytikion* of Holy Saturday.

faithful kneel in reverence...and the priest processes accompanied by candles and incense, and comes to the Altar.'[43]

The Cherubic Hymn, the processional candles, the fans, and in general the solemnity of the Great Entrance, help us to experience the reality of Christ's coming. They make manifest 'the entry of the saints and all the righteous, who are entering together with the Holy One of the holy ones. He is invisibly preceded by cherubic powers, angelic hosts, bodiless choirs and ranks of immaterial beings singing praise and providing an escort for Christ the great King who comes for the mystical Sacrifice.'[44]

Accompanied by the angelic hosts, Christ enters into the Holy of Holies holding our life, the life of the whole world, in His spotless hands. The precious Gifts are man and the world who through Christ are being returned to God, and the Great Entrance symbolises this return and the dedication of them to Him.

* * *

The Church exhorts us: *Let us now lay aside all worldly cares.* So we entrust our whole life to Christ as He is being sacrificed, and through death He brings our life to His Resurrection. But whereas the offering of our life to Christ is merely an image of death, 'our revivification is life in very truth'.[45]

As the celebrant was carrying out the Service of Preparation (Proskomide), we consigned our entire life to the precious Gifts: our sorrows and our joys, our enemies and our friends, the living and the departed are now in the hands of Christ. And He offers all of us to God the Father.

---

[43] St Nicholas Cabasilas, *Comm. Liturgy*, 24, *PG* 150.420AB. Until the 6th century, the transfer of the eucharistic Gifts to the Altar was a simple operation: the deacons would choose suitable offerings from the *prosphora* (the loaves of bread brought by the faithful), and take them to the Altar where they would hand them over to the bishop. It was then — during the chanting of the Cherubic Hymn — that the Preparation of the Gifts would be celebrated.

[44] St Germanus, *Contemplation*, *PG* 98.420A.

[45] St Nicholas Cabasilas, *Comm. Liturgy*, 4, *PG* 150.380A.

At this time, we beseech Christ: *Remember me, Lord, in Your Kingdom* (Luke 23: 42). That is, we ask Him to bring us out of the oblivion (*lethe*) of death and place us in the Truth (*a-letheia*)[46] and in Life, which are nothing other than Himself, so that we too may remember Him in the Mystery of His *anamnesis*, the Divine Liturgy.

* * *

The transfer of the precious Gifts from the holy Prothesis to the Altar 'signifies the Lord's entry into Jerusalem from Bethany'. The King of Kings enters the Holy City. The celebrant becomes the colt upon which no passion has ever sat (cf. Luke 19: 30) and is therefore accounted worthy to carry the King of glory. Instead of spreading garments before him (cf. Luke 19: 36), the faithful spread their very selves; they fall to the ground. And prepared in spirit, they welcome Christ:

> With our souls cleansed and in spirit carrying branches,
> with faith let us sing Christ's praises like the children,
> crying with a loud voice to the Master:
> Blessed are You, O Saviour, who have come into the world
> to save Adam from the ancient curse...
> O Word, who have ordered all things for our good, glory to You.[47]

Taking Your most pure Body down from the Tree

The placing of the Gifts on the Altar and the closing of the Royal Doors are the final actions of the Great Entrance.

As the priest places the holy Cup and Paten on the Holy Table, he recites the *troparion* 'The noble Joseph taking Your most pure

---

[46] Greek ἀλήθεια (*a-letheia*), meaning 'truth', is a negative form from the same root as λήθη (*lethe*), meaning 'forgetfulness', 'oblivion'; both relate to the verb λανθάνω (*lanthano*), meaning 'to escape notice'. –Trans.

[47] St Germanus, *Contemplation*, PG 98.420D; Palm Sunday, Matins (tr. Mother Mary and Kallistos Ware, *The Lenten Triodion*, p. 493 [adapted]).

Body down…'. The Paten, on which the Lamb being offered is placed, symbolises the hands of Sts Joseph and Nikodimus, 'who perform Christ's burial'.[48] The *Aer*, the cover placed over the precious Gifts, is a symbol of the winding sheet in which Joseph wrapped the immaculate Body of Christ, while the incense recalls the sweet spices used for His burial. Finally, the closing of the Royal Doors symbolises the sealing of the Tomb that held Life.

The celebrant performs the task of the saints who buried Christ. In a state of contrition, he contemplates with them at this time 'Him who decks Himself *with light as with a garment* [Ps. 103: 2]'. Lamenting 'in grief and tender compassion' he says: 'Woe is me, my sweetest Jesus! When but a little while ago the sun saw You hanging on the Cross, it wrapped itself in darkness, the earth quaked with fear and the veil of the temple was rent in twain. And now I see You for my sake submitting of Your own will to death. How shall I bury You, my God? How shall I wrap You in a winding sheet? How shall I touch Your most pure Body with my hands? What song at Your departure shall I sing to You, O compassionate Saviour? I magnify Your sufferings; I sing the praises of Your burial and Your Resurrection, crying: O Lord, glory to You.'[49]

Every Christian should imitate Joseph, who 'took the Body of Jesus, wrapped it in a clean winding sheet and placed it in a new tomb [cf. Matt. 27: 59–60] — which is to say, in a new person. Let each one of us therefore take diligent care not to sin, so as not to show contempt for God who dwells within us and expel Him from our soul.'[50] The soul of every Christian believer becomes a 'new tomb' which will receive the all-holy Body of Christ.

---

[48] St Germanus, *Contemplation*, PG 98.421C.
[49] *Aposticha*, *Doxastikon*, Holy Friday Vespers, *The Lenten Triodion*, pp. 615–16 (adapted).
[50] *To Mega Gerontikon* [*Sayings of the Elders*], vol. 3, (Panorama, Thessaloniki: Ieron Hesychastirion Genesion Theotokou, 1997), 'On discernment' 177, p. 168.

The Priest then puts away the censer and says to the Deacon: *Remember me, my brother and fellow celebrant.*

Deacon: *May the Lord God remember your priesthood in his Kingdom, always, now and for ever, and to the ages of ages.*

Then the Deacon bows his head and says: *Pray for me, holy Master.*

The Priest replies: *The Holy Spirit will come upon you, and the power of the Most High will overshadow you.*[51]

Deacon: *The Spirit himself will concelebrate with us all the days of our life. Remember me, holy Master.*

Priest: *May the Lord God remember you in his Kingdom, always, now and for ever, and to the ages of ages.*

Deacon: *Amen.* And he kisses the Priest's right hand, then goes out and stands in his usual place, before the Royal Doors, and says the Litany of the Proskomide.

The Holy Spirit concelebrates

As Christ enters the Holy City, the Comforter enters as well. At the Great Entrance, together with the angelic powers and the saints, 'the first to enter during the bloodless Sacrifice and rational worship is the Holy Spirit. In our mind's eye we see Him in the fire, the incense and in the fragrant smoke. The fire signifies His divinity, while the fragrant smoke signifies the presence of Him who came invisibly and made us fragrant through the mystical and bloodless worship.' Christ is the celebrant of mankind's salvation, in the Holy Spirit: 'Christ's visitation, and the Holy Spirit goes before Him. Christ's coming in the flesh, and the Holy Spir-

---

[51] Luke 1: 35.

it is inseparable from Him... Intimacy with God comes through the Holy Spirit.'[52]

In the Church, everything is a gift from the Comforter: 'Through the Holy Spirit comes our restoration to Paradise, our ascension into the Kingdom of heaven, our return to divine adoption, our courage to call God our Father, our being made partakers of the grace of Christ, our being called children of light, our sharing in eternal glory, and, in a word, our being brought into a state of all *fullness of blessing* [Rom. 15: 29], both in this world and in the world to come.'[53]

Now the priest invokes the Holy Spirit, and prays that the Spirit *will overshadow* the deacon with His grace. And in response to the priest the deacon prays: *The Spirit Himself will concelebrate with us.*

The Comforter *intercedes for us with sighs too deep for words* (Rom. 8: 26). He acts as our mediator, and our prayers are a gift from Him: *No one can say 'Jesus is Lord' except by the Holy Spirit* (1 Cor. 12: 3). The very event of the assembly is a gift of the Holy Spirit: 'It is the Comforter who summons the Church to assemble and hear the teaching.' In the assembly of the Church, the Comforter concelebrates with the priest and reveals Christ to the faithful: in His wisdom, the All-holy Spirit guides them and leads them by the hand 'to perfect knowledge, face to face, and initiation into the great God and Saviour of all, Christ'.[54]

* * *

Holy people are aware of the Holy Spirit concelebrating, and can physically see His overshadowing. *The Spiritual Meadow* records the following incident:

---

[52] St Germanus, *Contemplation*, PG 98.420AB; St Basil the Great, *On the Holy Spirit*, 19.49, PG 32.157AB.

[53] Ibid. 15.36, PG 32.132B.

[54] St Basil the Great, *On Psalm 48*, 1, PG 29.433A; St Maximus the Confessor, *Dogmatic Book for Marinus the Deacon*, PG 91.73A.

'Ten miles from the town of Aegeae there is a church of St John the Baptist. A holy elder, a hieromonk of great virtue, used to live there as a hermit. Well, one day the villagers went to the bishop with a complaint about him: "Dismiss this elder, for he is making things difficult for us. On Sundays, there are times when he begins the Liturgy at three in the afternoon! He's not observing the established order for the holy assembly."

'So the bishop summoned the elder, and said: "Monk, why do you behave like this? Don't you know the order of the services of the Church?" And the elder replied: "It is true, Your Eminence, that is the case... But I don't know what to do. On Sunday, after the Service of Matins is finished, I stand by the Holy Table, and until I see the Holy Spirit overshadowing the Altar, I do not begin the Divine Liturgy...".

'The bishop was amazed at the elder's virtue, and told the local residents about it. So they went away in peace, glorifying God.'[55]

---

[55] John Eucratas, *Leimonarion* [*The Spiritual Meadow*], 27, PG 87iii.2873BC.

4. THE LITANY OF THE PROSKOMIDE AND THE CREED

S tanding before the Royal Doors and facing the sanctuary, the Deacon intones the Litany: *Let us complete our prayer to the Lord.*

Choir: *Lord, have mercy.* And so after each of the following petitions.

Deacon: *For the precious Gifts here set forth, let us pray to the Lord.*

For this holy house, and for those who enter it with faith, reverence and the fear of God, let us pray to the Lord.

For our deliverance from all affliction, wrath, danger and constraint, let us pray to the Lord.

Help us, save us, have mercy on us, and keep us, O God, by your grace.

That the whole day may be perfect, holy, peaceful and sinless, let us ask of the Lord.

Choir: *Grant this, O Lord.* And so after each of the petitions that follow.

Perfection without end

Everyday life, with its dangers, its worries, its many and various sorrows and trials, is not external to the Divine Liturgy. In the spiritual realm, man does not lose his material dimension: both soul and body are filled with God's peace.

So in the petitions that the deacon now begins, we ask of the Lord that the present day should be peaceful, that our guardian

angel should be an angel of peace, that the whole world should enjoy peace, and that the end of our lives should be peaceful. In the Divine Liturgy, the peace of God becomes the song of the faithful: 'Beloved peace, sweet in name and in reality... Beloved peace, my constant concern and my adornment.'[1]

* * *

The spiritual life is an unceasing journey towards perfection. This journey is truly unceasing, because virtue has no end: 'Virtue has one limit — limitlessness.' And dispassion, which is the ultimate goal of the work of the virtues, is the perfection which has no end: it is 'the perfect, but still unfinished, perfection of the perfect'.[2]

This definition of perfection is explained by St Ephrem: 'Those who are dispassionate, progressing insatiably further and further towards their ultimate desire, make perfection endless... And perfection certainly is perfect by the measure of human powers, but it is also without end, because it is always surpassing itself in its daily progress, and is raised ever higher by its ascent towards God.'[3]

St Macarius of Egypt refers to spiritual perfection and the fruits it offers to man: 'Once the soul attains to the perfection of the Holy Spirit, that is to say, completely purified of all passions and united to the Comforter Spirit in inexpressible communion,...then it becomes all light, all eye, all spirit. It becomes all joy, repose, delight; all love, all compassion, all goodness and kindness [cf. Gal. 5: 22].'[4]

---

[1] St Gregory the Theologian, *Homily 22*, 1, PG 35.1132A.

[2] St Gregory of Nyssa, *Life of Moses 1*, PG 44.301B; St John Climacus, *Ladder of Divine Ascent*, 29.3, PG 88.1148C.

[3] See Sts Kallistos and Ignatius Xanthopoulos, *On those who choose to live in Hesychia*, 87, *Philokalia* [Greek edition] (Athens: Astir, 1957–63), vol. 4, p. 281.

[4] *Macarian Homilies*, 18.10, PG 34.641A.

During the assembly of the Liturgy, we ask for perfection because 'perfection comes from the divine and perfecting gifts'[5] of the eucharistic Mystery.

> Deacon: *For an angel of peace, a faithful guide, a guardian of our souls and bodies, let us ask of the Lord.*

A guardian angel

From the moment of Baptism, each Christian is protected by a guardian angel. The celebrant entreats the Lord on behalf of each person being baptised: 'Yoke to his life a radiant angel.' The Lord Himself talked about our guardian angels when He said of little children: *Their angels always behold the face of my Father, who is in heaven* (Matt. 18: 10).

The Prophet David assures us: *The angel of the Lord encamps around those who fear Him, and delivers them* (Ps. 33: 8). And St Basil interprets this verse as follows: 'Everyone who has believed in the Lord has an angel always near him, unless we drive him away by our evil deeds. For just as smoke makes bees withdraw and foul smells drive away doves, so sin, lamentable and stinking, drives away the angel who is guardian of our lives. If you have in your soul works worthy of angelic protection...God will place by you protectors and keepers, and will surround you with an angelic guard. And note the power of the angelic nature: that one angel is likened to an entire encampment... Just as walls are built around cities and deter enemy attacks from all quarters, so likewise does the angel' protect you on all sides like a bulwark.[6]

---

[5] St Dionysius the Areopagite, *Church Hierarchy*, 3.1, PG 3.424D.

[6] *On Psalm 33*, 5, PG 29.364BC.

One day, when St Macarius was in Constantinople, he encountered a noble young man weeping outside a den of vice. The youth had his face buried in his hands, and wailed and made such lamentation that you would think heaven itself wept with him. So Macarius went up to him and asked him to explain the reason for his sadness. The youth answered: 'Glorious servant of God, I am by nature an angel. As every Christian receives an angel from God at the time of his Baptism, it was given to me to protect this man here. But I am filled with sorrow when I see him sinning, as he is doing now in this den of vice. How could I not lament over the image of God which has been reduced to such darkness?'

'Why don't you admonish him?' asked the saint.

And the angel replied: 'I have no right to go near him. Since he began to sin, he is the slave of the demons, and I have no authority over him.'[7]

In this petition, we ask the Lord that our life should not be such as to drive our guardian angel away. For after the Lord, he is our hope of salvation:

> After God, I have placed in you all my hope of salvation,
> my guardian, my protector and my help.
> Bring with you choirs of angels
> as fellow-intercessors and helpers
> and together intercede with God on my behalf.[8]

---

[7] Cf. St Macarius, *PG* 34.221AC.

[8] St John Euchaites, *Canon to the Guardian Angel*, ode 9.

Deacon: *For pardon and forgiveness of our sins and offences, let us ask of the Lord.*
For those things that are good and profitable for our souls, and peace for the world, let us ask of the Lord.

Things profitable for our souls

Those things that are good and profitable which we ask of the Lord are not what worldly people call 'good and profitable'. Because 'for believers "things profitable" mean something different, not what the broad mass of people think they mean.'[9] A Christian knows that the soul exists and there is another life, and he sees everything through the prism of eternity.

Nevertheless, we Christians often do not know what is profitable for our souls, and that is why we ask Christ to give us whatever He judges to be in our interests. St John Chrysostom says: 'You yourself do not know what is in your best interests — unlike God, who knows your interests very well. Often you ask for things that are harmful and dangerous; yet God, who is more concerned with your salvation, does not pay attention to your request, but in every case takes care of your interests.' So the believer is not upset when he does not receive what he asked for, because he believes that the Lord 'orders all things out of love for man in the depths of His wisdom, and distributes to all what is profitable to them'.[10] And whether or not he receives an answer to his request, he gives thanks and glorifies God's love.

If we do not receive from God what we ask, it is because we ask for a stone and not for the Bread of life (cf. Matt. 7: 9). 'Let all your

---

[9] St John Chrysostom, *On 2 Corinthians*, 2.8, PG 61.404.
[10] *On Psalm 145*, 6, PG 55.526; *Octoechos*, Tone 8, Saturday Matins, *kathisma*.

petitions be spiritual, and then without fail you will receive what you ask' stresses St John. The Lord Himself exhorts us not to ask for trivial things because, as He has assured us, *one thing is needful* (Luke 10: 42).[11] And we in turn ask in the Divine Liturgy for the heavenly Bread, which is Christ. This is the One Thing which profits us — in Greek, *sym-pherei*, which literally means 'brings together'. It brings us all together close to the heavenly Father.

> Deacon: *That we may live out the rest of our days in peace and repentance, let us ask of the Lord.*
>
> *For a Christian end to our life, painless, unashamed and peaceful, and a good defence before the dread judgement seat of Christ, let us ask of the Lord.*
>
> *Commemorating our all-holy, pure, most blessed and glorious Lady…*
>
> Choir: [*All-holy Theotokos, save us.*] *To you, O Lord.*

Death: the beginning of a better life

A person who lives in the Church is not afraid to look squarely at the fact of death. He has prepared himself through repentance, and through the Divine Liturgy he lives the life to come even now. Such a person 'knows that the time that follows repentance is full of joy and delight. The joy of his heart mocks at death, and hell has no dominion over it, because this joy never ends.'[12]

For those who have truly repented and come to love Christ, death is not an entry into the darkness of non-existence but the doorway to the Bridal Chamber of the Master, a birth into the new

---

[11] *On Matthew*, 23.4, PG 57.312–313.

[12] St Symeon the New Theologian, *Catechesis 23*, SC 113, p. 22.

life. When St Ignatius the Godbearer was on his way to Rome, where he had been sentenced to be thrown to the lions, he wrote to the Christians there who were trying to have his sentence changed: 'For me, dying for Jesus Christ is better than reigning to the ends of earth... I seek after Him who died for our sake. I desire Him who rose for our sake. My birth is approaching. Forgive me, my brethren. Do not prevent me from living; do not desire my death! Do not give to the world one who desires to belong to God. Allow me to receive pure light. When I reach there [to God], then I shall be a man of God.' For the saints, what we call life is death, and our so-called death leads to life: 'It is a good thing for me to sink from this world and go to God, so that I may rise before His face.'[13]

* * *

In *The Spiritual Meadow* we read of the repose of a certain elder: 'In the region of Arselaon lived Abba Michael. When he fell gravely ill and was about to die, he said to his disciple Eustathius: "My child, bring me water so that I can wash my hands and receive Communion." Once he had taken Communion, he said: "You know, my child, that this place is dangerous and precipitous because of the steep slope where the grave is; and if I die up here, you will put yourself at risk taking me down and burying me. So help me and we can go down slowly." Once they had got down to the grave, the elder said a prayer, embraced his disciple and said to him: "May you have peace, my child, and pray for me." And he lay down in the grave, and departed to the Lord full of joy and delight!'[14]

The saints who have 'accomplished the liturgy of [their] life' depart to the Lord filled with peace. They approach death 'joyful and radiant', because death is 'the beginning of a better life, the prelude to a more spiritual way of living and a transition from

---

[13] *To the Romans*, 6, 2, PG 5.692B–693A, 688B.
[14] Cf. *To Gerontikon tou Sina* [*Sayings of the Fathers of Sinai*] (Thessaloniki: Sina Monastery, 1988), p. 184.

lower things to higher things'. For the saints, death is 'the beginning and the way to a change for the better'.[15]

The world is 'subject to change...and corruption through the
passing of time'. But death leads the saint to 'an ever-moving stability and a stable and changeless form of movement generated
eternally round that which is the one, unique and always the
same', that is to say, God.[16]

> While the Deacon is reciting the Litany, the Priest
> says in a low voice the following Prayer of the Prosko-
> mide:
>
> *Lord, God almighty, who alone are holy and does*
> *accept a sacrifice of praise from those who call on you*
> *with all their heart, accept and receive also unto your*
> *holy Altar the supplication of us sinners, and enable us*
> *to offer you gifts and spiritual sacrifices for our sins*
> *and the acts of ignorance on the part of the people.*
> *And count us worthy to find grace in your sight, that*
> *our Sacrifice may be well pleasing to you and that the*
> *good Spirit of your grace may rest upon us and upon*
> *these Gifts here set forth, and upon all your people.*
>
> (aloud) *Through the compassion of your only-*
> *begotten Son, with whom you are blessed, together*
> *with your All-holy, good and life-giving Spirit, now*
> *and for ever, and to the ages of ages.*
> Choir: *Amen.*

---

[15] Saturday before Pentecost, Vespers, *sticheron*; St John Chrysostom, *On
Matthew*, 38.4, *PG* 57.433; *On Hieromartyr Babylas*, 1, *PG* 50.529; St Gregory
of Nyssa, *On Pulcheria*, *PG* 46.877A.

[16] St Maximus the Confessor, *To Thalassius*, 65, *PG* 90.760A (*Philokalia*, vol. 2, p.
272, § 48).

Sins and acts of ignorance

In this prayer, which is called the Prayer of the Proskomide (Offering), the celebrant asks the Lord to make him worthy to offer the Holy Gifts for his own sins and for whatever has been committed in ignorance by the people.

It is not, of course, without significance that the prayer differenciates between sin and sin that is committed through ignorance. The sins of the people are termed *acts of ignorance*. The Liturgy then is offered to God for the sins of the priest and for whatever the people have done out of ignorance.

We are all sinners. But while in the case of the laity it is possible to sin out of ignorance, to sin out of ignorance is not permissible for a priest. Even the most insignificant of sins on the part of a priest are great 'not by their nature, but because they are exacerbated by the priestly dignity of him who dares to commit them'. As God told the Israelites, when the High Priest sins it is as if the entire people sin (cf. Lev. 4: 1–3). That is why, in such a case, it is laid down that the same propitiatory sacrifice should be offered *if the whole congregation of Israel sin through ignorance* [Lev. 4: 13–4]. This fact shows that 'the wounds of the priest need more assistance, that is, as much as the wounds of all the people together'.[17]

The celebrant, as a human being *entangled in carnal desires*, offers the Holy Anaphora *for himself and for the people's sins committed in ignorance* (Heb. 9: 7). Only Christ was without sin, and He has cleansed us from every sin — *He had by Himself purged our sins* (Heb. 1: 3). That is precisely why the celebrant falls before the Lord, asks remission of sins and beseeches Him that the Holy Spirit may dwell in the hearts of the faithful, so that the Sacrifice may be acceptable in His sight.

---

[17] St John Chrysostom, *On the Priesthood*, 6.11, PG 48.687.

Priest: *Peace be with you all.*
Choir: *And with your spirit.*

Peace prepares the way for love

In earlier times, when the Liturgy began with the Entrance with the Gospel Book followed by the readings, the priest's first word was the offering of peace. He would thereafter offer the peace of God several times. This is also done today: when the celebrant reads the Gospel, when he gives a blessing or announces the kiss of love and after he has performed the Sacrifice, he says, *Peace be with you all.*[18]

The priests say this blessing 'from the beginning of the Mystery...because being at peace among ourselves and with God is to be understood as the source and starting-point of every good thing'. When we are at peace, we are close to God. And as long as we are close to Him, we enjoy His peace to an ever greater degree. The Son and Word of God enters into us and 'makes our hearts serene'.[19]

The priest offers the peace of God 'because this is the mother of all good things... It is this that prepares the way for love.' In fact, 'what is most important for us is the peace of Christ, which brings with it, as its sister, love among ourselves'.[20]

We receive the blessing of peace and we make our way towards love. We make our way towards an encounter with Christ, who is Peace and Love.

---

[18] Cf. St John Chrysostom, *On Colossians*, 3.4, PG 62.322–3.

[19] St Cyril of Alexandria, *On John*, 12.1, PG 74.708BC; Pentecost, Matins, Canon, ode 1.

[20] St John Chrysostom, *On Colossians*, 3.4, PG 62.322; St Cyril of Alexandria, *On John*, 11.2, PG 74.473A.

Deacon: *Let us love one another, that with one mind we may confess:*

Choir: *Father, Son, and Holy Spirit, Trinity consubstantial and undivided.*

And the kiss of love is exchanged.

The kiss of love

After the Consecration of the Holy Gifts, we shall commune in Christ. But we cannot progress to unity with God if we are not united with our fellow-travellers journeying towards the Kingdom. If Christ is not among us, He is not going to enter within us. So the communion of love among the faithful comes first, in order that Holy Communion may follow. This is why the celebrant exhorts us: *Let us love one another.*

Love between ourselves is also a precondition for confessing our faith: *Let us love one another, that with one mind we may confess.* We are images of God in Trinity, and in order truly to confess the *Trinity undivided* we must also be undivided among ourselves — we must live a life of love.

It is not possible, however, to achieve love for our neighbour as long as our souls are divided between God and the world. Desires for material goods and possessions become the cause of quarrels and division between us and our brothers and sisters. 'It is not possible for those who are divided from their own selves to be gathered together and partake in peaceable union with God. For if we are illumined by the contemplation and knowledge of the one God, and come to be unified to this single and divine assembly, we shall no longer succumb to the desires which divide us.'[21]

---

[21] St Dionysius the Areopagite, *Church Hierarchy*, 3.3.8, PG 3.437A.

It is these desires that give rise to attachment to material things and hostility towards our fellow man.

*   *   *

The response of the faithful to the exhortation *Let us love one another* is an act: the act of the kiss of love. In the liturgical community, between the fellow guests at the Supper, 'the most divine kiss is sacredly enacted'.[22] The kiss of love is not a mere liturgical symbol but a liturgical experience, a sacred action. The liturgical kiss is not the *image* of the love which unites the faithful but the *experience* of that unity. It is the bond of love uniting those who offer the rational worship; it unites them among themselves and with the Word of God.

The kiss of love symbolises 'the concord and rational identity' between the faithful 'on account of which those who are worthy become familiar with God the Word... For the mouth [with which the kiss of love is given] is a symbol of rational expression [for through the mouth we express ourselves with words] and it is through rationality that all intelligent [logical] beings who share in it are closely bound to each other and to the first and unique Word, the cause of all rationality.'[23]

Every action in the Divine Liturgy is an everyday happening transfigured. The kiss of love takes on new dimensions: 'We are a temple of God. So when we kiss each other, we are kissing the

---

[22] St Dionysius the Areopagite, *Church Hierarchy*, 3.3.8, PG 3.437A. The *Apostolic Constitutions* describe how the kiss was performed in early times: 'Let the clergy kiss the bishop, the lay men the laymen, and the women the women' (*Ap. Const.*, 8.11, PG 1.1089C). Today, the kiss of love is performed between concelebrating priests.

[23] St Maximus the Confessor, *Mystagogy*, 17, PG 91.696A. 'Word', 'rational' and 'logical' all derive in Greek from the same root, λόγος (*logos*), which in addition to the Johannine usage (John 1: 1 and 14) indicating God from eternity – the Creative Word, who became incarnated in the man Jesus Christ – conveys the God-given human faculty of coherent, i.e. rational, thought and expression. Real concord between 'logical' beings and their union with God does not take place only through words, but primarily through the rational powers of the soul.

threshold and the entrance of the holy Temple.' Matter is sanctified and flesh receives the blessing of the Holy Spirit. 'Many
times,' said one elder, 'as the deacon was saying "Kiss one another", I would see the Holy Spirit on the lips of the monks.'[24]

The liturgical kiss is the manifestation of love: 'The kiss is a
sign that the souls have become as one and banish all rancour.' It
is also an expression of the unity of the faithful: 'The kiss unites
our souls and transforms us all into one body' — into members of
the Body of Christ. The faithful are united in a bond of love and
together construct the Body of Christ (cf. Eph. 4: 12): 'Love builds,
and this takes place as the faithful are knit together and united
among themselves, and together make up' the Body of the
Church.[25]

In its eschatological interpretation, the kiss of love 'prefigures
and foreshadows the concord among all the faithful, their oneness of mind and rational identity, in faith and love, which will
come about when the inexpressible good things to come are revealed.'[26]

Deacon: *The doors, the doors! With wisdom let us
attend.*
And the Priest, lifting the veil, waves it over the
Holy Gifts while the Creed is said.

---

[24] St John Chrysostom, *On 2 Corinthians*, 30.2, PG 61.606; *To Mega Gerontikon*,
[*Sayings of the Elders*], vol. 4 (Panorama, Thessaloniki: Ieron Hesychastirion to
Genesion tes Theotokou, 1999), p. 362. Cf. *Apostolic Constitutions*, supra.

[25] St Cyril of Jerusalem, *Mystagogical Catechesis* 5.3, PG 33.1112A; St John
Chrysostom, *On the Betrayal of Judas*, 1.6, PG 49.382; *On Ephesians*, 11.4, PG
62.85.

[26] St Maximus the Confessor, *Mystagogy*, 17, PG 91.693D–696A.

People: *I believe in one God, Father almighty, maker of heaven and earth, and of all things visible and invisible.*

And in one Lord, Jesus Christ, the only-begotten Son of God, begotten of the Father before all ages, Light from Light, true God from true God, begotten not made, consubstantial with the Father, through him all things were made. Who for us and for our salvation came down from heaven, and was incarnate of the Holy Spirit and the Virgin Mary and became man.

He was crucified also for us under Pontius Pilate, and suffered and was buried; and he rose again on the third day, in accordance with the Scriptures, and ascended into heaven and is seated at the right hand of the Father, and will come again in glory to judge the living and the dead, and his Kingdom will have no end.

And in the Holy Spirit, the Lord, the giver of life, who proceeds from the Father, who together with the Father and the Son is worshipped and glorified; who spoke through the prophets.

In one holy, catholic and apostolic Church.

I confess one Baptism for the forgiveness of sins.

I await the resurrection of the dead and the life of the age to come. Amen.

The doors, the doors!

After the dismissal of the catechumens, the doors of the church would be closed and deacons and sub-deacons would stand at the doors, so that the faithful could not go out and unbelievers or heretics could not come in. It says in the *Apostolic Constitutions*: 'Let the doors of the church be guarded, lest any unbeliever or

uninitiated person should come in. And if a brother or sister from a different region arrives, with a letter of recommendation, let the deacon make enquiry about them...in case they should be sullied by heresy.'[27]

Just as the church has doors which we should watch so that the uninitiated do not come in, so the human being, who is a living temple of God, has the 'doors' of his senses, which must be on guard at this sacred moment so that sin does not enter. For there are many ways in which we may sin: with our eyes, our hearing, our senses of smell, taste or touch, our tongue or our reasoning. And then the words of the Prophet are fulfilled, that *death has come through the small doors* (Jer. 9: 21). This is why the celebrant proclaims, '*The doors, the doors! With wisdom let us attend*, which means, when we are present at the Divine Liturgy, we should keep ourselves pure from any lascivious glance, from condemning our brethren, from foul language and vain talk, uncontrolled laughter and every falsehood... Then we are indeed standing *aright* and with *fear* of God at the Divine Liturgy.'[28]

The closing of the doors of the church signifies the closing of our senses and the elimination of worldly thoughts from our mind. Thus liberated from the images of this vain world, man attains to the vision of divine states of being. The Word leads the soul 'to gaze upon things intelligible'.[29]

In the eschatological perspective of the world, the closing of the church doors 'shows the passing away of material things and

---

[27] *Apostolic Constitutions*, 2.57–8, PG 1.737B–740A. In the liturgy of the *Apostolic Constitutions*, immediately after the kiss of love the deacon says: 'None of the catechumens, none of the hearers, none of the unbelievers, none of the heterodox' (8.12, PG 1.1092A). The exclamation, 'The doors, the doors!...' developed out of this command; the exclamation therefore had, and should have, a practical purpose.

[28] St Maximus the Greek, in: Grigoriou Monastery, *Agios Maximos o Grekos, o Photistes ton Roson* [*St Maximus the Greek, Enlightener of the Russians*], (Athens: Armos, 1991), p. 125.

[29] St Maximus the Confessor, *Mystagogy*, 13, PG 91.692B.

the entry of those believers who are worthy into the intelligible world, that is the bridal chamber of Christ, which will come about after that fearsome parting and the yet more fearsome sentence' of the Judge.[30]

Enumerating the gifts of God

After the doors are closed, the faithful gathered around the Lord's Table confess their faith in the Trinitarian God and in His love. Right faith is an essential prerequisite for the celebration of the eucharistic Mystery.

The Creed is the enumeration of God's gifts, and man's thanksgiving. Faced with the divine gifts which we have received from the Lord, there is nothing else that we can offer 'except to confess His great benefactions and thank Him for them'. The confession of the Creed signifies 'the mystical thanksgiving which we shall offer in the next life for the wondrous events and ways in which the all-wise providence of God has dealt with us, by which we have been saved'.[31] And at the same time, it will be the proof that God's love for man has borne fruit.

[30] St Maximus the Confessor, *Mystagogy*, 15, *PG* 91.693C.
[31] St John Chrysostom, *On Genesis*, 9.5, *PG* 53.80; St Maximus the Confessor, *Mystagogy*, 18, *PG* 91.696B.

5. THE HOLY ANAPHORA

Deacon: *Let us stand aright; let us stand with fear; let us attend, that we may offer the Holy Anaphora in peace.*
Choir: *A mercy of peace, a sacrifice of praise.*

Let us stand with fear

With the Holy Anaphora, which now begins, we reach the most sacred moment of the Divine Liturgy. That is why the deacon calls on us to pay attention to how we stand, both in soul and body: *Let us stand aright; let us stand with fear.* In St John Chrysostom's time, this exclamation took a slightly different form: 'Stand up; let us stand aright.'[1]

St John interprets the meaning of this exhortation as follows: We should 'elevate our base and earth-bound thoughts and rid ourselves of the spiritual paralysis induced by the cares of this life, so that we can present our souls upstanding before God... Think in whose presence you are, and with whom you will call upon God — with the Cherubim... So no one should take part in these sacred and mystical hymns indolently... On the contrary, one should expel all things earthly from one's mind and transport oneself totally to heaven, and then offer the all-holy hymn to the God of glory and majesty as if standing before the very throne of glory and flying with the Seraphim. That is why the deacon

---

[1] The corresponding exclamation in the *Apostolic Constitutions* reads: 'Stand up; let us be standing with fear and trembling to make our offering to the Lord' (*Constitutions*, 8.12, *PG* 1.1092A).

exhorts us to *stand aright* at this moment... In other words, to stand with fear and trembling, with a sober and watchful heart.'[2]

The Divine Liturgy is called an *anaphora*, meaning an 'offering up' in Greek, because we ourselves and our precious Gifts are offered up — raised up to God. And we must 'stand with reverence and fear at the terrible moment of the Holy Anaphora, for with whatever disposition of soul and whatever thoughts each person has at that time as he stands before God, he is raised up to the Lord with that same disposition.'[3]

The precious Gifts are not simply offered on the earthly Altar, but are raised up to the Altar above the heavens. We are all called to be raised up to the realm of undisturbable peace, and our translation to that realm must take place *in peace*. 'Great peace and quiet is needed' at this moment and place.[4] When the Holy Anaphora is offered on the Altar above the heavens, angelic powers stand round about in fear and trembling. They cover their faces in reverence and sing in praise of the triple Sun of the Godhead.

A mercy of peace, a sacrifice of praise

To the celebrant's exhortation to offer the Holy Anaphora *in peace*, the faithful reply: 'We offer it in peace and in love towards the Lord and our brother. We offer a *mercy of peace*. We offer *mercy*, that is, love, which is the fruit of peace.' Indeed, 'when no passion disturbs the soul, nothing prevents it being filled with mercy'.[5]

God tells us through the Prophet Hosea that the offering of our love to Him and to our brethren is preferable to a sacrifice that is offered without love: *I desire mercy and not sacrifice* (Hos. 6: 6). Furthermore, 'all the commandments of the Old Testament

---

[2] *On the Incomprehensible*, 4.5, PG 48.734.

[3] St Anastasius of Sinai, *Homily on the holy Synaxis*, PG 89.833BC. The Greek word ἀναφορά (*anaphora*) comes from the verb ἀναφέρω (*anaphero*) and means an upward movement, an elevation.

[4] St John Chrysostom, *On the Birthday of Jesus Christ*, 7, PG 49.361.

[5] St Nicholas Cabasilas, *Comm. Liturgy*, 26, PG 150.424B.

concerning sacrifices and whole burnt offerings are contained in the commandment of mercy and love'.[6] In consequence, it is not possible to offer the sacrifice of glorifying God before we have offered the sacrifice of our love. The sacrifice offered with love is a sacrifice well pleasing to God. It is a sacrifice that glorifies and hymns His own love: *a sacrifice of praise.*

The sons of the Kingdom, whose hallmark is peace, offer a *mercy of peace* and *a sacrifice of praise.* 'Mercy towards everyone who is suffering misfortune and needs help. But a *mercy* of peace. When we love the peace that is extended towards all, when we have demolished all enmity and conflict with everyone, then we offer the true sacrifice of praise.'[7]

This is the sacrifice that God asks of us: *Sacrifice to God, a sacrifice of praise* (Ps. 49: 14). 'In other words, a sacrifice of thanksgiving, of sacred hymns and of deeds that glorify God… You should live in such a way that your Lord is glorified. This is also what Christ taught when He said: *Let your light so shine before men that they may see your good works and glorify your Father who is in heaven* [Matt. 5: 16]… So let your life be such that your Master is glorified, and then you will have offered the sacrifice in its entirety.'[8]

The faithful Christian knows what sort of sacrifice is well pleasing to God, and addresses His love in these words: 'I will glorify You from my heart, from the altar of my soul. And for Your sake I will offer the sacrifice of praise, which is preferable to a myriad of whole burnt offerings. I will celebrate it for You, the perfect God.'[9]

In the Divine Liturgy, we offer the supreme *sacrifice of praise.*

---

[6] St Basil the Great, *On Isaiah*, 1.27, PG 30.172C.

[7] St Maximus the Greek, in: Grigoriou Monastery, *Agios Maximos o Grekos, o Photistes ton Roson* [*St Maximus the Greek, Enlightener of the Russians*], (Athens: Armos, 1991), p. 125.

[8] St John Chrysostom, *On Psalm 49*, 5, PG 55.248.

[9] St Basil the Great, *On Psalm 115*, 5, PG 30.113B. The whole burnt offering (in which the whole of the sacrificed animal was burnt on the altar) was the highest sacrifice according to the Law of Moses.

Through Christ, the faithful *offer up a sacrifice of praise to God continually, that is the fruit of lips that confess His name* (Heb. 13: 15). At the Holy Anaphora, the faithful offer 'prayers, hymns, thanksgiving. These are the "fruit of the lips"... And "confessing His name" means that we give Him thanks for everything, and especially for what He has suffered for us.'[10]

The Lord loves this *sacrifice of praise* because therein lies the road to man's salvation: *A sacrifice of praise honours me, and there is the way whereby I will show him my salvation* (Ps. 49: 23). 'Communion in the Body and Blood of the Master is rightly called "God's salvation"...because it was given for redemption from sins.'[11] At the Divine Liturgy, we offer God a *sacrifice of praise*, and God offers us His *salvation*, which is Christ (cf. Luke 2: 30).

> **Priest:** *The grace of our Lord Jesus Christ, and the love of God the Father, and the communion of the Holy Spirit be with you all.*[12]
> **Choir:** *And with your spirit.*

A trinitarian gift

At the Divine Liturgy we become partakers of the gifts of the Holy Trinity: from the source, which is *the love of God the Father*, through the way and door, which is *the grace of our Lord Jesus Christ, the communion of the Holy Spirit* comes upon the assembly of the Church and upon each believer individually.

---

[10] St John Chrysostom, *On Hebrews*, 33.4, PG 63.229–230.

[11] St Hesychius of Jerusalem, in St Nikodimus of the Holy Mountain, *Ermeneia eis tous 150 psalmous* [*Commentary on the 150 Psalms*], vol. I (Thessaloniki: Orthodoxos Kypseli, 1979), p. 720.

[12] 2 Cor. 13: 13.

This prayer 'offers us the good things of the Holy Trinity... *grace* from the Son, *love* from the Father, *communion* from the Holy Spirit. The Son's providence for us is *grace*, because He offered Himself as our Saviour without our contributing anything, and indeed when we were debtors. Because the Father has been reconciled with mankind through the Passion of His Son and shown love to those who were hostile to Him, His offering to us is called *love*. And finally, because He *who is rich in mercy* [Eph. 2: 4] should share His good things with His reconciled enemies, the Holy Spirit accomplishes this by descending upon the Apostles. That is why the Holy Spirit's goodness towards men is called *communion*.'[13]

The Divine Liturgy is the communion of human beings in the grace of the trinitarian God. The life which is offered to man, and brings him alive, is a gift from the Holy Trinity: 'Our life is given by God, through Christ, in the Holy Spirit.'[14] In general, every divine blessing that comes upon man is a gift of the Holy Trinity. For 'whatever is of the Holy Trinity is indivisible. Where there is the communion of the Holy Spirit, it is found also to be that of the Son. And where there is the grace of the Son, there is also that of the Father and the Holy Spirit.' So 'there is one gift and one authority of the Father, and of the Son, and of the Holy Spirit'.[15]

* * *

The people's response (*and with your spirit*) to the blessing given by the celebrant signifies that the faithful participate actively in the celebration of the Divine Liturgy. In relation to this

---

[13] St Nicholas Cabasilas, *Comm. Liturgy*, 26, PG 150.424B. St Nicholas explains why this prayer is necessary, given that all good things were given to human beings when Christ came to earth: 'So that we may not lose these things once we have received them, but may keep them to the end. This is why the celebrant does not say "may they be given to all of you", since they have already been given, but "may they be with all of you".'

[14] St Basil the Great, *Against Eunomius*, 3.4, PG 29.664C.

15 St John Chrysostom, *On 2 Corinthians*, 30.2, PG 61.608 and *On John*, 86.3, PG 59.471.

St John Chrysostom says: 'The celebrant does not touch the Gifts which lie before him until he has invoked the grace of the Lord upon you, and you have replied, *And with your spirit*. With this response, you remind yourselves...that the Gifts offered are not the work of man; rather, it is the grace of the Holy Spirit, which is present and hovers over all, that prepares this mystical Sacrifice.'[16]

> Priest: *Let our hearts be on high.*
> Choir: *We have them with the Lord.*

The miracle of the liturgical transfiguration

The Gospel account of the Transfiguration of Christ reads: *Jesus took Peter and James and John and led them up a high mountain apart by themselves; and He was transfigured before them* (Mark 9: 2). The same thing happens at the Holy Anaphora, which is the miracle of the liturgical transfiguration: *the grace of our Lord Jesus Christ* 'takes' us out of the world in which we live, and 'leads us up' [in Greek *anapherei* – the verb from which *anaphora* derives] the high mountain of *the love of God the Father*, where the mystery of *the communion of the Holy Spirit* is celebrated.

When God asked the patriarch Abraham to sacrifice Isaac, He said to him: *Take your son, your only son Isaac whom you love, and go to the high land and offer him there as a burnt offering* (Gen. 22: 2). It is up to this high land that the celebrant exhorts us also to go, so that we may offer the eucharistic Anaphora. Let us then imitate the patriarch Abraham, who did not allow either his slaves or his animals to approach the place of sacrifice. St John

---

[16] *On Pentecost 1*, 4, *PG* 50.458–9.

Chrysostom explains: 'You too should not allow any of the slavish and base passions to accompany you [to the place of the Holy Anaphora]. Go alone up the mountain where he ascended, there where nothing else is allowed to ascend... Let nothing disturb you at that moment, but become higher even than the heavens themselves.'[17] 'Keeping our hearts on high with God, let us observe that outstanding vision — our human nature, coexisting eternally with the immaterial fire of the Godhead.'[18]

Let our hearts be on high, says the priest. By the words *on high*, he indicates the place where the encounter between the soul that loves God and Christ the bridegroom happens. This is not a predetermined place. We are talking about a divine ladder which rests on the holy Altar, the top of which is inaccessible to human sight. The saints are characterised by an eternal motion. They move from the Altar to the vision of the uncreated light, and back to the Altar, which is filled with light. For upon it Christ — the Light of the world — lays down 'His illuminating Body'[19] for the nourishment and life of the world.

The soul climbs up unceasingly. And the further up it goes, the higher it longs to go. The ascent kindles its desire, and the food of the Divine Eucharist increases its hunger for mystical contemplation. St Symeon the New Theologian, who looked upon the beauty of the uncreated light and was nourished on the food of incorruption, uses a unique image: 'I do not know which gives me greater delight, the sight and enjoyment of the purity of the rays of the Sun, or the drinking and the taste of the wine in my mouth. I want to say the latter [the taste of the wine], and yet the former [the rays of the Sun] attracts me and seems sweeter. And when I turn to them, then I enjoy still more the sweetness of the taste of the wine. So the sight [of the rays] does not lead to satiety,

---

[17] *On 2 Corinthians*, 5.4, *PG* 61.432–3.

[18] St Gregory Palamas, *Homily 21*, *PG* 151.285B.

[19] Ibid. *In Defence of the holy Hesychasts*, 1.3.25, *Chrestou* I, p. 436.

nor can I have enough of drinking [that wine]. For when it seems
that I have drunk my fill, then the beauty of the rays sent forth
makes me thirst greatly, and again I find myself hungry and
thirsty.'[20]

The soul ascends so as to encounter God, and the effort it ex-
pends to do so gives it strength. It discovers new powers within itself as it climbs the liturgical Tabor: 'It makes its way ever upwards, continuously renewing its powers from the heights it has
attained so far.' At this point man moves beyond reason: so as to
satisfy his desire, he does not ask to see God as he himself is able
to but as God actually is. And God's divine love for mankind satisfies this desire for that vision by showing the impossibility of
the request, for 'it is characteristic of true contemplation of God
that the desire of the one who gazes steadfastly upon Him never
ends'.[21]

We have them with the Lord, the faithful reply to the celebrant. With this response, they assure him that they have already
ascended 'up to the heights…to the throne of God'.[22] Their hearts
are on high, *where Christ is, seated at the right hand of God*
(Col. 3: 1).

---

[20] *Catechesis 23, SC* 113, p. 24.

[21] St Gregory of Nyssa, *Life of Moses 2, PG* 44.401A, 404A.

[22] St Methodius of Olympus, *Symposium*, 8.10, *PG* 18.153A.

Priest: *Let us give thanks to the Lord.*
Choir: *It is meet and right.*

Let us give thanks to the Lord

We are now ready to proceed to the offering of the Sacrifice. The way we make the offering is by giving thanks to the Lord, and this is what the celebrant now emphasises. Christ Himself taught us the eucharistic way, the way of thanksgiving, in which to celebrate the Mystery: 'Jesus took bread, gave thanks for, broke it, and gave it to them saying, Take, eat; this is my Body which is given for you... He took the cup, and gave thanks, and gave it to them, saying, Drink of it, all of you [cf. Matt. 26: 26–7, cf. Luke 22: 19].'[23]

The best way to guard God's gifts is to keep them in mind and to give thanks for them. 'The terrible Mysteries which are celebrated at every assembly of the faithful, and which afford abundant salvation, are called the Eucharist [literally, 'Thanksgiving'] because they are the recollection of many benefactions, they show us the culmination of divine Providence, and in every way they prepare us to give thanks to God... That is why, at the time when this Sacrifice is being made, the priest exhorts us to give thanks to God for the whole world, for the past and the present, for all that has taken place, and for all that will take place in the future. This thanksgiving of ours liberates us from earth and transports us to heaven. It transforms us from humans into angels.'[24]

We give thanks to God for His benefactions; and the Eucharist itself is a new benefaction from God, for, while it adds nothing to Him, it 'makes us more His own'.[25]

---

[23] Cf. St John Chrysostom, *On Matthew*, 82.1, *PG* 58.738.
[24] Ibid. 25.3, *PG* 57.331.
[25] Ibid.

It is meet and right.

To the priest's exhortation to give thanks to the Lord, the faithful reply: *It is meet* [or 'worthy'] *and right*. This response signifies that they agree that the Divine Eucharist should be celebrated: 'Once all the faithful have given their agreement and exclaimed *It is meet and right*, the priest offers the Divine Eucharist to God.'[26]

The response of the faithful shows the unity of the Body of Christ. It also shows that their presence is essential for the Mystery to be celebrated. 'The thanksgiving to God is made in common, for it is not the priest alone who gives thanks, but all the people too. The priest speaks first, and he begins the Eucharist once all have agreed that this is enacted worthily and with just cause.'[27] At the Eucharist, the entire congregation takes part and proceeds together with the celebrant.

As we make our way towards the new Life, we sing the new song together with the saints: *...the four living creatures and the twenty-four elders fell down before the Lamb... And they sang a new song, saying, Worthy are you to take the book and to open its seals, for You were slain and by Your Blood ransomed men to God from every tribe and tongue and people and nation... And I looked, and I heard around the throne the voice of many angels saying... Worthy is the Lamb who was slain, to receive power and wealth and wisdom and might and honour and glory and blessing... And the four living creatures said, Amen! and the elders fell down and worshipped* (**Rev.** 5: 8–14).

---

[26] St Nicholas Cabasilas, *Comm. Liturgy*, 27, *PG* 150.425A.
[27] St John Chrysostom, *On 2 Corinthians*, 18.3, *PG* 61.527.

Priest (in a low voice): *It is meet and right to hymn you, to bless you, to praise you, to give you thanks, to worship you in every place of your dominion; for you are God, ineffable, incomprehensible, invisible, inconceivable, ever existing, eternally the same; you and your only-begotten Son and your Holy Spirit. You brought us out of non-existence into being, and when we had fallen you raised us up again, and left nothing undone until you had brought us up to heaven and granted us your Kingdom that is to come.*

For all these things we give thanks to you, and to your only-begotten Son and your Holy Spirit; for all the benefits that we have received, known and unknown, manifest and hidden.

We thank you also for this Liturgy which you have been pleased to accept from our hands, though there stand around you thousands of archangels and myriads of angels, the Cherubim and the Seraphim, six-winged and many-eyed, soaring aloft upon their wings.

For all these things we give thanks to You

The Holy Anaphora reveals to us God's constant loving providence towards man: *You brought us out of non-existence into being, and when we had fallen you raised us up again, and left nothing undone until You had brought us up to heaven and granted us Your Kingdom that is to come.* Initially, God brought man into existence ('being'). Then, through the entire plan of the divine economy, he restored him to a blessed existence ('well-being'). Finally, he offers him His Kingdom, which is eternal blessed existence ('eternal well-being').

St Maximus writes that rational creatures 'were first given the

principle of being, interwoven with their essence. Secondly, they were given that of blessed existence [well-being], according to their free choice... And thirdly, they have been given abundantly and by grace the principle of eternal blessed existence [eternal well-being].'[28]

Giving an allegorical interpretation of the creation story, the same saint says: 'The sixth day is the complete fulfilment, on the part of those practising the ascetic life, of the natural activities which lead to virtue. The seventh day is the conclusion and cessation, in those leading the contemplative life, of all natural thoughts about inexpressible spiritual knowledge. The eighth day is the transposition and transmutation to deification of those found worthy... The sixth day betokens the inner essence of the being of created things. The seventh signifies the mode of the well-being of created things. The eighth day denotes the inexpressible mystery of the eternal well-being of created things.' 'The eighth and first, or rather, the one unending day, is the manifest and all-radiant coming of God... God [then] gives eternal and blessed existence [eternal well-being] through communion with Himself, because it is He alone that in the proper sense exists, and exists eternally, and exists in blessedness.'[29] Man's communion with the Creator is the only eternal and blessed manner of being. This is the deification of man and his entry into the heavenly Kingdom.

It is this upward movement of God's love towards His supreme creation that is shown to us by the Holy Anaphora.

* * *

God, impelled by His love, created the world and man 'since the divine goodness had to overflow and spread.'[30] He created man and placed him near to Himself, to sing in praise of His glory. And

---

[28] *Ambigua*, 154, *PG* 91.1392A.

[29] *Two Hundred Texts on Theology*, 1.55–6, *PG* 90.1104BC (*Philokalia*, vol. 2, p. 125); *Ambigua*, 154, *PG* 91.1392D.

[30] St Gregory the Theologian, *Homily 38*, 9, *PG* 36.320C.

when man fell away through sin, God raised him up and brought him to heaven.

Christ became man, and 'left nothing undone until he had accomplished and suffered everything...until He had raised up the adversary and enemy [man, in other words] to God Himself and made him His friend... In a sense Christ took the first-fruits of human nature and raised them up as a gift to God our Master. It was as it happens when the corn in the fields is ripe: someone takes a few ears of corn and makes a little sheaf and offers it to God, and by that small offering he brings God's blessing on the entire field. Christ did the same thing here: through that one body, that first-fruit [which He assumed], He brought God's blessing upon the whole human race... So He offered to the Father the first-fruits of our nature. And the Father so admired this gift — both for the great worth of Him who made the offering, and because it was an offering without blemish — that He received it in His hands, set it beside Him and said, *Sit at my right hand* [Ps. 109: 1]. To what creature did God say, *Sit at my right hand*? It was the creature that had once heard the words, *You are dust, and to dust you shall return* [Gen. 3: 19]... Think how low man had fallen, and how high he has risen. There was no lower point to which man could sink than this to which he had already sunk, nor one any higher than where Christ had raised him up!'[31]

We give thanks to God for what we know and what we do not know, for His gifts both manifest and unseen, for His providence at every moment of our lives. 'I thank You, All-holy King, because before I was born You who alone are immortal, who alone are all-powerful, who alone are good and love mankind, came down to earth from Your holy height and took flesh and were born of the Holy Virgin, in order to refashion me and bring me to life and free me from the sin of our forefathers, and to prepare for me a way up to heaven. Then after I was born and had grown a little, You re-

---

[31] St John Chrysostom, *On Ascension*, 2–3, PG 50.445–7.

newed me through the refashioning of Holy Baptism, and adorned me with the grace of Your Holy Spirit, and gave me a radiant guardian angel... But I took no account of all these favours that You did for me...but once again threw myself, wretch that I am, into the pit and defilement of foul thoughts and deeds. And having fallen again into that pit, I fell among the thieves of the soul who were hiding there... And even though I in my insensibility was happy being their captive, yet You, my Master, could not bear to see me making such a spectacle of myself...but You had compassion, You had mercy on me...and stretched out to me Your immaculate hand.'[32]

We give thanks to God for everything. We thank Him for the Divine Liturgy itself, which He accepts from us. God could have ordained that the immaculate angelic powers should celebrate the Holy Eucharist, yet He accounted us humans worthy to perform this task, and accepts the offering from our unclean hands.

We thank God for the Divine Eucharist, and after the Eucharist, He bestows on us yet more grace since 'thanksgiving from the recipient spurs the giver to offer gifts greater than before'. And the blessed chain goes on: grace–thanksgiving–grace... We become aware of grace flooding over us: 'For the person who is grateful to his Maker becomes a receptacle of God's goodness and an instrument of His praise.'[33] We give thanks and glorify His holy name infinite times:

As You are my God, O Good One,
You had pity on me when I was fallen
and were well-pleased to descend to me,
raising me through the Crucifixion, that I may cry to You:
Holy, Lord of glory, incomparable in goodness.[34]

---

[32] St Symeon the New Theologian, *Thanksgiving 2*, SC 113, p. 330–34.
[33] St Isaac the Syrian, *Asc. Hom.*, 2, p. 10; St Irenaeus, *Against Heresies*, 4.11.2, SC 100, p. 501.
[34] *Octoechos*, Tone 1, Sunday Matins, Canon, ode 3.

Priest (aloud): *Singing, crying, shouting the Triumphal Hymn, and saying:*

Choir: *Holy, holy, holy, Lord of Sabaoth;*[35] *heaven and earth are full of your glory. Hosanna in the highest. Blessed is he who comes in the name of the Lord. Hosanna in the highest.*[36]

The Triumphal Hymn

The seal with which we stamp the *prosphora*, the oblation bread, for the Divine Liturgy bears the letters ΙΣ ΧΣ – ΝΙ ΚΑ, meaning 'Jesus Christ conquers', and proclaims the victory of Christ. And the hymn we sing as we make the offering also extols Christ's victory. It is called the Triumphal Hymn. It is the hymn of jubilation and profound gratitude to the Lord of the angelic powers, to 'the incorruption that conquered death'.[37]

The Triumphal Hymn is a combination of the angelic hymn which Isaiah heard when he received his calling as a prophet, and the hymn with which the people received the *Theanthropos* in the Holy City of Jerusalem 'as he was going to His voluntary Passion'. By singing this hymn at the Divine Liturgy, we are imitating both the angels and the people of the Holy City. We are praising and glorifying the Triple Sun of the Lord's dominion, and receiving the 'King of Kings', who 'comes to be slain and to be given as food for the faithful'.[38]

St John Chrysostom compares the Triumphal Hymn which we sing at the Divine Liturgy with the triumphal song sung by the Hebrews when they were liberated from the tyranny of the Egyp-

---

[35] *Sabaoth*: a Hebrew circumlocution for God, meaning 'Lord of Hosts'.

[36] Isa. 6: 3, Matt. 21: 9.

[37] St Methodius, *Symposium*, 3.7, *PG* 18.72B.

[38] Holy Monday Matins, Lauds; Cherubic Hymn for Holy Saturday.

tians.[39] The comparison shows that the triumphal song in the
Liturgy 'is much more splendid... For it is not Pharaoh who has
been overcome, but the Devil. It is not material weapons that
have been destroyed, but it is evil that has been abolished... We
are not going out towards the promised land, but emigrating to
heaven. We do not eat manna, but are nourished on the Body of
the Master. We do not drink water from a rock, but Blood from
the side of Christ.'[40]

* * *

On the lips of the angelic powers, the Triumphal Hymn, as
they sang it round about the holy throne of God, had a double significance. It was a hymn of praise to the Trinitarian God, and at
the same time a prophecy: 'This hymn is not only a doxology, but
also a prophecy of the good things that were going to spread
throughout the world... *The whole earth is full of His glory* [Isa.
6: 3]... When was the earth filled with the glory of God? When
that hymn came down from heaven to earth, and mankind on
earth formed one choir with the heavenly powers, raising the
same melody to God and offering a common hymn of glory.'[41]

The significance of the Triumphal Hymn on our own lips is
comparable. It is a doxology for Christ's victory which has already
been accomplished, and a prophecy concerning the second and
glorious coming of the Victor. It is the good news of the final coming of the Son of man, which will be preceded by the Cross, the
sign of His victory. 'Then all the nations and peoples from all ages
will fall down before Him and without objection will offer worship, and there will be one wonderful symphony of praise: The
saints will sing hymns, as they have always done, while the impi-
ous will of necessity make supplication. Then indeed the Tri-

---

[39] *Let us sing to the Lord, for gloriously has He been glorified...* (Exod. 15: 1–19).
[40] *On Psalm 46*, 2, PG 55.210.
[41] St John Chrysostom, *Commentary on Isaiah*, 6.3, PG 56.71.

umphal Hymn will be sung by all with one voice — by the victors
and by the vanquished.'[42]

Just as Christ the Victor is He *who is and who was and who is
to come* (Rev. 1: 4), so too His victory existed, exists and will exist
without interruption. Similarly, the hymn in celebration of His
victory will be sung unceasingly. At the heavenly Liturgy there
will be a constant movement of angels and humans around God
as they glorify the one Godhead in three Persons.[43]

Angels and men give glory together

The Triumphal Thrice-holy Hymn is a manifestation of the unity
of the heavenly and earthly worlds. Angels and men give glory together.

Speaking of the hymn, St John Chrysostom asks: 'Did you
recognise this voice? Is it yours, or that of the Seraphim? It is both
yours and that of the Seraphim, thanks to Christ who destroyed
the *middle wall of enmity* [Eph. 2: 14] and made peace between
heaven and earth [cf. Col. 1: 20]... Before, certainly, this hymn was
sung only in heaven, but when the Lord graciously descended to
earth, He also brought this melody to us. That is why, when the
High Priest stands before the Holy Table,...he does not simply
summon us to this hymn of praise, but first recalls the Cherubim
and brings to mind the Seraphim, and then exhorts all to raise
the strain that provokes such fear and trembling. Having dis-
tracted our thoughts from earth by reminding us of those who
sing with us, it is as if he calls to each of us, saying: "You are
singing with the Seraphim, abide therefore with the Seraphim;
open your wings with them, and fly with them together around
the royal throne."'[44]

In the Liturgy of the Kingdom, the angelic hosts appear as *four*

---

[42] St Gregory of Nyssa, *On holy Pascha*, 3, PG 46.653B.
[43] Cf. St Maximus the Confessor, *Mystagogy*, 19, PG 91.696C.
[44] *Homily on Isaiah 6*, 3, PG 56.138.

living creatures, full of eyes in front and behind: the first living creature like a lion, the second living creature like an ox, the third living creature with the face of a man, and the fourth living creature like a flying eagle. And the four living creatures, each of them with six wings, are full of eyes all round and within, and day and night they never cease to sing: Holy, holy, holy is the Lord God almighty, who was, and is, and is to come (Rev. 4: 6–8).

The four living creatures with many eyes symbolise the angelic powers and the whole of creation. The king of birds (the eagle), the king of domestic animals (the ox), the king of wild animals (the lion) and the king of creation (man) sing the Triumphal Hymn day and night to the Almighty Lord: '*Singing* is the eagle; *crying* is the ox; *shouting* is the lion; *saying* is man.'[45] All of creation participates in glorifying God.

* * *

Heaven and earth have now been unified. Angels, humans and material creation, the intelligible, the rational and the material world, all join together in singing the hymn to the *Theanthropos's* victory:[46] 'It is truly meet and right, proper and our bounden duty, to praise You, to hymn You,…who are hymned by the heavens and the heavens of heavens and all their powers, the sun and moon and the whole choir of stars, the earth, the sea and all that is in them, the heavenly Jerusalem, the festival of the elect, the Church of the firstborn whose names are written in heaven, the souls of the Righteous and of the Prophets, the souls of the Martyrs and Apostles, Angels, Archangels, Thrones, Dominions, Principalities and Authorities and fearsome Powers, the Cherubim with many eyes and the six-winged Seraphim…with unceasing lips and never-silent strains of theology, singing the Triumphal Hymn to Your magnificent glory in vibrant voices, cry-

---

[45] St Germanus, *Contemplation*, PG 98.429D.
[46] Cf. St Maximus the Confessor, *Mystagogy*, 13, PG 91.692C.

ing, giving praise, shouting, and saying: *Holy, holy, holy, Lord of Sabaoth.'*[47]

Those whose spiritual senses are awakened are able to perceive the participation of all of creation in the hymn of praise. We read in *The Spiritual Meadow* that on Mount Sinai, the mountain where God walked, 'on the day of Pentecost, a Liturgy was being celebrated on the holy peak. When the priest exclaimed, "Singing the Triumphal Hymn to Your magnificent glory in vibrant voices", all the mountains replied with a fearsome roar, repeating three times: *Holy, holy, holy.* This roar and its reverberation lasted some half an hour. But it was not heard by all, but only by those who had *ears to hear* [Matt. 11: 15] the hymn of the angels.'[48]

Priest (in a low voice): *We too with these blessed Powers, Master, Lover of mankind, cry out and say: Holy are you and All-holy, you and your only-begotten Son and your Holy Spirit. Holy are you and All-holy, and magnificent is your glory, who did so love your world as to give your only-begotten Son, that everyone who believes in him might not perish, but have eternal life.*[49] *And, when he had come and had fulfilled the whole dispensation for us, on the night in which he was betrayed, or, rather, gave himself up, for the life of the world,*[50] *he took bread in his holy, most*

---

[47] Liturgy of St James.

[48] John Eucratas and Sophronius the Sophist, *Leimonarion to palaion* [*The ancient Spiritual Meadow*], 3rd edn (Volos: Agioreitiki Bibliothiki, 1959), p. 60. The exclamation 'Singing the triumphal hymn' is in the form used in the Liturgy of St James. It is probable that this was the Liturgy celebrated in the 6th century on Sinai on the day of Pentecost. Cf. *To Gerontikon tou Sina* [*Sayings of the Fathers of Sinai*] (Thessaloniki: Sina Monastery, 1988), p. 60.

[49] John 3: 16.

[50] John 6: 51.

pure and unblemished hands and, when he had given thanks and had blessed, sanctified and broken it, gave it to his holy disciples and Apostles, saying:

(aloud) *Take, eat; this is my Body, which is broken for you for the forgiveness of sins.*[51]

Choir: *Amen.*

Priest (in a low voice): *Likewise after supper he also took the cup, saying:*

(aloud) *Drink from this, all of you; this is my Blood of the New Testament, which is shed for you and for many for the forgiveness of sins.*[52]

Choir: *Amen.*

God so loved the world

The magnitude of the gift that God the Father gave the world shows the greatness of His love: You *did so love Your world as to give Your only-begotten Son.* He gave His only-begotten Son to the world which was as dead, so that life could come anew. 'It was not that He was unable to deliver us in some other way, but in this way he showed us His exceeding love. He drew us to Himself through the death of His only-begotten Son. And if He had had anything more precious than Him, He would have given that for our sake in order to bring our race back to Him!'[53]

'*God so loved the world* [John 3: 16]: notice how much wonderment is contained in this. Reflecting on the magnitude of what he had to convey, John the Evangelist could not but say, *so loved...* Tell us, blessed John, how much is that "so loved"? Tell us the measure; tell us the magnitude; teach us of the superabun-

---

[51] Matt. 26: 26; 1 Cor. 11: 24.

[52] Matt. 26: 27–8; Luke 22: 20.

[53] St Isaac the Syrian, *Asc. Hom.*, 71, pp. 345–6.

dance. *God so loved the world that He gave His only-begotten Son.*' 'Each word has great significance...and [the whole] demonstrates the exceeding greatness of the divine love. For the distance separating God and mankind was vast, infinite even. The immortal God who is without beginning, the boundless greatness, *loved* those who were formed from earth and dust, who were filled with innumerable sins. He *loved* the ungrateful, those who were constantly contravening His divine will.'[54]

The sacrifice of Christ is the manifestation of divine love: *In this the love of God was made manifest among us, that God sent His only-begotten Son into the world, that we might live through Him. In this is love, not that we loved God but that He loved us and sent His Son to be the expiation for our sins* (1 John 4: 9–10).

The sacrifice of Christ is accomplished

At the Last Supper, Christ celebrates sacramentally His sacrifice on the Cross. He offers His holy Blood, and by calling it the *blood of the New Covenant* [or 'Testament'], 'He shows that He is going to die. That is why he talks about a testament, a will. And indeed He recalls the earlier Covenant [the Old Testament], because that too was ratified by blood [cf. Heb. 9: 18–21].'[55] At the Last Supper, we see the past (the Old Testament), the present (the New Testament) and the future (His imminent death) coexisting in the person of Christ.

In the Liturgy of St James, before the Consecration of the Holy Gifts, the people sing with compunction: 'Your death, O Lord, we proclaim, and Your Resurrection we confess.' The Divine Eucharist is the sacramental 'living out' of Christ's sacrifice. During the celebration 'Christ the Master is present, and His death is accomplished, the awful Sacrifice'. 'Revere this sacred Table,' says

---

[54] St John Chrysostom, *On Genesis*, 27.1, PG 53.241; *On John*, 27.2, PG 59.159, cf. Gen. 18: 27: *I am but dust and ashes.*
[55] St John Chrysostom, *On Matthew*, 82.1, PG 58.738.

St John Chrysostom, 'revere the Sacrifice that lies upon it, which is Christ slaughtered for us.'[56]

The Lord was given over to death for our sake, or, rather, He gave Himself up willingly (cf. Matt. 26: 21). In Scripture 'it is said that He was betrayed, but it is also written that He gave Himself up [cf. Eph. 5: 2]'. Christ 'suffered death on our behalf and for our sake, willingly. We see Him going to His death voluntarily, even though He could easily have avoided the Passion.'[57] On the night of the Last Supper, Christ was handed over to the chief priests by Judas, *or, rather, gave Himself up, for the life of the world.*

At the Last Supper, Christ offers the disciples His all-holy Body already *broken*, and His holy Blood already *shed*. In a manner beyond the grasp of the human mind, the Lord anticipates the events of His betrayal and the Cross. By giving the Twelve His holy Body as food, 'He shows with clarity that the sacrifice of the Lamb has already been accomplished'.[58] The Last Supper is also called the Mystical Supper because it has revealed to us the saving Sacrifice; it has initiated us into the mystery of that Sacrifice.

The Divine Eucharist 'is not an image and prefiguration of sacrifice, but an actual Sacrifice', because Christ is sacrificed and offered to the faithful. St John Chrysostom says: 'You are approaching an awesome and holy Sacrifice... Christ lies before you slain.'[59]

The sacrifice on Golgotha and the sacrifice of the Divine Eucharist are one, because 'we always offer the same Christ. We do not offer one sheep today and another tomorrow, but always the same one. Thus the sacrifice is one... The sacrifice that was offered then is the one we offer now, the sacrifice that is never ex-

[56] St John Chrysostom, *On Acts*, 21.5, PG 60.170 and *On Romans*, 8.8, PG 60.465.
[57] St Gregory the Theologian, *Homily 45*, 27, PG 36.660C; St Cyril of Alexandria, *On John*, 6, PG 73.1049B.
[58] St Gregory of Nyssa, *On the Pascha*, 1, PG 46.612C.
[59] St Nicholas Cabasilas, *Comm. Liturgy*, 32, PG 150.440C; *On the Betrayal of Judas*, 1.6, PG 49.381.

pended.' Christ 'having brought Himself as an offering once...He is ever being slain, sanctifying those who partake.'[60]

The Divine Eucharist is the Mystery of Christ's death on the Cross. So as we participate in this Mystery, we taste the fruits of Christ's sacrifice.

Through the Cross of Christ, 'death was abolished, resurrection was granted to us, the gates of Paradise were opened...we became children of God'.[61] Man was freed from enslavement to the Devil, and his original beauty with which he was endowed when first created was restored: 'When Christ ascended the Cross and died and rose again, the freedom of mankind was firmly established, and form and beauty [that of the first-created man] were fashioned.' Man and the cosmos were sanctified for all ages: 'A few drops of blood re-create the entire world.'[62]

On the holy Altar we see the root that put forth the Tree of Life: God's love for man. We ask ourselves, 'What could compare with this love?... What mother ever loved so tenderly? What father so loved his children? Who has ever loved their beloved with such mad desire?'[63]

Upon the Table of Life we encounter the loving Father, who 'through the Passion of His Son was reconciled with the human race, and showed love to His enemies'.[64] Divine love is at once the root and the fruit of the Cross.

The Last Supper and the Divine Eucharist

The Divine Eucharist is the sacramental extension of the Last Supper. It is not a formal repetition of it, but the Last, the Mystical

---

[60] St John Chrysostom, *On Hebrews*, 17.3, PG 63.131; Service of Preparation for Holy Communion, Canon, ode 9.

[61] St John of Damascus, *On the Orthodox Faith*, 4.84, PG 94.1128D–1129A.

[62] St Nicholas Cabasilas, *On the Life in Christ*, 2, PG 150.537C; St Gregory the Theologian, *Homily 45*, 29, PG 36.664A.

[63] St Nicholas Cabasilas, *On the Life in Christ*, 6, PG 150.645D–648A.

[64] Ibid. *Comm. Liturgy*, 26, PG 150.424C.

Supper itself, for the same Christ offers and is offered. St John
says, 'believe that even now this is the Supper at which Christ was
present. In no way is that Supper different from this Mystery...
For it is He that offers both the one and the other.' The saint
speaks categorically because what he says stems from the experience of his holy life: 'He who performed the Mystery at the Last
Supper, He it is who now accomplishes the Mystery of the Divine
Liturgy... This Holy Table is the same Table as that of the Last Supper, and is nothing less.'[65]

The presence of Christ, the light that shone at the Last Supper,
shines also at every eucharistic Supper. This presence is its divine
adornment: 'Now, too, Christ is present; He who adorned that
Table now adorns this one.' Having offered the sacrifice of Himself, Christ 'does not cease from His priesthood, but ever celebrates
the Divine Liturgy for our sakes', and intercedes with God for us.[66]

Solomon the wise spoke prophetically of the Supper of life:
*Wisdom has built her house...she has also set her table. She has
sent her servants to call to the cup with an exalted proclamation,
saying... Come, eat of my bread and drink of the wine I have
mixed for you... That you may reign for ever* (Prov. 9: 1–6). The
things Solomon speaks of 'are symbols of what is now celebrated
at the Divine Liturgy... Our generous God is ready [to be offered],
the divine Gifts are before us. The mystical Table is laid. The life-
giving Cup is full. The King of glory sends forth the invitation to
the Supper, the Son of God receives the guests... The personified
Wisdom of God the Father, which has built Herself a temple not
made by hands, distributes Her Body in the form of bread and offers Her life-giving Blood in the form of wine. What a fearful mystery!... What incomprehensible condescension! What unfathomable compassion!'[67]

---

[65] *On Matthew*, 50.3, *PG* 58.507; 82.5, *PG* 58.744.

[66] St John Chrysostom, *On the Betrayal of Judas*, 1.6, *PG* 49.380; St Nicholas
Cabasilas, *Comm. Liturgy*, 28, *PG* 150.428B.

[67] St Cyril of Alexandria, *On the Mystical Supper*, *PG* 77.1017CD.

To participate in Christ's Supper is to see and taste His love: *Taste and see that the Lord is good* (Ps. 33: 9). John the Evangelist begins his account of the Last Supper by saying that this was the expression of Christ's endless love for His disciples: *Before the feast of the Passover, Jesus...having loved His own who were in the world, He loved them unto the end* (John 13: 1). And having set Himself before them as the food of immortality, He gives the new commandment of love: *A new commandment I give to you, that you love one another even as I have loved you* (John 13: 34). Then he goes on to reveal the magnitude and the character of His love for us, and explains the first *even as* (John 13: 34) with a second: *Even as the Father has loved me, so have I loved you; abide in my love* (John 15: 9).

When we participate in the Supper of the Eucharist, we are participating in the Supper of divine Love and are called to abide in that love.

Priest (in a low voice): *Remembering therefore this commandment of salvation and all that has been done for us: the Cross, the Tomb, the Resurrection on the third day, the Ascension into heaven, the Sitting at the right hand, the Second and glorious Coming again,*

(aloud) *we offer you your own of your own, in all things and for all things.*

Choir: *We praise you, we bless you, we give thanks to you, O Lord, and we pray to you, our God.*

Remembrance of Christ

Having offered His disciples His holy Body and precious Blood, Christ gave them the commandment: *Do this in remembrance of*

me (Luke 22: 19). In this way He teaches us that true remembrance of Him is not merely a thought but an act: the celebration of the Mystery of His Supper. And so that we should not regard this remembrance of Him as a mere symbol, He said clearly: *Take, eat my body… Drink my Blood.*

These words of Christ and the recollection of the entire divine economy lead us into the eucharistic offering: *Remembering therefore this commandment of salvation and all that has been done for us…we offer You Your own of Your own.* At the Divine Liturgy, 'the memory of Christ's sacred works is ever renewed' through words and through actions. Through the Eucharist, we carry out precisely that sacred action that Christ our Master carried out. We offer the Holy Anaphora 'in commemoration of His death'. We do not simply think about the sacrifice of Christ, we live it: 'The Sacrifice that was offered then [by Christ] is the one we offer now, the Sacrifice that is never expended… We are always enacting the same Sacrifice.'[68]

One of the reasons the Lord instituted the Eucharist is for us to actually *live* the remembrance of Him, because this leads us to thanksgiving: 'Christ said, *Do this in remembrance of me* [Luke 22: 19], revealing to us why He gave us this Mystery,…which is in itself [reason] enough to move us to reverence. For when you consider what your Master suffered for you, you will become a greater lover of wisdom', more spiritual, that is to say.[69] It is from the remembrance of the benefaction that the thanksgiving — the Eucharist — springs forth, and it is the Eucharist that makes us 'greater lovers of wisdom': it makes us even more lovers of Christ who is the *Wisdom of God* (1 Cor. 1: 24).

Through the mouth of St John Chrysostom, Christ explains the meaning of this remembrance: 'Just as you kept the Jewish

---

[68] St Dionysius the Areopagite, *Church Hierarchy*, 3.3.12, *PG* 3.441C; St John Chrysostom, *On Hebrews*, 17.3, *PG* 63.131.

[69] St John Chrysostom, *On 1 Corinthians*, 27.4, *PG* 61.230. In patristic writing, *philosophia* or 'love of wisdom' denotes spiritual life.

Passover in order to remember the wonders that took place in Egypt, so you should keep this [my Passover] in order to remember me.' 'As Moses says, "This day shall be for you an eternal remembrance" [cf. Exod. 12: 14], so also Christ says, "in remembrance of me, until I come" [cf. 1 Cor. 11: 26].'[70]

Given that we live in expectation of Christ, the Divine Liturgy, the Mystery of the remembrance of Him, is the foretaste of the Kingdom which is to come.

Remembrance of Christ's Kingdom

Christ said at the Last Supper: *I shall not drink again of this fruit of the vine until that day when I drink it new with you in my Father's Kingdom* (Matt. 26: 29). So it follows that the Divine Liturgy, which is the foretaste of the Supper of the Kingdom, unites the Last Supper with the Kingdom of God. In the time between the Last Supper and the future Kingdom, the Divine Liturgy is celebrated — the life-giving remembrance of the Supper, of *all that has been done for us,* and of the Kingdom itself.

In the Divine Liturgy, we experience things to come as already present. We recall sacramentally what has taken place and what has not yet been accomplished, and we refer to these things as 'having been done': *Remembering… all that has been done for us: the Cross, the Tomb, the Resurrection on the third day, the Ascension into heaven, the Sitting at the right hand, the Second and glorious Coming again*, we offer the eucharistic Sacrifice.

Through the Liturgy, we enter into a different time which is not measured by the usual divisions of past, present, and future. The future (that is, the Kingdom which is coming) throws light on the past, and is offered to us as a luminous present reality. Thus in the Liturgy the first and the last, the beginning and the end, the Alpha and the Omega are present simultaneously: 'That life

---

[70] *On Matthew*, 82.1, *PG* 58.739.

which is to come has in some way been poured into this present life and mingled with it.' We look for the resurrection of the dead and we live already in heaven: 'This Mystery transforms earth into heaven.'[71]

In the grace of the Divine Liturgy, things to come are things *done*, because Christ is 'above space and time and the particularity of events'.[72] In the Liturgy we experience the mystery of Christ, who came and is *coming and now is* (John 4: 23).

We offer to You Your own of Your own

Man received the world from the hands of God as a gift full of divine blessings. Wanting to express his gratitude, and not having anything to offer in return, he thus gives back to God His own gift. So the world which was the vehicle of God's love for man now returns to God, and becomes the vehicle of man's thanksgiving to God.

We offer to God the gift that He gave us, placing upon it the seal of our gratitude. The tilling of the soil, the sowing and harvesting, the kneading of the bread and the treading of the grapes is man's seal upon God's world. The wheaten bread, the pure wine, the unadulterated oil are the world that returns to God, laden with the labours, the worries, the joys and hopes of mankind.

Yet this gift of God's is not the only blessing He gives us, or even the greatest. For if, through the first creation, God revealed His love to man by offering him the world as a gift, in the new creation He revealed His love by offering man His own self as a gift! That is why now, in the new Sacrifice, we offer God the very same offering that he offered us, that of Christ.

The Gifts which we bring to the Altar as an offering have the capacity to express, in a correspondingly worthy manner, our

---

[71] St Nicholas Cabasilas, *On the Life in Christ*, 1.1, *PG* 150.496C; St John Chrysostom, *On 1 Corinthians*, 24.5, *PG* 61.205.

[72] St Clement of Alexandria, *Stromata II*, 2, *PG* 8.937A.

gratitude for His love, which was made manifest in both the original creation of the world and in the new creation in Christ. And those same Gifts also indicate the freedom that Christ has bestowed on us by offering Himself *as a ransom for many* (Matt. 20: 28). This is precisely expressed in what the priest says to Christ in the Liturgy of St Gregory the Theologian, just before the Consecration: 'I offer You these symbols of my freedom.'[73]

The person who has come to love the Lord ardently expresses his love by offering creation to the Creator as a eucharistic gift, a gift of thankfulness. And holding the Gifts in his hands, his intellect ascends to the heights of God through the Holy Anaphora. 'It ascends in very truth...it hears the unspeakable words [cf. 2 Cor. 12: 4] and sees invisible things. And it becomes entirely wrapped in the miracle of it...and it rivals the tireless angelic choir, having truly become another angel of God upon earth. And through itself it leads on every created thing to God.'[74]

Through man and with man, creation comes to the heavenly Altar. It too receives the sanctifying grace of the Paraclete and becomes a locus of encounter between the created and the Uncreated; creation becomes Eucharist. And man partakes of the 'eucharisted food'[75] — Christ — and is made christ.

* * *

God's love for man is so great that He receives from us the gifts which He Himself gave us, '...for when we offer Him things which are in reality His own He accepts them as if they were ours'.[76] And we confess the ineffable debt we owe to His love.

We offer to You Your own of Your own and *we give thanks to You.* 'We offer to You, God and Father, that same offering which

---

[73] *PG* 36.712A.

[74] St Gregory Palamas, *To the nun Xenia*, 59, *Philokalia*, vol. 4, p. 317.

[75] St Justin, *First Apology*, 66, *PG* 6.427C.

[76] St Maximus the Confessor, *To Thalassios*, 51, *PG* 90.481D (*Philokalia*, vol. 2, p. 211, § 7).

Your only-begotten Son dedicated to You. And as we offer it we give thanks to You, because He too gave thanks to You as He dedicated it. We do not add anything of our own to this bringing of gifts: for these Gifts are not our own work, but belong to You, the Creator of all; nor did we conceive this manner of worship... That is why these things that we offer You, from among Your own gifts which You have given us, are Yours in all and every respect.'[77]

As we offer to the Lord these things which are His own, we thank Him *in all things and for all things*. We thank Him in every place and time, for every one of His benefactions, *always and for all things in the name of our Lord Jesus Christ* (Eph. 5: 20).

Priest (in a low voice): *Again we offer you this spiritual worship without the shedding of blood, and we ask, pray, and implore you: send down your Holy Spirit upon us and upon these Gifts here set forth.*
Deacon: *Master, bless the holy Bread.*
The Priest blesses the holy Bread, saying: *And make this bread the precious Body of your Christ.*
Deacon: *Amen. Master, bless the holy Cup.*
The Priest blesses the Chalice, saying: *And that which is in this Cup, the precious Blood of your Christ.*
Deacon: *Amen. Master, bless both the Holy Gifts.*
The Priest, blessing both the Holy Gifts, says: *Changing them by your Holy Spirit.*
Deacon: *Amen, amen, amen.*

77 St Nicholas Cabasilas, *Comm. Liturgy*, 49, PG 150.481D–484A.

The descent of the Paraclete

In the Liturgy of St James, the following dialogue takes place between the celebrant and the people before the Anaphora begins. The celebrant says: 'Magnify the Lord with me, and let us exalt His name together.' And the people reply: *The Holy Spirit will come upon you and the power of the Most High will overshadow you* (Luke 1: 35). The response of the people recalls the dialogue between the Theotokos 'full of grace' and the Angel Gabriel at the Annunciation.

Every Divine Liturgy is a new Annunciation. The Church's petition, *send down Your Holy Spirit upon us,* in a way repeats the words of the Ever-Virgin Mary: *Behold the handmaid of the Lord, be it unto me according to Your word* (Luke 1: 38). And the Annunciation of the Theotokos Church is accomplished.

Through the Divine Eucharist, the holy Church becomes a Mother Theotokos. The Paraclete descends upon the Church and upon the Precious Gifts, and in a sacramental manner, the Word of God is conceived, and the Timeless One is born and is offered *for the life of the world* (John 6: 51). The Church receives the fulfilment of *those things that were told her from the Lord* (Luke 1: 45): *This is my Body... This is my Blood* (Matt. 26: 26–8).

* * *

In order for the Mystery of the Divine Eucharist to be celebrated, the Lord gave the Apostles and their successors 'the power that would enable them to accomplish it', that is to say, the Holy Spirit. 'This Mystery is a work of the descent of the Holy Spirit, because He did not descend once only and then abandon us, but He is and will be with us for ever... It is He that performs the Mysteries through the hand and the tongue of the priests.'[78]

The descent of the Holy Spirit *upon us and upon these Gifts here set forth* is God's response to the petition of His children. It

---

[78] Ibid. 28, *PG* 150.428AB.

is the assurance that God regards us as His children and that our gifts have been received by His love. 'When you see the Holy Spirit descending bounteously, do not have any doubt about our reconciliation with God,' writes St John Chrysostom.[79]

Through the Divine Liturgy, 'we are able to celebrate Pentecost all the time'. The descent of the Paraclete is the eucharistic Pentecost: 'This moment in the Mystery manifests the moment of Pentecost.'[80]

The presence of the Paraclete brings the people of God together around the Holy Table. 'He welds together the whole institution of the Church': 'If the Holy Spirit were not present, the Church would not have been founded, but since the Church does exist, it is evident that the Holy Spirit is present.'[81]

St Symeon the New Theologian, concealing his own identity, says that he heard the following from someone else: 'I never celebrated without seeing the Holy Spirit, just as I saw Him coming to me when the bishop ordained me priest... I saw Him simple, without form, but surely as light. And as I wondered...the Holy Spirit said to me secretly: "This is how I come to all the Prophets, the Apostles, the saints and the elect of God living even today. For I am the Holy Spirit of God." '[82]

Priest (in a low voice): *That those who partake of them may obtain vigilance of soul, forgiveness of sins, communion of the Holy Spirit, fullness of the Kingdom of heaven, boldness to approach you, not judgement or condemnation.*

---

[79] *On Pentecost 1*, 3, *PG* 50.457.

[80] St John Chrysostom, *On Pentecost 1*, 1, *PG* 50.454; St Nicholas Cabasilas, *Comm. Liturgy*, 37, *PG* 150.452B.

[81] Sunday of Pentecost, Vespers, *sticheron*; St John Chrysostom, *On Pentecost 1*, 4, *PG* 50.459.

[82] *Practical and Theological Chapters, PG* 120.685D–668A.

Also we offer you this spiritual worship for those who have gone to their rest in faith, Forefathers, Fathers, Patriarchs, Prophets, Apostles, Preachers, Evangelists, Martyrs, Confessors, Ascetics, and every righteous spirit made perfect in faith;

(aloud) *Above all for our most holy, pure, most blessed and glorious Lady, the Theotokos and Ever-Virgin, Mary.*

Choir: *It is truly meet to call you blessed, Theotokos, the ever-blessed and all-immaculate, and Mother of our God. More honourable than the Cherubim and infinitely more glorious than the Seraphim, who without corruption gave birth to God the Word; you, truly the Theotokos, we magnify.*

It is truly meet to call you blessed, Theotokos

We offer the Divine Eucharist on behalf of all the saints, and *above all* on behalf of the Most Holy Theotokos, the Mother of God, so as to honour them and also to thank God for granting them to us as intercessors for our salvation. The very existence of the saints is a eucharist — a thanksgiving — from man to God for His benefactions, but it is particularly so with regard to the Most Holy Mother of God which is why we honour and bless her in a special way.

The Lady Theotokos is the supreme creation of God's love. Within the created order, she is the 'exceptional and outstanding and absolutely deiform fulfilment worked by God's creative Wisdom'. 'She alone is the boundary between created and uncreated nature. No one can approach God except through her and the Intercessor born of her. And none of God's gifts can be given to angels or to men except through her!' So it is right that she is the

shared boast of angels and mankind, and that she is praised in heaven and on earth. This is shown by the hymn to the Mother of God, the *Axion Estin* (*It is truly meet*), which is sung at this sacred moment. The first part of this hymn was revealed by the Archangel Gabriel to an Athonite monk. The Archangel sang it then for the first time, followed by the well-known strophe *More honourable than the Cherubim*.[83]

Addressing God the Father, the celebrant and the faithful said, *It is meet and right to hymn You...* Addressing the Mother of God, the faithful are now singing, *It is truly meet to call you blessed, Theotokos...*, for she is 'god after God, the one who is second in rank after the Trinity'.[84] Angels and humans unite in a common choir to magnify her who is *truly the Theotokos*.

There are many names by which we sing the praises of the All-holy Virgin, but her primary appellation is Theotokos, 'Birth-giver of God'; 'for this name expresses the entire mystery of the divine economy. If she who gave birth is Theotokos, then He who was born of her is most certainly God [*Theos*], but certainly He is also man. For how could the pre-eternal God be born of woman unless he had become a man?'[85] In naming the Virgin Theotokos, we are at the same time proclaiming the mystery of Christ that is celebrated at the Divine Liturgy.

Provider and nourisher of the faithful

The All-immaculate Lady became the 'life-giving earth' which brought forth Christ, the vivifying wheat on which all things are nourished: 'bearing for the world the wheat of life which nourishes all things'. She became the earth which brought to fruition

---

[83] Theophanes, *Theotokos*, p. 8; St Gregory Palamas, *Homily 53*, 23, *Oikonomou*, p. 159; *Synaxarion* of St Nikodimus of the Holy Mountain, 11 June.

[84] St Nikodimus of the Holy Mountain, *Theotokarion*, Sunday evening, *prosomoion** in Tone 5.

[85] St John of Damascus, *On the Orthodox Faith*, 3.56, PG 94.1029C.

the Bread of immortal life. From her immaculate womb was formed the all-holy Body of the Master. Thus the Ever-Virgin became 'a divine Table, which offers...the flesh and Blood of Him who came forth from her in an inexpressible manner'.[86]

At every Divine Liturgy, the Lady Theotokos is not only the Holy Table but also 'the steward and bounteous provider who serves the divine and divinising food... In a word, it is she who provides all the wonderful and uncreated gifts of the Holy Spirit, those given in this life as well as those still held in reserve' to be revealed in the age to come.[87]

By her submission to the pre-eternal counsel of God, the Ever-Virgin was found worthy to become the nourisher of her Creator. And her Son, repaying that debt, gave her the grace to become 'the nourisher of every spiritual and rational nature [of angels and men]. For as with food, drink, enjoyment and hidden delight of every kind, He made her worthy to provide them abundantly with the gifts of the Holy Spirit.'[88]

The Divine Liturgy is the marriage feast of Christ the Bridegroom (cf. Rev. 19: 9, Matt. 22: 2–4). To this feast of thanksgiving and praise, St John the Forerunner calls in the people and is the leader of the Bride, Christ is the Bridegroom and master of the ceremony,[89] and the Bride unwedded the provider and nourisher of the guests.

---

[86] *Octoechos*, Tone 4, Tuesday Matins, Canon, ode 8; Theophanes, *Theotokos*, pp. 22, 30.

[87] Theophanes, *Theotokos*, p. 204.

[88] Ibid. p. 172.

[89] St Cyril of Alexandria, *On John*, 2.1, PG 73.264B.

6. DIPTYCHS* AND PRAYERS

Priest (in a low voice): *For holy John the Baptist, Prophet and Forerunner, the holy, glorious and wholly blessed Apostles, for Saint* [name] *whose memory we keep today, and for all your Saints, through whose supplications do you, O God, visit us.*

Remember too all those who have fallen asleep in hope of resurrection to eternal life (here the Priest remembers whom he will of the dead by name), *and give them rest where the light of your countenance watches.*

Also we beseech you to remember, O Lord, all Orthodox bishops, who rightly expound the word of your truth, the whole order of presbyters, the diaconate in Christ, all the hieratic and monastic orders.

Also we offer you this spiritual worship for the whole world, for the holy, catholic and apostolic Church, for those living in purity and reverence; for our faithful Christian sovereigns, for their whole court and army. Grant them, Lord, peace in their kingdom that we too, in their tranquillity, may lead a calm and peaceful life in godliness and reverence.[1]

(aloud) *Remember first, O Lord, our Archbishop* [name], *and grant that he may serve your holy Churches in peace, safety, honour, health, and length of days, rightly expounding the word of your truth.*[2]

---

[1] 1 Tim 2: 2.   [2] 2 Tim 2: 15.

In memory of the saints

The Divine Liturgy is the remembrance of Christ's life. For that very reason, it is at the same time a remembrance of the lives of those in whom Christ lived, the lives of the Christ-bearing saints.

Each day of the yearly liturgical cycle is dedicated to the memory of the saints who went to their rest in Christ on that day. It is the day on which they reached the end of their journey, the culmination of their struggles, their perfection through the Holy Spirit: 'On this day, Saint [name] was perfected'. The word for 'perfected' in Greek used here, τελειοῦται (teleioutai), comes from the root τέλος (telos), meaning 'the end', and so simultaneously it expresses the coming to the end of earthly life as well as the attainment of perfection (teleiosis) in Christ, to which the saints alone attain: 'We call martyrdom "being perfected" not because the martyr has reached "the end" of his life just like other people, but because he manifested a perfect work of love' for Christ.[3]

Like a good and loving mother, the Church shows her children the divine love that burnt in the hearts of the saints which enabled them to achieve the unachievable. At the Table of Life, in which we participate, the holy lives of the saints and their holy relics are set out for our spiritual delight. In the service of Matins, which precedes the Divine Liturgy, we hear of their prodigious struggles. 'The saints wearied themselves, and we rejoice; they struggled, and we are jubilant. The crown is theirs, and we share their glory; or rather, the glory belongs to the entire Church... The Martyrs are our own members. So *if one member suffers, all suffer together; if one member is honoured, all rejoice together* [1 Cor. 12: 26]. The head is crowned, and the rest of the body exults. One person becomes an Olympic victor, and the whole multitude rejoices.'[4]

---

[3] Clement of Alexandria, *Stromata IV*, 4, PG 8.1228B.

[4] St John Chrysostom, *Encomium on the holy Martyr Romanos 1*, 1, PG 50.605–6.

The faithful have good reason to celebrate. The prayers of the saints are the support and protection of the body of the Church. 'The compassion of the saints is such that they are not concerned only about themselves, but beseech the Lord for the entire world as if it were one household. They beseech Him on behalf of the whole host of mankind as if it were one body.'[5]

The life and the love of the saints is an invitation to eucharistic fellowship. Their presence is a spiritual magnet; it holds the faithful together. They summon us to the eucharistic assembly and bring us together in one place around the Lord's Table. In this divine gathering we thank God for the saints whom He has given us as protectors, guides and examples for our lives, and for the glory with which He extolled them and continues to do so. We also thank the saints themselves because they are beneficial to us in every way and lead us to God.

The fact that the saints become the reason why we glorify God's all-holy name is the most welcome offering that can be given to them. When they were alive, they strove to do everything for the glory of Christ, and now they rejoice from heaven when God is glorified because of them.

If, while the saints were on earth, 'they were continuously giving thanks to God and doing everything for His glory when the heavenly good things were still only a object of hope for them, how should we expect them to behave now? For on the one hand their gratitude is now much greater because they have become perfect in every virtue, and on the other they no longer hope for the good things of heaven but from their own experience know the Lord's generosity... That is why they can never have their fill of praising God and do not consider that their thanksgiving alone is sufficient, but desire that angels and men should unite with them in praising Him so that their debt of gratitude to Him will

---

[5] St John Chrysostom, *On Psalm 9*, 8, *PG* 55.134.

be repaid closer to its value, since the magnitude of the thanksgiving becomes greater as the number of those who give praise increases.'[6]

Visit us, O God

The Incarnation of the Word is God's visitation to humans: 'Our Saviour from on high has visited us.'[7] When we now ask of God that He should visit us, we are asking Him to extend His visitation, that is, to experience, through the Divine Liturgy, the Mystery of His becoming man. We beg the Lord to extend His visitation until His Second Coming, and to remain with us not as a mere visitor but as the Master of the house.

Between the first visitation of the Word and His Second Coming, there is the present age. We Christians struggle to love the Lord, because love helps us to live the mystery of His visitation: *If a man loves me, he will keep my word, and my Father will love him, and we will come to him and make our home with him* (John 14: 23). Love perpetuates God's visitation and transforms man into a dwelling-place of God and a dweller in God: *God is love, and he who abides in love abides in God, and God abides in him* (1 John 4: 16). When we participate in the Mystery of divine love — in the Eucharist and Holy Communion — we are celebrating the Mystery of God's visitation in the world and in our lives. As Christ says: *He who eats my flesh and drinks my blood abides in me, and I in him* (John 6: 56).

An offering for the world

In the Service of Preparation, the celebrant commemorated his bishop, the concelebrating clergy, the brethren living and de-

---

[6] St Nicholas Cabasilas, *Comm. Liturgy*, 48, PG 150.472D–473A.

[7] Christmas Matins, *exapostilarion*.

parted. As he commemorated their names, he placed particles from the seal of the *prosphora* corresponding to them close to the Lamb, the image of Christ who is offered. Now, after the Consecration, the offering has been accomplished and Christ Himself is present. So we beseech Him still more fervently on behalf of our fathers and brethren, those near and those far, the living and the departed. The commemoration of our brethren at this time 'proclaims the terrible mystery that God gave Himself for the world'.[8]

We offer You this rational worship for the whole world. The Eucharist is the Ecumenical Council of the Church. Even if there is only one brother present to participate in the celebration of the Divine Eucharist, the whole ecumene is present in that assembly of the celebrant and the brother. The Holy Anaphora is offered *for the whole world*, because upon the Holy Table is Christ, 'the propitiatory Victim for the whole world'. With Him present, the celebrant and faithful form the universal Church. All things are illumined by the light of His love. The 'whole of creation is made new and divinised'.[9]

> **Priest (in a low voice):** *Remember, Lord, the city* (or the holy monastery) *in which we dwell, and every city and land, and the faithful who dwell in them. Remember, Lord, those who travel by land, air, or water, the sick, the suffering, those in captivity and their salvation. Remember, Lord, those who bring offerings, those who care for the beauty of your holy Churches, and those who remember the poor, and send down upon all of us your mercies.*

---

[8] St John Chrysostom, *On Acts*, 21.5, *PG* 60.170.
[9] Ibid. *On 1 Corinthians*, 41.5, *PG* 61.361; 8 September, Matins, *kathisma*.

> (aloud) *And grant that with one voice and one heart we may glorify and praise your all-honoured and majestic name, of the Father, and of the Son, and of the Holy Spirit, now and for ever, and to the ages of ages.*
> Choir: *Amen.*

With one voice and one heart

In order for the liturgical community to glorify the *all-honoured and majestic name* of the Trinitarian God, it must have one voice and one heart. It often happens that people living outside the Church and the Divine Liturgy can agree on something and pursue it with one voice. Their voices are in unison, but not the beating of their hearts; their deeper purposes are not in tune with the words of their mouths.

In the Church, however, a different order prevails. In the praise offered at the Eucharist, the mouths and hearts of the faithful are in harmony. By the grace of the Holy Spirit the faithful become one voice, one heart. *Being of one accord, and of one mind* (Phil. 2: 2). Unity in love is a *perfect gift coming down from above* (Jas. 1: 17).

The earliest Christians experienced this love to the highest degree: a throng of people with one heart. St Basil urges us: 'Let us try to imitate the earliest Christian community, the way they had all things in common, their manner of life, their soul, the way they had concord of mind, a common table, inseparable brotherhood! What unfeigned love they had, making their several bodies appear as one and uniting their separate souls into one harmonious unity!'[10] In this atmosphere of unifying love, the multitude of the faithful are 'like the strings of a lyre. They are many, but in con-

---

[10] *Homily in Famine and Drought*, 8, PG 31.325B.

sonance they make *one* delightful melody.'[11] We become one mouth which sings in praise of Love, one heart which beats for Love.

> The Priest blesses the people with his hand, saying: *And the mercies of our great God and Saviour, Jesus Christ, shall be with you all.*[12]
>
> Choir: *And with your spirit.*
>
> Deacon, standing before the Royal Doors: *Having commemorated all the Saints, again and again in peace let us pray to the Lord.*
>
> *For the precious Gifts here set forth and sanctified, let us pray to the Lord.*
>
> *That our God, who loves mankind, having accepted them on his holy and immaterial Altar above the heavens as a sweet-scented spiritual fragrance, may send down upon us in return his divine grace and the gift of the Holy Spirit, let us pray.*

As a sweet-scented spiritual fragrance

We are certain that the precious Gifts have been accepted on the heavenly Altar *as a sweet-scented spiritual fragrance*, because Christ is 'the myrrh of Divinity'[13] and *the savour of His anointing oils is above all perfumes* (S. of S. 1: 3).

Before His Incarnation, the Word was 'myrrh kept within'. Through His Incarnation, He empties Himself and becomes *myrrh poured out* (S. of S. 1: 3). And the Lady Mother of God who carried

---

[11] St John Chrysostom, *On perfect Love and Compunction*, 2, PG 56.281.

[12] Cf. 2 John v. 3, Titus 2: 13.

[13] St Gregory of Nyssa, *On the Song of Songs*, 1, PG 44.784A.

Christ in her womb became 'the vessel of the fragrant myrrh': 'As a spiritual perfume flask, the Virgin bears Christ, who is like inexhaustible myrrh, and through the Spirit she comes to pour it forth in the cave [of Bethlehem], so as to fill our souls with its fragrance.'[14]

The coming of the divine Myrrh into the world made man a partaker of its fragrance. Before the Word became flesh, human nature itself formed a wall between man and God for 'He was God only, and our nature was human only'. Our human nature was like a clay vessel for containing myrrh which keeps the myrrh confined within it. With the Incarnation of Christ, however, the vessel itself became Myrrh, and so there is no longer any obstacle to our union with God: 'It is as though the vessel were by some means to become the myrrh it contains. No longer then could the myrrh not be imparted to those outside, no longer would it remain within the vessel or by itself. In the same way, since our nature has been deified in the Saviour's Body, nothing separates the race of men from God.'[15]

Through Christ's Incarnation, the path to deification was opened for the human race. The vessel itself became Myrrh; man is deified and becomes by grace *christ*, the anointed one. Jesus was called Christ (corresponding to the Hebrew term *Messiah*) as the one who is par excellence anointed by God.

At every Divine Liturgy, Christ, the holy Myrrh, is emptied out, and makes the world fragrant with 'scents inspired by God'. The eucharistic gathering becomes fragrant, as does each of the faithful. For if you but speak the name of Christ, 'you are at once flooded with fragrance'. Glorifying the Creator imparts fragrance to the heart that praises Him: 'The heart that glorifies its Creator is a savour of fragrance to the Lord.' That is why our soul says to the

---

[14] St Nicholas Cabasilas, *On the Life in Christ*, 3, *PG* 150.569C; 5 February, Matins, Canon, ode 8; 20 December, Matins, Canon, ode 9.
[15] St Nicholas Cabasilas, *On the Life in Christ*, 3, *PG* 150.572AB.

Master: 'My myrrh is corruptible; Yours is the myrrh of life. For Your name is myrrh, poured out upon those who are worthy.'[16]

The Divine Liturgy is the Mystery of the emptying out of the divine Myrrh. Those who sit at the Table are drawn by His fragrance: *We will run after You for the fragrance of Your anointing oils* (S. of S. 1: 4). They commune in Christ, and leave the Divine Liturgy as myrrh-bearing souls. They themselves become the *sweet fragrance of Christ* and the *fragrance of life unto life* (2 Cor. 2: 15–16).

> **Deacon:** *For our deliverance from all affliction, wrath, danger and constraint, let us pray to the Lord.*
>
> **Choir:** *Lord, have mercy.*
>
> **Deacon:** *Help us, save us, have mercy on us and keep us, O God, by your grace.*
>
> *That the whole day may be perfect, holy, peaceful and sinless, let us ask of the Lord.*
>
> **Choir (and after each petition):** *Grant this, O Lord.*
>
> *For an angel of peace, a faithful guide, a guardian of our souls and bodies, let us ask of the Lord.*
>
> *For pardon and forgiveness of our sins and offences, let us ask of the Lord.*
>
> *For those things that are good and profitable for our souls, and peace for the world, let us ask of the Lord.*
>
> *That we may live out the rest of our days in peace and repentance, let us ask of the Lord.*
>
> *For a Christian end to our life, painless, unashamed, and peaceful, and a good defence before the dread judgement seat of Christ, let us ask of the Lord.*

---

[16] 5 February, Matins; St John Chrysostom, *On Colossians*, 9.3, *PG* 62.364; *Epistle of Barnabas*, 2.10, *ANF* 1, 138; Holy Tuesday, Compline.

> *Having asked for the unity of the faith*[17] *and the communion of the Holy Spirit, let us entrust ourselves and one another and our whole life to Christ, our God.*
> Choir: *To you, O Lord.*

The unity of the faith

Unity of faith is a precondition for being accepted into the unity of the Divine Eucharist. So before we approach the Cup of life, we ask the Lord to keep us in the unity of the faith. The Church is the one Body of Christ. It must therefore have one soul, one heart, one voice. 'For this is unity of faith: that we are all one, when we all understand the bond [of faith and love] in the same way.'[18]

The one faith makes it possible for us to be nourished with the one Bread of life. St Ignatius writes: 'You should gather with one faith and in the name of Jesus Christ...celebrating with one Bread, which is the medicine of immortality.' Having received this one, holy and apostolic faith, the Church 'preserves it with care... She believes in it in the same way, as if she had but one soul and one heart. She preaches, teaches and passes on the tradition in accordance with this faith, as if she had but one mouth... Just as the sun, that creation of God, is one and the same for the whole world, so also the proclamation of truth shines everywhere and illumines all people who wish to come to knowledge of the truth.'[19]

---

[17] Eph. 4: 13.

[18] St John Chrysostom, *On Ephesians*, 11.3, *PG* 62.83. Cf. St Nikodimus of the Holy Mountain, *Ermeneia eis tas 14 epistolas apostolou Pavlou*, [*Commentary on the 14 Epistles of the Apostle Paul*], vol. 2 (Thessaloniki: Orthodoxos Kypseli, 1990), p. 434.

[19] *Ephesians*, 20, *ANF* 1, p. 58. Cf. *PG* 5.661A; St Irenaeus, *Against Heresies*, 1.10.2, *SC* 264, pp. 159–60.

All things are in common in the Church: our faith is common, our hope is common, our love too is common. The Church, as St Maximus writes, is a type and image of God; God as Creator holds all His creations in unity through His infinite power and wisdom, and similarly the Church binds the faithful into one unity in accordance with the one grace and calling of faith.[20]

This bond uniting the faithful is engendered by Baptism, sanctified by Chrismation, and nourished and made to grow by Holy Communion. This is why only those who belong to the unity of the faith can take their places at the Mystical Supper. The Church denies the unbaptised the food that bestows incorruption, because she knows that 'if someone uninitiated presents himself dishonestly and takes Communion, he will eat eternal condemnation as his punishment'. Those who do not participate in the Truth cannot participate in the Life. Those who do not participate in the unity of the faith cannot enter into the communion of the Holy Spirit: 'Our faith is in accordance with the Eucharist, and the Eucharist confirms our faith.'[21] The common Cup presupposes a common faith.

For the same reason, those who have rejected or distorted the Orthodox faith in Christ cannot commune in Him. Holy Communion is not given either to the unbaptised or to the heterodox: 'It is not permitted for outsiders to approach the Divine Eucharist. And we should regard as outsiders those who are still unbelieving and unbaptised, as well as those who have been misled into a belief that is heterodox and incompatible with the faith of the saints.' The Church forbids heretics to participate in the Lord's Supper: 'We will not become sharers in the holy and life-giving Sacrifice with those who are wont to believe in doctrines other than those that are right and true but with our brethren and

---

[20] Cf. *Mystagogy*, 24, PG 91.705B.
[21] *Apostolic Constitutions*, 7.25, PG 1.1017B; St Irenaeus, *Against Heresies*, 4.18.5, *SC* 100, p. 611.

those of one mind, with whom there is unity of spirit and identity of faith.'[22]

The Church refuses to receive heretics to Holy Communion. She also refuses to have communion in worship with people of other confessions, that is, to pray with them. Some see this as harsh, and do not understand the love of the Mother Church. The Church, however, desires and prays for the return of every human being in repentance. And she recognises that a superficial 'communion' will harm the heterodox themselves, and will also shake the faith of some Orthodox believers.

Those who live in the unity of the faith are aware of the Church's love for mankind. They are aware that her motherly heart goes out to every human being, and they see how she burns with love for all: for unbelievers and catechumens, for those far from faith and those near.

Priest (in a low voice): *To you, O Master, Lover of mankind, we entrust our whole life and our hope, and we entreat, pray and implore you: count us worthy to partake of your heavenly and awesome Mysteries at this sacred and spiritual Table with a pure conscience, for the forgiveness of sins and pardon of offences, for communion of the Holy Spirit, for inheritance of the Kingdom of heaven and for boldness before you; not for judgement or condemnation.*

(aloud) *And count us worthy, O Master, with boldness and without condemnation to dare to call upon you, the God of heaven, as Father, and to say:*

---

[22] St Cyril of Alexandria, *On Worship in Spirit and Truth*, 11, 17; *PG* 68.761D, 1077C.

For communion of the Holy Spirit

Count us worthy to partake...for communion of the Holy Spirit, prays the celebrant. Communion in the holy Body and Blood of Christ is also communion in the Holy Spirit: 'For through both we are watered with one Spirit [cf. 1 Cor. 12: 13].' Christ Himself 'has given us to drink of His own Cup, He has given us to drink of the Holy Spirit'. Indeed, at the first celebration of the Mystery, Christ 'took the cup and mingled wine and water; He lifted it up to heaven and showed it to God the Father; and when He had given thanks, and blessed it, and sanctified it, and filled it with the Holy Spirit, He gave [His holy Blood] to His holy and blessed disciples.'[23]

At the Church's Supper, the celebrant, 'as he raises his hands to heaven and calls upon the Holy Spirit to come and sanctify the Gifts set forth', stands in the place of Christ. Then, 'with the descent of the Holy Spirit, the bread [offered] becomes the Bread of heaven'. And all who partake of 'the holy Body and Blood of the Lord become a dwelling-place of the Holy Spirit'.[24]

The Holy Spirit 'vivifies the whole universe... He stands in heaven and fills the whole earth... He dwells in His entirety in each person, and is in His entirety with God. He does not minister to the divine Gifts like a servant [as do the angels], but with authority distributes the gifts of grace.'[25]

Within the Church, the faithful receive the gifts of the Holy Spirit. More particularly, in the Divine Liturgy we receive the Paraclete Himself into our assembly and into our souls.

---

[23] St John Chrysostom, *On 1 Corinthians*, 30.2, *PG* 61.251; cf. St John Chrysostom, *On Matthew*, 45.2, *PG* 58.474; Liturgy of St James.

[24] Ibid. *On the name 'cemetery'*, 3, *PG* 49.398; *On John*, 45.2, *PG* 59.253; *Baptismal Catecheses*, 2.27, *SC* 50, p. 149.

[25] St Basil the Great, *Homily 15*, 3, *PG* 31.469B–472A.

Boldness before God

Christ is the High Priest who brings man as an offering to the heavenly Father, because in offering His all-immaculate Self, He has offered man. We become 'acceptable to God the Father inasmuch as it is Christ as Priest who brings us as an offering. For through Christ *we have obtained access* [Rom. 5: 2], and He has inaugurated for us the passage into true existence, having entered first into the Holy of Holies [cf. Heb. 6: 20] for our sake and shown us the true path.'[26]

Through His life, Christ inaugurated the path of true life. Man is now able to be regenerated in Christ and to become like the first-formed man, 'full of boldness towards God, delighting in His actual appearance, face to face'.[27]

Through the Blood of Christ, God's mercy was given to condemned mankind, and the way leading to the Father was opened: 'We give thanks to You, O Lord our God, that You have given us boldness to enter the Holy of Holies by the means of the Blood of Jesus, having inaugurated for us a new and living way through the veil of His flesh [cf. Heb. 10: 19–20].'[28]

So, since 'the Blood of Jesus gives us the boldness to enter the Holy of Holies', we dare to enter and fall down before the ocean of His mercies, and to address Him: *Our Father in heaven.*

People: *Our Father in heaven, may your name be hallowed, your Kingdom come, your will be done on earth as it is in heaven. Give us today our daily bread, and forgive us our debts, as we forgive our debtors; and do not lead us into temptation, but deliver us from the evil one.*

[26] St Cyril of Alexandria, *On Worship in Spirit and Truth*, 16, PG 68.1016B.
[27] St Gregory of Nyssa, *Great Catechism*, 6, PG 45.29B.
[28] Liturgy of St James.

Priest (aloud): *For yours is the kingdom and the power and the glory, of the Father, and of the Son, and of the Holy Spirit, now and for ever, and to the ages of ages.*[29]
Choir: *Amen.*

Now are we children of God

In the Lord's Prayer, we address God and we call Him *Father*. 'How exceedingly great is God's love for mankind!' writes St John Chrysostom. 'What words are adequate to give thanks to God who gives us so many good things? Examine, my beloved, the worthlessness of your and my nature. Think about what we are related to — earth, soil, clay, bricks, dust. For since we were made out of earth, we dissolve back into earth after death. So after considering all this, be amazed at the unfathomable richness of God's great goodness towards us. For you an earthen creature have been told to call Him, the heavenly One, Father — the mortal addressing the Immortal, the corruptible addressing the Incorruptible, the ephemeral addressing the Eternal!'[30]

St Gregory of Nyssa marvels at the honour afforded to man: 'What a soul must he, who calls God "Father", have! What boldness is required! What sort of conscience must a person have so that once he understands who God is, as far as this is possible for man,...he then dares to call Him his own Father!'[31] This highest honour was given to man by the Blood of Jesus. That is why the faithful pray, as the moment of communion in the immaculate Blood of Christ approaches: 'Make us worthy, O Master, Lord who loves mankind, with boldness, uncondemned, with a pure heart, an enlightened soul, a face unashamed and sanctified lips, to

---

[29] Matt. 6: 9–13.
[30] *On living in accordance with God*, 3, *PG* 51.44.
[31] *On the Lord's Prayer*, 2, *PG* 44.1140CD.

dare to call upon You the holy God and Father in heaven and to say: *Our Father in heaven.*'[32]

The beginning of the Lord's Prayer reveals the adoption by grace which we have received through Baptism. 'We are taught to proclaim the grace of our adoption, since we have been found worthy of addressing our Creator by nature as our Father by grace. Thus, venerating this title of our begetter by grace, we should strive to stamp the characteristics of the Father on our lives, sanctifying His name on earth, taking after Him as our Father, showing ourselves to be His children through our actions, and through all that we think or do glorifying the author of this adoption, who is by nature Son of the Father.'[33]

This adoption, which we enjoy in the present life within the Church, is the image of the eternal adoption which is to come. 'The holy and venerable invocation of the great and blessed God and Father is a symbol of the adoption which will be bestowed as a gift and charism of the Holy Spirit, and which will be bound up with man's substance and being. In that adoption, the coming of Grace will prevail over and cover every attribute of the human. All the saints — all those who already in this life, through the work of the virtues, have shone brightly and gloriously with the beauty of divine goodness — will be called sons of God and will actually be such.'[34]

The soul that sets out for the Kingdom of God adorned with divine beauty (because it has kept pure its correspondence to the image, and has attained to the likeness) is led by divine Grace to divine adoption. Through this adoption, the soul 'which, mystically and by grace, has God as its one and only Father, will be led to the Oneness of His secret hiddenness, leaving all things far behind. And it will experience things divine rather than knowing

---

[32] Liturgy of St James.

[33] St Maximus the Confessor, *On the Lord's Prayer*, *Philokalia*, vol. 2, p. 291.

[34] Ibid. *Mystagogy*, 20, *PG* 91.696CD.

them, to such an extent that it will no longer want to belong to itself.'[35]

On reaching the inner recesses of God the soul gives itself entirely to Him, 'who in His entirety graciously receives it entire into Himself, and in a divine manner places His whole self in it, and thus deifies it in its entirety'. All human efforts to do what is good come to an end: the soul is not active but passive. It ceaselessly receives from God the grace of His unending love: 'In the age to come, we shall undergo by grace the transformation unto deification and no longer be active but passive; and for this reason we shall not cease from being deified' by the Father who loves mankind.[36] As John the Evangelist writes: *Beloved, we are God's children now; it does not yet appear what we shall be, but we know that when He appears we shall be like Him* (1 John 3: 2).

Priest: *Peace be with you all.*
Choir: *And with your spirit.*

The Table of peace

Each Divine Liturgy is a new appearance of Christ resurrected. The first appearances of Christ after the Resurrection are described by John the Evangelist: *Then the same day at evening, being the first day of the week, when the doors were shut where the disciples were assembled for fear of the Jews, came Jesus and stood in the midst, and said unto them, Peace be unto you... Then were the disciples glad, when they saw the Lord. Then said Jesus to them again, Peace be unto you... And, after eight days, again His*

---

[35] St Maximus the Confessor, *Mystagogy*, 23, *PG* 91.701BC.
[36] Ibid. *PG* 91.701C; Ibid. *To Thalassius*, 22, *PG* 90.320D.

disciples were inside, and Thomas with them; then came Jesus, the doors being shut, and said, Peace be unto you (John 20: 19–26).

In both of these appearances, the Lord *stood in the midst* of the twelve. The same thing is repeated at every Liturgy: He stands *in the midst* of the assembly and gives us His peace. For the closer we come to the 'Table of peace', the more need there is for peace. 'You are about to receive a King when you receive Holy Communion. And when the King enters the soul, there should be ample calm, ample stillness, profound peace in our thoughts.'[37]

Deacon: *Let us bow our heads to the Lord.*
Choir: *To you, O Lord.*
Priest (in a low voice): *We thank you, O King invisible, who by your boundless power created all things, and in the abundance of your mercy brought them into being out of non-being. Do you yourself, O Master, look down from heaven on those who have bowed their heads to you; for they bow them not to flesh and blood, but to you, the awesome God. Therefore, O Master, bestow these Holy Gifts on all of us, for our good and according to the need of each: sail with those who sail, journey with those who journey, heal the sick, you who are the physician of our souls and bodies.*
(aloud) *Through the grace and compassion and love towards mankind of your only-begotten Son, with whom you are blessed, together with your All-holy, good and life-giving Spirit, now and for ever, and to the ages of ages.*
Choir: *Amen.*

[37] St John Chrysostom, *On the Betrayal of Judas*, 1.6, PG 49.381; *On the Incomprehensible*, 6.4, PG 48.756.

The bowing of heads

After the Lord's Prayer, the celebrant tells the faithful to bow their heads to Christ, so acknowledging Him as Master and Lord. The faithful bow their heads to God 'not only because He is by nature Master and Creator and God, but also as slaves who have been bought with the very Blood of His only-begotten Son'.[38]

By bowing our heads we show the Lord our submission like grateful servants, but as His friends and sons by grace we also show our thankfulness. For through Christ's sacrifice on the Cross, we have been made friends and sons of God: *Greater love has no man than this, that he lay down his life for his friends. You are my friends...no longer do I call you servants* (John 15: 13–15). 'The Lord of the servants became a mortal son of His own servant, namely Adam, so that the sons of Adam who are mortal might become sons of God.'[39]

* * *

We all have the same Father. Yet the uniqueness of the human person is not annihilated within the communion of the Church. All human beings are images of God, but each of us has his own character and his own struggle. That is why Christ is offered in Holy Communion *according to the need of each.*

The Master is one, the gifts are various. 'According to what is in our best interest the Saviour becomes different for each one of us. For those who need joy, he becomes a vine [cf. John 15: 1]. For those who need to enter, He stands as a door [cf. John 10: 7]. For those who need to offer up prayers, He is present as mediator and High Priest [cf. 1 Tim. 2: 5, Heb. 7: 26]. For those who have sins, He becomes a sheep, so as to be slaughtered for them [cf. John 1: 29]. He

---

[38] St Nicholas Cabasilas, *Comm. Liturgy*, 35, *PG* 150.448B.
[39] St Athanasius the Great, *On the Incarnate Manifestation of God the Word*, 8, *PG* 26.996B.

becomes all things to all men [cf. 1 Cor. 9: 22], while Himself remaining by nature what He is.'[40]

All commune in the same Bread of life. And each receives Him
whom he needs in his personal life: 'Those in sickness, the Physician; those in danger, the Rescuer; sinners, the Protector; the
poor, the Treasure; those in sorrow, the Consolation; wayfarers,
the Companion on the way; those at sea, the Helmsman: all receive Him who everywhere ardently anticipates their need.'
Through the Gifts set before us Christ becomes 'a rock of patience, a cause of consolation, a giver of strength, a provision of
good courage, an assistant in valour' for the journey of our life.
For He is 'the truly good and infallible road which does not lead
the traveller astray, but guides Him to God the Father who is truly the Good'.[41]

---

[40] St Cyril of Jerusalem, *Catechesis 10*, 5, *PG* 33.665AB.

[41] 6 December, Matins, *Doxastikon* at Lauds; Service for the Great Schema; St
Basil the Great, *On the Holy Spirit*, 8.18, *PG* 32.100C.

7. HOLY COMMUNION

Priest (in a low voice): *Give heed, Lord Jesus Christ our God, from your holy dwelling-place and from the glorious throne of your Kingdom; and come to sanctify us, you who sit on high with the Father and are invisibly present here with us; and grant to us with your mighty hand communion in your most pure Body and precious Blood, and through us to all the people.*

Then the Priest bows three times, saying each time: God, have compassion for me, a sinner, and have mercy on me.

Above I have you, and below I intermingle with you

Shortly before His Passion, Christ assured the disciples: *I go to the Father…yet a little while and the world will see me no more, but you will see me; because I live, you will live also* (John 14: 12, 19). The *world* means those who live outside the Divine Liturgy. They do not see Christ because they live in darkness. 'Christ says that He will be invisible and in no way seen by those of a worldly mind after He leaves the earth, that is, after His Ascension into heaven. He will, however, be visible to the saints.' At the Liturgy, Christ is *invisibly present*. Just as the body concealed His Divinity during the Incarnation of the Word of God, so 'the holy Bread is like a veil, hiding the Divinity within it'.[1]

---

[1] St Cyril of Alexandria, *On John*, 9, PG 74.264D–265A; St Gregory Palamas, *Homily 56*, 5, *Oikonomou*, p. 205.

At His Incarnation, Christ came to earth and became man without leaving the Father's throne: 'It was divine condescension, not a change of place.' Yet 'the wonderful thing was that He was at the same time living a human life as man, and giving life to all things as God the Word, and coexisting with the Father as the Son of God'.[2]

At His Ascension, the *Theanthropos* returned to the Father's throne together with His deified Body, which at the same time He left for us, and which He offers to us at every Liturgy. 'Elias left a sheepskin to his disciple, but the Son of God on ascending left us His own flesh! The Prophet, however, cast off his mantle, whereas Christ both left us His flesh *and* was exalted on high together with it.'[3]

Since His Ascension, the Lord sits with the Father in heaven and is present with the faithful at the Divine Liturgy. His presence fills earth and heaven. But now that man is united with Christ, he too is simultaneously on earth and in heaven together with Him: 'Above I have you, and below I intermingle with you.'[4] Above: in the bosom of God the Father; below: in the bosom of the Church our Mother. Both above and below, man lives in God's love.

The place and time of the Divine Liturgy are sanctified by Him who is 'above place and time and name and understanding'. Christ, who is in heaven, is also with us in the Divine Liturgy. He is not simply with us, but comes to dwell in us. 'All who partake in the holy Body of Christ, all who taste His Blood...taste Him who sits upon the heavenly throne, who is worshipped by angels, who is close to the immaculate Power' that is, God the Father.[5]

With His all-holy hands, the Lord gives Himself to the celebrant and through him to *all the people*. Christ is the *great joy* which through Holy Communion is given to *all the people* (Luke 2: 10).

---

[2] Akathist Hymn, stanza 15; St Athanasius the Great, *On the Incarnation*, 17, PG 25.125C.

[3] St John Chrysostom, *On the Statues*, 2.9, PG 49.46.

[4] Ibid. *On 1 Timothy*, 15.4, PG 62.586.

[5] St Clement of Alexandria, *Stromata V*, 11, PG 9.109A; St John Chrysostom, *On Ephesians*, 3.3, PG 62.27.

Deacon: *Let us attend.*

The Priest elevates the holy Bread and says aloud: *The Holy Things for the holy.*

Choir: *One is Holy, one is Lord: Jesus Christ, to the glory of God the Father. Amen.*[6]

The Choir then begins chanting the Communion Hymn* for the day.

The Holy Things for the holy

The *Holy Things* that are to be given as Communion to *the holy* are the holy Body and precious Blood of Christ. Christ is the only one who is by nature holy, the One and only Lord. We can be called *holy* only because we are participants in His holiness: 'The faithful are called *holy* on account of the Holy One in whom they participate and in whose holy Body and Blood they commune.'[7]

The elevation of the holy Body of Christ performed by the celebrant at this moment 'images His lifting up onto the Cross, His death by crucifixion, and indeed His Resurrection'. Christ 'is lifted up in the hands of the priest as upon the Cross'.[8]

The act of lifting up signifies that 'Communion in the immaculate Mysteries is not permitted to all indiscriminately... For Holy Things are to be given only to the holy, holy not meaning here only those who are perfect in virtue but also those who are struggling to attain that perfection... For there is nothing that prevents them too being sanctified through partaking of the Holy Mysteries.'[9]

---

[6] 1 Cor. 8: 6; Phil. 2: 11.

[7] St Nicholas Cabasilas, *Comm. Liturgy*, 36, PG 150.449A.

[8] St Germanus, *Contemplation*, PG 98.448B; St John of Damascus, *On the Immaculate Mysteries of which we partake*, 5, PG 95.409C.

[9] St Nicholas Cabasilas, *Comm. Liturgy*, 36, PG 150.448D.

The holy are not struggling only to rid themselves of sin, but also to acquire the Holy Spirit. Commenting on the phrase *the Holy Things for the holy*, St John Chrysostom says: 'With a loud voice and a terrible cry, the priest, raising his hand aloft like a herald standing up high and visible to all the people, cries out in a loud voice amidst that total silence, calling some to take Communion and barring others, not with his hand, but with his voice... When the priest says *the Holy Things for the holy*, he means: "Whoever is not holy, let him not approach." He does not say that one should be simply pure of sin, but *holy*. For the holy person is distinguished not just by being free of sins, but also by the presence of the Holy Spirit and a wealth of good works. He is saying, "I do not merely want you to be free of filth, but to be white and beautiful... Whoever is like that, let him approach and touch the royal Cups." '[10]

One is Holy, one is Lord: Jesus Christ

To the priest's exclamation *the Holy Things for the holy*, the faithful reply: *One is Holy, one is Lord, Jesus Christ, to the glory of God the Father*. The response of the faithful is a confession that through 'the only-begotten Son who became incarnate and was crucified, we have been sanctified and saved from death and have obtained immortality'.[11] For 'no one possesses sanctity through their own efforts, nor is it a work of human virtue, but comes to all from Him and because of Him. In the same way, if you put many mirrors in the sunlight, each will shine and radiate light, so that one would think there are many suns, while in

---

[10] *On Hebrews*, 17.5, PG 63.133. In his homily the saint is censuring those who are content with preparing themselves during Great Lent as a mere formality for taking Communion on Easter Day only and who subsequently continue their heedless lives. The saint says that a Christian must struggle without ceasing so as to commune at all times.

[11] St Symeon of Thessaloniki, *On the holy Liturgy*, 99, PG 155.297D.

reality there is but one sun that illumines everything. Similarly, when the only Holy One pours Himself out into the faithful, He becomes visible in many souls and brings forth many holy people, yet He alone is the Holy One.'[12]

'The profession *One is Holy* made by all the people at the end of the mystical rite…reveals the gathering and union, beyond all reason and understanding, with the mysterious Oneness of the divine simplicity of those who have been mystically and wisely made perfect in God, a union that will take place in the incorruptible age of the spiritual world. In that world, those made perfect will behold the light of the invisible and supremely ineffable glory and together with the heavenly powers will become susceptive to divine purity.'[13]

Christ is 'the very source and very root of all good, the very Life, the very Light and very Truth. He does not keep His wealth of good things to Himself, but pours it out for everyone, and after overflowing remains full.'[14] The very source of holiness transmits to all, angels and humans, the myrrh of holiness: He sanctifies the whole Church, and all who keep the receptacle of their soul and body pure receive the fullness of His holiness.

One is Holy, one is Lord, Jesus Christ, to the glory of God the Father. Before Christ, no man was able to glorify God fittingly. The Lord alone was able to say to the Father, *I have glorified You upon earth* (John 17: 4). 'How did He glorify Him? Simply by manifesting His own holiness before men, once He had showed Himself to be holy as the Father Himself is holy.'[15]

We become partakers of this holiness of Christ's when we participate at the Eucharistic Table. As the moment of Holy Communion approaches, the Church issues the invitation: 'If any is holy,

---

[12] St Nicholas Cabasilas, *Comm. Liturgy*, 36, PG 150.449BC.

[13] St Maximus the Confessor, *Mystagogy*, 21, PG 91.696D–697A.

[14] St John Chrysostom, *On John*, 14.1, PG 59.91.

[15] St Nicholas Cabasilas, *Comm. Liturgy*, 36, PG 150.449CD.

let him come. If any is not, let him repent. *Maran atha* [the Lord is coming] [cf. 1 Cor. 16: 22]. Amen.'[16]

> The Deacon says to the Priest: *Master, break the holy Bread.*
> The Priest breaks the Lamb into four parts, saying: *The Lamb of God is broken and distributed, broken yet not divided, ever eaten yet never consumed, but sanctifying those who partake.*

The Lamb of God is broken

At the first Divine Liturgy to be celebrated on earth, Christ broke the Bread into pieces and gave it to His disciples saying: *Take, eat: this is my Body which is broken for you* (1 Cor. 11: 24). This action of the Lord's is repeated at every Liturgy and is called the Fraction* or breaking of the holy Body. The celebrant divides the Lamb of God into four parts, he places them on the Paten in the form of a cross, and once he himself has received Communion he will then give Communion to the faithful.

This 'dividing into pieces of the Lamb reveals the slaughter of the Honoured One'.[17] At the Crucifixion, the soldiers did not break Christ's legs — as they did with the thieves crucified with Him — *that the Scripture might be fulfilled, a bone of Him shall not be broken* (John 19: 36, cf. Exod. 12: 10). In the sacrifice of the Liturgy, however, the Lord is broken into pieces and offered to the faithful. St John Chrysostom underlines: 'What Christ did not suffer on the Cross, He undergoes at the offering for your sake, and He endures to be broken so that all may be filled.'[18]

---

[16] *Didache*, 10.6, *ANF* 7, p. 380.
[17] St Eutychius of Constantinople, *On holy Pascha*, 3, PG 86.2396A.
[18] *On 1 Corinthians*, 24.2, PG 61.200.

The Fraction is the act that reveals Christ par excellence: it was *in the breaking of bread* (Luke 24: 35) that the two disciples recognised Him in Emmaus, and the earliest Christians used the term 'breaking of bread' for the Eucharist (cf. Acts 2: 42, 20: 7). Through the breaking of the Bread, 'the undivided Christ is divided up and shared out for our sake, so that we may all become partakers of Him. And while being indivisible, He is divided for us, uniting us with Himself and making us one, as He prayed for' in His prayer to God the Father (cf. John 17: 11).[19]

* * *

Christ is 'He who truly is', 'that which is partaken of by everyone, and is not diminished by the participation of the partakers.'[20] 'Let us suppose that there is one source of fire, and from it are lit ten thousand lamps, and twice that number... Does not the fire remain integrally the same despite having passed on its energy to so many lamps?' Christ is the source of spiritual fire 'which is in no way diminished by being passed on to others, but remains complete in itself while forever welling forth and imparting good things to all'.[21]

Christ is broken in pieces, but He is not divided. After the breaking, every part of the holy Bread is Christ in His entirety. 'He is distributed, but remains undivided and whole. He is to be found and recognised in His entirety in each separate part that is cut out.' Those who partake worthily at the sacred Table all receive Christ in His entirety, and He fills us in our entirety. 'So that those [who receive Communion] can be called and can actually be gods by grace, thanks to God who in His entirety has filled them totally and has left no part of them empty of His presence.'[22] Christ is

---

[19] St Symeon of Thessaloniki, *On the holy Liturgy*, 99, *PG* 155.300AB.

[20] St Gregory of Nyssa, *Life of Moses* 2, *PG* 44.333C.

[21] St John Chrysostom, *On John*, 14.1, *PG* 59.91.

[22] St Germanus, *Contemplation*, *PG* 98.449B; St Maximus the Confessor, *Mystagogy*, 21, *PG* 91.697A.

wholly present in each of us. He is wholly present in the whole of the Church, in all the length and breadth of the earth to all ages.

From His fullness have we all received (John 1: 16). We receive the fullness of Life and compose the holy Church, *which is His body, the fullness of Him who fills all in all* (Eph. 1: 23). Material foods are exhaustible by nature. But the Lamb of God is He who is *ever eaten yet never consumed.* His sacrifice is 'inexhaustible'.[23] For it is the never-exhausted food of never-ending divine Life and Love.

> Deacon: *Master, fill the holy Cup.*
> The Priest takes the portion of the Lamb bearing the initials IΣ and makes the sign of the cross with it above the holy Chalice and places it in it, saying: *Fullness of the Cup, of faith, of the Holy Spirit.*[24]
> Deacon: *Amen.*

Christ is one

Following the celebrant's proclamation *the Holy Things for the holy,* three actions are performed in succession: first the celebrant elevates the holy Body of Christ, then he breaks It, and now he unites It with the holy Blood.

The union of the holy Body with the holy Blood of Christ signifies 'that Christ is one, even though He is made visible both in the holy Bread and in the holy Cup. It also signifies that the same Christ is [for the faithful] both a support through the holy Bread, and gladness through the Cup [cf. Ps. 103: 15].'[25]

---

[23] St John Chrysostom, *On Hebrews*, 17.3, PG 63.131.

[24] The words *of the Cup, of faith,* and *of faith, full* on the next page, are later additions, dating from the 18th century (Trembelas, *Leitourgiai*, pp. 135–7).

[25] St Symeon of Thessaloniki, *On the holy Liturgy*, 99, PG 155.300B.

Fullness...of the Holy Spirit: Christ fills us with the Holy Spirit. 'For what is the benefit and the result of Christ's Passion and His words and deeds? Considered in relation to us humans, it is nothing other than the coming of the Holy Spirit upon the Church.'[26]

Deacon: *Master, bless the hot water.*

The Priest blesses it, saying: *Blessed is the fervour of your Holy Things, always, now and for ever, and to the ages of ages. Amen.*

The Deacon pours the hot water into the Chalice in the form of a cross, as the Priest says: *The fervour of faith, full of the Holy Spirit. Amen.*

The fervour of the Holy Spirit

Having performed the union of the holy Body and Blood of Christ, the celebrant pours the hot water (the *zeon*,* as it is called) into the Chalice. 'As once *blood and water* came forth from the living divine side [cf. John 19: 34], full of warmth, so now at the time of Holy Communion the very hot water that is poured into the holy Cup completes the symbolism of the Mystery.'[27]

St Nikodimus writes on this point: 'The miracle of the Lord's undefiled side was twofold, not only because it gave forth *blood and water*...but also because it gave them forth warm and living, for that side was living and life-giving...by reason of its hypostatic union with the life-giving Divinity. Thus, in representation of the first miracle, it was ordained that wine and water should be put

---

[26] St Nicholas Cabasilas, *Comm. Liturgy*, 37, PG 150.452B.
[27] St Germanus, *Contemplation*, PG 98.449B.

into the Chalice, and, from the very beginning, in representation of the second miracle...that during the singing of the Communion Hymn this water should be put into the Chalice hot and simmering — not cold or lukewarm — so that the priest himself and the others who partake of the warm Body and Blood will feel that they are receiving them as they once came forth from the life-giving side of the Saviour... The holy *zeon*, as the name indicates, should be boiling when it is poured in — so that the Chalice is warmed by it — for *zeon* means "boiling water".'[28]

As he performed the union of the holy Body and Blood, the celebrant said: *Fullness of the Cup, of faith, of the Holy Spirit.* Now, as he pours the *zeon* into the Chalice, he says: *The fervour of faith, full of the Holy Spirit.* Everything underlines the coming of the Paraclete. 'This hot water, because it is both water and shares the nature of fire [through boiling], signifies the Holy Spirit, who is called water and also appeared as fire descending on the disciples of Christ [cf. John 7: 38–9, Acts 2: 3].'[29]

The celebrant with the Chalice in his hands is holding a 'source of the Spirit'. So we bring our mouths 'to the nipple of the spiritual Cup like infants at the breast, in order to draw out the grace of the Holy Spirit'. And 'our mouths are filled with spiritual fire'.[30]

---

[28] Commentary on the 32nd Canon of the Sixth Ecumenical Council, *Pedalion* [*The Rudder*], 6th edn (Athens: Astir, 1957), pp. 248–9.

[29] St Nicholas Cabasilas, *Comm. Liturgy*, 37, *PG* 150.452B.

[30] St John Chrysostom, *On Matthew*, 82.6, 5, *PG* 58.745, 744, 743. The early Christians received Communion in the holy Blood by drinking from the chalice. The image of the suckling infant is very characteristic, because the believer communes in the life-giving Blood of the Lord as it ran from His wounded side.

Priest (in a low voice): *I believe, Lord, and I confess that you are truly the Christ, the Son of the living God, who came into the world to save sinners, of whom I am the foremost. Also I believe that this is indeed your most pure Body, and this indeed your precious Blood. Therefore I beseech you, have mercy on me and forgive me my offences, voluntary and involuntary, in word and in deed, in knowledge and in ignorance, and count me worthy to partake uncondemned of your most pure Mysteries for the forgiveness of sins and for eternal life. Amen.*

See, to divine Communion I draw near;
My Maker, burn me not as I partake,
For you are fire consuming the unworthy;
But therefore make me clean from every stain.

Of your mystical Supper, Son of God, receive me today as a communicant; for I will not tell of the Mystery to your enemies; I will not give you a kiss, like Judas; but like the thief I confess you: Remember me, Lord, in your Kingdom.

See the deifying Blood, O man, and be afraid,
For it is a coal that burns the unworthy.
It is the Body of God, and deifies and nourishes me;
It deifies my spirit and wondrously nourishes my mind.

You have beguiled me with longing, O Christ, and with your divine love have changed me. But burn up my sins with immaterial fire, and count me worthy to be filled with delight in you, that I may leap for joy, O Good One, and magnify your two comings.

Into the radiance of your Saints how shall I enter, unworthy as I am? For if I dare to enter the bridal chamber with those who are worthy, my robe will betray me because it is not a wedding garment, and I will be bound and cast out by the angels. Cleanse, O Lord, the filth of my soul, and save me in your love for mankind.

Master, lover of mankind, Lord Jesus Christ, my God, let not these Holy Mysteries be for my condemnation because of my unworthiness, but rather for the cleansing and sanctification of both soul and body, and as a pledge of the life and Kingdom to come. It is good for me to cleave to God, to place in the Lord the hope of my salvation.

Of your mystical Supper...

Communion prayers

The prayers that are now said by the celebrant, and which should be said by everyone who is preparing to receive Communion, are the last of a series of prayers called the Service of Preparation for Holy Communion. This service is read in three parts. The first part is the Canon* for Holy Communion, whose acrostic is the alphabet in Greek, and it is read the previous evening during Compline.* The second part is read in the morning and consists of three psalms, three *troparia* and nine prayers by various holy Fathers. The third part consists of the prayers read at this point by the celebrant.

The first prayer of this third part is a confession of faith and hope in Christ's love: *I believe, Lord, and I confess that You are*

the Christ, the Son of the living God, who came into the world to save sinners, of whom I am the foremost.

This phrase is based on the words of St Paul: *The saying is sure and worthy of full acceptance, that Jesus Christ came into the world to save sinners, of whom I am the foremost; but I received mercy for this reason, that in me first Jesus Christ might display His perfect patience* (1 Tim. 1: 15–16). St John Chrysostom explains the Apostle's words using an example: 'Let us suppose that there is a large city, all of whose citizens are malefactors. Some more and some less, but all deserve condemnation. Now suppose that there is one among them who more than any other deserves every punishment, because he has committed every sort of evil. If therefore someone says that it is the king's will to pardon them all, they will not believe it until they see that man, the greatest malefactor of all, receiving his pardon. Then no one will be left with any doubts. This is also what St Paul says: "Wanting to assure human beings that He forgives all their transgressions, God chose the greatest sinner of all... So let no one have doubts about his salvation, since I have been saved."'[31]

With the assurance that Jesus Christ will show His *perfect patience* also to us sinners, we ask Him to make us worthy to approach without condemnation the Cup of His love.

Employ a mother's boldness, All-pure Lady

In addition to these prayers which make up the Service of Preparation for Holy Communion, the holy Fathers also wrote many other such preparatory prayers. One of these prayers, written by St Philotheos, Patriarch of Constantinople, and addressed to the Mother of God, goes as follows:

'O truly immaculate and most pure Virgin and Theotokos! Wonder terrible to the angels and inexplicable to mortals, or,

---

[31] *On 1 Timothy*, 4.2, PG 62.522.

rather, to both awesome indeed and beyond comprehension: the first-fruit of our race, the exceedingly pure vessel of the Godhead, the workshop of our salvation; through utter goodness, exceeding all understanding and words, you brought forth for us one of the Trinity, our Lord Jesus Christ, who is perfect God and perfect man, so that with the stuff of humankind He might save our nature from its fall of old and bring it once again to its original dignity. You are the restoration of those who fall even after this saving divine economy of God the Word; by your exceeding solicitude, you deliver even me from such a multitude of dangers, I who am unworthy of any help or providence, since by my arbitrary will I constantly sin in every time and place and matter. Look even now upon my wretchedness, and visit me as is your wont, for I am constrained, and know not what will become of me: if I look at the multitude of my innumerable evils, I perceive myself far from the terrible Mysteries and altogether unworthy; if I long refrain from approaching these Mysteries because I would be receiving them unto condemnation, I become wholly subject to the enemy. I therefore cast the countless multitude of my iniquities upon the ocean of the unsearchable compassion of your Son and God; and putting you forward as a mighty intercessor, I now take courage and draw near. Employ therefore a mother's boldness towards Him, All-pure Lady, and make Him merciful towards me, I beseech you.

'Yea, All-pure One, be my protector, and do not abhor me who am embroiled in many sins, though I have abused myself through all my senses, in actions and words and movements of the mind, in countless aspects of my way of life and conduct and in carefully-crafted demonic pretences. Manifest yourself even at this hour as my co-worker, and implore the Lord who is easily reconciled and forbearing not to reject me and prove me to be devoid of His grace. Rather, may He overlook my many transgressions, and through His holy flesh and precious and life-giving Blood may He sanctify, enlighten and save me, and make me a son of

light: may I walk and direct my steps towards His holy commandments, not turning once more to sin and being defiled.

'That without condemnation I may become a partaker of the pure and terrible gift and receive even here sureties of the more perfect gift to come; so that I may be both delivered from eternal punishment and attain eternal life, through you, my firm hope and protector, glorifying and magnifying Father, Son and Holy Spirit, the All-holy and blessed Trinity, unto the ages of ages. Amen.'[32]

The Priest then says to the Deacon: *Brother and fellow-celebrant, forgive me a sinner.*

Deacon: *May the Lord God remember your priesthood in his Kingdom, always, now and for ever, and to the ages of ages. Amen.*

Priest: *God, have compassion for me, a sinner, and have mercy on me* (three times). Then he approaches the Holy Gifts and, with fear and trembling, takes a portion of the holy Bread and says: *Behold, I draw near to Christ, our immortal King and God. To me, the unworthy Priest* [name], *is granted communion in the precious and all-holy Body of our Lord and God and Saviour, Jesus Christ, for the forgiveness of my sins and for eternal life.*

He then summons the Deacon, saying: *Deacon, draw near.*

The Deacon, as he approaches, says: *Behold, I draw near to Christ, our immortal King and God. Grant me, Master, the unworthy Deacon* [name], *communion in the precious and all-holy Body of our Lord and*

---

[32] St Nikodimus of the Holy Mountain, *Apanthisma lian katanyktikon Efchon* [*Anthology of emotive Prayers*] (Volos: Agioreitiki Bibliothiki, 1963), p. 50.

God and Saviour, Jesus Christ, for the forgiveness of my sins and for eternal life.

The Priest gives the Deacon a portion of the holy Bread and says: *To you, the reverent Deacon* [name], *is granted communion in the precious and all-holy Body of our Lord and God and Saviour, Jesus Christ, for the forgiveness of your sins and for eternal life.*

Then the Priest takes the Chalice and says: *To me, the unworthy Priest* [name], *is granted communion in the precious, all-holy, all-pure and living Blood of our Lord and God and Saviour, Jesus Christ, for the forgiveness of my sins and for eternal life.* And he drinks three times from the Chalice, then kissing the Chalice and lifting it up, he says: *This has touched my lips: it will take away my iniquities and cleanse my sins.*[33]

Then he says: *Deacon, again draw near.*

The Deacon approaches, saying: *Behold, again I draw near to Christ, our immortal King and God. Grant me, Master, the unworthy Deacon* [name], *communion in the precious, all-holy, all-pure and living Blood of our Lord and God and Saviour, Jesus Christ, for the forgiveness of my sins and for eternal life.*

The Priest takes the Chalice and communicates the Deacon three times, saying: *To you, the reverent Deacon* [name], *is granted communion in the precious, all-holy, all-pure and living Blood of our Lord and God and Saviour, Jesus Christ, for the forgiveness of your sins and for eternal life.* Then the Deacon kisses the Chalice, and the Priest lifts it up, saying: *This has touched your lips: it will take away your iniquities and cleanse your sins.*

---

[33] Isa. 6: 7.

This has touched my lips

When the celebrant has communed with fear and trembling in the all-holy Body and immaculate Blood of the Lord, he kisses the Chalice and says: *This has touched my lips: it will take away my iniquities and cleanse my sins.*

These words were spoken by an angel to the Prophet Isaiah when at the time of his calling to the office of prophet, *there was sent to* [him] *one of the Seraphim, and in his hand he held a burning coal which he had taken with tongs from the altar and he touched* [his] *lips* (Isa. 6: 6–7). The burning coal was a symbol of Christ. 'As a burning coal is wood by nature but has been totally filled with fire and has the power and efficacy of fire, so it is with Christ... Even though in accordance with the divine economy He was, and appeared as, a human being like us, yet the whole fullness of the Godhead dwelt within Him [cf. Col. 2: 9]... So it is very appropriate for Emmanuel to be represented by a burning coal, since if He touches our lips, He will certainly take away all our sins and cleanse all [our] iniquities.'[34]

The angel did not dare to touch the burning coal, the symbol of Christ, with his hand, but used tongs. The celebrant, however, takes Christ Himself into his hands, to his lips, and into himself. St John Chrysostom observes: 'If you take into account that the Holy Things [the holy Body and Blood of the Lord] set forth here are so precious that even the Seraphim are far from being worthy to touch them, and then reflect on your Lord's love for mankind, you will be amazed that the grace of the holy Body and Blood does not spurn descending even to our worthlessness. Bearing this in mind, O human, and considering the magnitude of the gift, raise yourself up once and for all, abandon the earth and ascend to heaven.'[35]

Our attachment to earthly things is an obstacle to Holy Com-

---

[34] St Cyril of Alexandria, *On Isaiah*, 4, *PG* 70.181BD.
[35] *Homily on Isaiah 6*, 3, *PG* 56.139.

munion bearing fruit in us. St Symeon the New Theologian writes: 'To those who have not risen above the senses, this Bread appears according to the senses to be [merely] bread, but to the spiritual understanding it is Light which cannot be contained or approached... So when you eat the divine Bread and drink the Wine of gladness, if you are not aware that you have experienced immortal life and have received into yourself that Bread illuminant and fiery,...do you think you have communed in Life? Do you think you have touched the unapproachable fire of the Godhead or that you have partaken in any degree in the eternal Light? This has certainly not happened to you, since you do not perceive in your soul any of the things we have spoken of. That Light illumines you, but you are blind. The fire warms you, but does not touch you. And the Life came to you, but did not unite Itself to you.'[36]

In order to receive eternal life into ourselves, let us approach Holy Communion with a pure soul and 'with burning desire. Let us cross our hands [one upon the other], and receive into them the Body of the Crucified One. And after touching it with our eyes, our lips and our foreheads, let us partake of the divine Coal. Thus the fire of our love will be ignited by the divine Coal, and burn up our sins and illumine our hearts; and through participation in the divine fire, we shall catch on fire and be deified.'[37]

After the Priest and the Deacon have received Communion, the Deacon, holding the Paten above the Chalice, carefully transfers the portions of the holy Bread from it into the Chalice, saying: *Let us who have*

---

[36] *Ethical Discourse 14, SC* 129, p. 440.
[37] St John of Damascus, *On the Orthodox Faith*, 4.86, *PG* 94.1149AB. See also n. 22 to p. 183 above.

beheld the Resurrection of Christ worship the holy Lord Jesus, who alone is without sin. We venerate your Cross, O Christ, and we praise and glorify your holy Resurrection. For you are our God; we know no other besides you, and we call upon your name. Come, all believers, and let us venerate Christ's holy Resurrection. For behold, through the Cross joy has come to all the world. Ever blessing the Lord, we praise his Resurrection: for by enduring the Cross, he destroyed death by death.

Shine, shine, O new Jerusalem, for the glory of the Lord has risen upon you. Dance now and rejoice, O Zion. And do you, pure Theotokos, delight in the rising of your Child.

How divine, how dear, how very sweet is your voice; for you have promised faithfully to be with us to the end of the age, O Christ. Holding fast to this as an anchor of hope, we the faithful rejoice.

O Christ, great and most holy Passover; O Wisdom and Word and Power of God, grant us to partake of you more perfectly in the day of your Kingdom which knows no evening.[38]

And he carefully wipes any particles remaining on the Paten into the Chalice, saying: *Wash away, Lord, by your holy Blood the sins of your servants here remembered, through the prayers of the Theotokos and all your Saints. Amen.* If, however, there are many who wish to commune, he wipes the particles into the Chalice after the faithful have communicated.

---

[38] The Paschal Hours; Easter Matins, Canon, ode 9.

We can always be celebrating Easter

Our participation in Holy Communion is 'a true confession and remembrance that the Lord died and rose again, in our stead and for our sake'.[39] This reality is now confirmed by the celebrant, who, after receiving Communion, recites four troparia of the Resurrection as he places the holy Body of Christ in the Chalice.

In the Divine Liturgy, we have seen the Resurrection of Christ celebrated liturgically in the eucharistic assembly. Now, through Holy Communion, we experience that Resurrection in our very being, 'since Christ the Master Himself rises within us, dressed in glistening garments and radiating the brightness of incorruption and of the Godhead'.[40]

St Paul assures us that every time we partake of Christ's holy Body and Blood, we are proclaiming His death (cf. 1 Cor. 11: 26). So, since 'we can always be proclaiming the death of the Lord, we can always be celebrating Easter'.[41] Every assembly for the Liturgy is the Resurrection of Christ, and every Communion is the resurrection of the person who participates in it. 'Resurrection of the soul is union with Life. A dead body is not considered alive, nor can it be alive, unless it receives into itself a living soul that without mingling is commingled with it; and so it is with the soul. If the soul is not united, in some inexpressible way and without confusion, with God who is the true eternal Life, it is not able to live on its own and in itself.'[42]

When the believer receives Communion without condemnation, his whole life 'is an Easter, a Passover: it is a transition from things visible to things intelligible...to the state in which we shall be pure, and shall enjoy eternally and in purity the most pure Sacrifice — Christ — in God the Father and the Holy Spirit. For

---

[39] St Cyril of Alexandria, *On John*, 12, PG 74.725D.
[40] St Symeon the New Theologian, *Catechesis 13*, SC 104, p. 198.
[41] St John Chrysostom, *On Pentecost 1*, 1, PG 50.454.
[42] St Symeon the New Theologian, *Catechesis 13*, SC 104, pp. 194–6.

there we shall see Christ always and be seen by Him; we shall be with Christ and shall reign with Him.'[43]

> The Deacon then turns to the people and says: *With fear of God, with faith and love, draw near.*
> Choir: *Amen, amen, amen. Blessed is he who comes in the name of the Lord.*

Preparing to draw near

The celebrant now invites us to draw near in order to receive Christ into ourselves. This is the most sacred moment of our lives, and we take care that our spiritual and physical attitude should be appropriate to the event that we are experiencing.

St John Chrysostom says: 'When you are about to draw near to this divine and terrible Table in this sacred mystagogy, you should draw near with fear and trembling, with a pure conscience, with fasting and prayer, and without making a noise, without trampling and pushing those around you — such disorder is a sign of utter madness and contempt for the Holy Mysteries.'[44] And he asks: 'Tell me, man, why are you agitated? Why are you in a hurry? Are you under pressure from the need to get on with your work? At that moment can it even cross your mind that you have work to do?... Is it not the sign of a heart of stone that at that moment you think you are standing on earth rather than being part of a choir of angels?'[45]

The experience of liturgical events leads us to reverence, and reverence attracts God's mercy. The rites performed in the Divine

---

[43] St Symeon the New Theologian, *Ethical Discourse 14, SC* 129, p. 442.
[44] *On the Birthday of Jesus Christ,* 7, PG 49.360.
[45] *On the holy Baptism of Jesus Christ,* 4, PG 49.370.

Liturgy 'are Mysteries in actuality and name, and where Mysteries are performed there is a profound silence. Let us therefore partake in the sacred offering silently, in a very orderly manner, and
with the appropriate reverence. In this way we shall attract God's
love even more, we shall purify our souls and we shall attain eternal good things.'[46]

In order, however, to draw near in the proper manner at the
time of Holy Communion, we need to have prepared ourselves in
advance. For 'even though God gives us all the Holy Mysteries
freely without our having offered anything to Him, for truly they
are free gifts, He nevertheless requires that we should be fit to receive and to preserve them, and He does not give us sanctification
and blessing if we are not so disposed... He made this clear in the
parable of the sower. *The sower went forth* [Matt. 13: 3], He says,
not to plough the earth, but to sow, thus showing that the
ploughing and all the preparation should be our contribution.'[47]

By preparing ourselves as well as we possibly can, we reap
'greater benefit from the divine Mysteries. For according to the
greater or lesser preparation that a person has made, he receives
greater or lesser grace from Holy Communion.'[48] Spiritual preparation consists in cultivating in ourselves faith, fear of God and
love. And this effort requires prayer, fasting, confession and constant repentance.

With faith, fear of God and love

Faith, fear of God and love define the manner in which we ought
to approach the Cup of life and commune in Christ.

Faith is the starting point for life in Christ. Through faith we
are born in Christ, and through faith we exist and live in Christ.

---

[46] Ibid. *PG* 49.372.

[47] St Nicholas Cabasilas, *Comm. Liturgy*, 1, *PG* 150.369AB.

[48] St Nikodimus of the Holy Mountain, *Pnevmatika Gymnasmata* [*Spiritual Exercises*], Study 26, iii, 6th edn (Thessaloniki: Rigopoulos, 1971), p. 220.

'The whole economy and the condescension of the Son of God took place for this purpose, so that through faith in Him and the keeping of His commandments He might make us partakers of His Divinity and His Kingdom.'[49]

Faith is 'seeing things invisible as if they were visible'. At the Divine Liturgy, the believer sees Christ who is invisibly present. 'His very Body is before us...not only for us to touch, but for us to eat and be filled. Let us then draw near with faith, since all of us have some illness. For if such power has been transmitted to those who but touched the hem of His garment [cf. Matt. 14: 36, Luke 8: 46–7], how much more power will they who have Him in His entirety within them receive? To draw near to Christ with faith, however, does not only mean receiving Holy Communion, but also to touch it with a pure heart, as if we were approaching Christ Himself.'[50]

* * *

Faith gives rise to *fear of God* when the heart is free from the cares of daily life. St Isaac writes that 'fear of God is the beginning of virtue. It is called the offspring of faith, and is sown in the heart when the mind is removed from the distraction of the world.'[51]

Fear of God is of two kinds: 'The first is generated in us by the threat of punishment. It is through such fear that we develop in due order self-control, patience, hope in God and dispassion; and it is from dispassion that love comes. The second kind of fear is linked with love itself and constantly produces reverence in the soul, so that is does not grow indifferent to God because of the intimate communion of its love.'[52]

---

[49] St Symeon the New Theologian, *Ethical Discourse 3*, SC 122, p. 418.

[50] St John Chrysostom, *Baptismal Catecheses*, 2.9, SC 50, p. 138; *On Matthew*, 50.2, PG 58.507.;

[51] *Asc. Hom.*, 1, p. 3.

[52] St Maximus the Confessor, *Four Hundred Texts on Love*, 1.81, PG 90.977D (*Philokalia*, vol. 2, p. 62).

When man reaches this state, he does not fear anything other than falling from the height of love. That is why, after communing in Christ, who is Love, we ask Him: *Establish us in the fear of You*. We ask for the fear that grips the soul of one perfect in virtue: 'Such a person possesses true love...and this perfect love leads him to perfect fear. He fears and keeps God's will, no longer because he fears punishments or to avoid hell, but...because he has tasted the sweetness of being with God, and he is afraid of losing it and being deprived of that sweetness. So this perfect fear, which arises out of this perfect love, drives out the introductory fear [that which is experienced by beginners]. And for this reason it is said that *perfect love casts out fear* [1 John 4: 18].'[53]

* * *

When a person feels his heart overflowing with love for Christ, he feels the necessity of communing and being united with Love. The moment when a person receives the Lord into himself is the movement of divine love which is offered and of human love which draws near to receive the offering. Christ's holy Body and Blood are eternal love. St Ignatius says: 'I desire the Bread of God...and for my drink I desire His Blood, which is love incorruptible.' Christ 'was not content to become man, to be buffeted and killed, but He also commingles Himself with us. He changes us into His own Body, not only in faith, but in reality.' Christ 'desires to come into our hearts by means of this Mystery... O love truly divine and inexorable! Or I should rather call you flames of love rising up to heaven!'[54]

The holy Fathers urge us to respond to this divine love: 'Dedicate yourself entirely to God by means of this Mystery, receiving with love that beloved Jesus, who out of His exceeding love or-

---

[53] Liturgy, Prayer of Thanksgiving after Holy Communion; Abbas Dorotheus, *Discourse 4*, 1, PG 88.1657D–1660A.
[54] *On Romans*, 7, PG 5.693B; St John Chrysostom, *On Matthew*, 82.5, PG 58.743; St Nikodimus of the Holy Mountain, *Spiritual Exercises*, Study 26, ii, p. 217.

dained such a beloved sacrament, that a heavenly and covetable union should take place between God who loves and you who are loved.'[55]

We show our love and gratitude to our Benefactor, and are inundated with new gifts. We are already tasting the heavenly Kingdom. 'Let us love Christ as we should love Him. This love of ours for Him is itself the great reward [which God gives us]: this is the Kingdom and sweet pleasure, this is enjoyment, glory and honour, this is light, this is the great happiness which words cannot describe nor mind conceive.'[56] 'The love of God is Paradise... When we find love, we are nourished on heavenly Bread... One who has found love eats Christ every day and every hour, and from this becomes immortal... Blessed is he who eats the Bread of love, which is Jesus [cf. John 6: 58]... Love is the Kingdom which the Lord promised to His disciples in a veiled manner, saying that they would eat in His Kingdom. So what is it that says they will "*eat and drink at the Table of* [His] *Kingdom* [Luke 22: 29–30]" if not love? For love is able to nourish man in place of food and drink. Love is the wine that makes glad the heart of man [cf. Ps. 103: 15]. And he is blessed who has drunk of that wine.'[57]

The Divine Liturgy is the Kingdom of God, and the food at the Supper of the Kingdom is love. Through repentance and fear of God, we traverse the sea of this life and arrive at love. 'Repentance is the ship, fear is its helmsman and love is the divine harbour. So fear places us in the ship of repentance, conveys us across the sullied sea of life and brings us to the divine harbour which is love, to which all those who are weary and heavy laden attain through repentance [cf. Matt. 11: 28]. Once we arrive at love, we have arrived at God.'[58]

---

[55] St Nikodimus of the Holy Mountain, *Spiritual Exercises*, Study 26, ii, pp. 217–8.

[56] St John Chrysostom, *On Romans*, 5.7, *PG* 60.431.

[57] St Isaac the Syrian, *Asc. Hom.*, 46, pp. 223–4.

[58] Ibid. pp. 224–5.

The Priest gives Communion to the people, saying to each communicant: *The servant of God [name] is granted communion in the precious and all-holy Body and Blood of our Lord and God and Saviour, Jesus Christ, for the forgiveness of sins and for eternal life.*

While Communion is being given the Choir chants the following *troparion*: *Of your mystical Supper, Son of God, receive me today as a communicant; for I will not tell of the Mystery to your enemies; I will not give you a kiss, like Judas; but like the thief I confess you: Remember me, Lord, in your Kingdom.*

He calls His sheep by name

As the celebrant gives the holy Body and Blood of the Lord to each person, he addresses him or her by name, by the name given them when they were baptised in the name of the Father, and of the Son, and of the Holy Spirit, and became sons of God by grace.

Holy Communion marks the moment of our personal encounter with the Lord. Through the lips of the celebrant, Christ the Good Shepherd calls His sheep one by one: *He calls His sheep by name* (John 10: 3). The faithful approach Him and receive from His most pure hands the food that gives incorruption. 'When you see the priest giving you the Holy Mysteries, do not think that it is the priest doing this; believe rather that the hand stretched out is that of Christ.'[59]

Christ is not only the Shepherd, but also the door for the sheep, the true gateway to life. And through Him the sheep go in and out and find food (cf. John 10: 9), which again is Christ Himself. 'What shepherd feeds his sheep on members of his own

---

[59] St John Chrysostom, *On Matthew*, 50.3, PG 58.507.

body? And why do I say shepherd? There are many mothers who, after the pangs of childbirth, hand their children over to wet-nurses. Yet Christ could not endure to do that, but Himself nour-ishes us with His own Blood and in every way intertwines us with Himself... Through the Holy Mysteries [that is, His Body and Blood], He mingles Himself with each believer, and those He has begotten [in Baptism] He feeds with His own Self, not handing them over to anyone else.'[60]

We and Christ are one

If the Divine Liturgy in its totality is the ocean of God's grace and love, if throughout the Liturgy we are receiving the gifts of grace, then at the moment of Holy Communion we receive the very Giv-er of these gifts, Christ Himself: 'In truth, we are not partaking of one of His gifts, but of His very Self.'[61]

Through Holy Communion, we become one Body with Christ: 'You take into you the Lord Himself, you are mingled with His holy Body, you are intermixed with the Body that is in heaven', says St John Chrysostom.[62] The all-pure Blood of the Master is mingled with our blood and transforms our souls. 'It makes [our souls] vigorous and pure and leads them to the infinite beauty' of the divine Archetype. We humans were created in God's image, and 'this Blood vivifies the royal image in us. This Blood produces an indescribable beauty, and does not allow the nobility of the soul to wither, because it is constantly watering and nourishing it... This Blood is the salvation of our souls: by this the soul is washed and made beautiful, by this it is enkindled; it causes our intellect to shine more brightly than fire, and our soul to glitter more than gold.'[63]

---

[60] St John Chrysostom, *On Matthew*, 82.5, *PG* 58.744.
[61] St Nicholas Cabasilas, *On the Life in Christ*, 4, *PG* 150.584D.
[62] *On Colossians*, 6.4, *PG* 62.342.
[63] St John Chrysostom, *On Hebrews*, 16.2, *PG* 63.125; *On John*, 46.3, *PG* 59.261.

When Christ comes into us, he does not sanctify our soul alone but our whole being. For by Holy Communion, 'Body [is mingled] with body, Blood with blood... What great mysteries are these! What a miracle, that the mind of Christ should become one with our mind, that His will should be amalgamated with our will, His Body with our body, His Blood with our blood! What is our mind like when the divine mind prevails over it; what is our will like when the divine will predominates; and what becomes of the dust [our body] once the fire [of the Godhead] overcomes it!'[64] The distribution of the pure Mysteries 'makes those who partake worthily to be similar — by grace and by participation — to Him who is the causal Good'.[65]

Motivated by love, God has given us the Mystery of Holy Communion in order for us to be deified. Christ sacrificed 'Himself on our behalf through His death on the Cross, and He continually offers Himself up, giving His immaculate Body to us daily as a soul-nourishing feast, so that by eating it and by drinking His precious Blood we may through this participation consciously grow in spiritual stature...and [be] refashioned in a purer form... Thus we do not belong to ourselves, but to Him who has united us to Himself though this immortal meal...'.[66]

St Symeon the New Theologian extols the Lord after Holy Communion:

What is this measureless compassion of Yours, O Saviour?
How have You accounted me worthy to become one of Your
    members
— I who am impure, a prodigal, a harlot?
How have You dressed me in a garment most bright,
glistering with the radiance of immortality
and making all my members into light?

---

[64] St Nicholas Cabasilas, *On the Life in Christ*, 4, PG 150.584D–585A.

[65] St Maximus the Confessor, *Mystagogy*, 21, PG 91.697A.

[66] St Nikitas Stithatos, *One Hundred Texts on the Inner Nature of Things*, 94, *Philokalia*, vol. 4, p. 135.

For Your Body, pure and divine,
is wholly radiant, wholly intermixed
and commingled ineffably with the fire of Your Divinity...
I have been united, I know, also with Your Divinity
and have become Your most pure Body,
a member shining forth, a member truly holy,
a member glittering from afar, and radiant, and shining.[67]

This inexpressible mystery of God's union with man is described by St John Chrysostom in one phrase: 'We and Christ are one!'[68]

Christ nourishes us in both worlds

Holy Communion is a foretaste of the Kingdom of God: Christ is given to us *that whoever believes in Him should not perish, but have eternal life* (John 3: 16). Through Holy Communion, the Kingdom which is to come dawns in our souls.

Our departed brethren who have been saved also receive a foretaste of the Kingdom, for they too receive sanctification from Holy Communion. 'That which brings delight and bliss for those who are in that place, whether you call it Paradise or the bosom of Abraham...or the Kingdom itself, is nothing other than this holy Cup and this holy Bread... That is why the Lord described the joy of the saints in the age to come as a Supper (cf. Luke 14: 16), to show that there is nothing there greater than this Holy Table!'[69]

The Divine Liturgy is an assembly of the children of God, who are waiting for their Lord to return *from the marriage banquet, so that they may open the door for Him as soon as He comes and knocks.* And then the Lord *will gird Himself and have them sit at table, and He will come and serve them* (Luke 12: 36–7). We await

---

[67] *Hymn 2*, 1–17, *SC* 156, pp. 176–8.
[68] *On Hebrews*, 6.3, *PG* 63.58.
[69] St Nicholas Cabasilas, *Comm. Liturgy*, 43, 45, *PG* 150.461CD, 465B.

Him who is coming, and at the same time we partake of Him. We participate in the joy that is to come. So death is nothing other than our transition from this temporary life to eternal Life, a transition from the Table of the Eucharist to the Banquet Table of the Kingdom: 'For the grace of the Table is one, and one the Host who nourishes us in both worlds', that of the living and that of the departed.[70]

When all have communicated, the Priest says: *O God, save your people, and bless your inheritance.*[71]

Choir: [*God is the Lord, and he revealed himself to us.*[72]] *We have seen the true Light; we have received the heavenly Spirit; we have found the true faith, worshipping the undivided Trinity; for the Trinity has saved us.*[73]

The Deacon says to the Priest: *Master, exalt.*

The Priest places the Chalice on the Holy Table and censes it three times, saying each time: *Be exalted, O God, above the heavens; and your glory over all the earth.*[74]

The Priest, facing the Holy Table, lifts the Chalice and says in a low voice: *Blessed is our God*, and he then turns to the people, showing them the Chalice, and continues, aloud: *Always, now and for ever, and to the ages of ages.* He then carries the Chalice to the holy Prothesis.

Choir: *Amen, [amen, amen. For the forgiveness of*

[70] St Nicholas Cabasilas, *On the Life in Christ*, 4, PG 150.625B.
[71] Ps. 27: 9.
[72] Ps. 117: 27.
[73] Vespers of Pentecost, *idiomelon*.
[74] Ps. 56: 6.

sins and for eternal life.] And the troparion: Let our mouth be filled with your praise, O Lord, that we may sing of your glory, for you have counted us worthy to partake of your holy, divine, immortal and life-giving Mysteries; keep us in your sanctification, as we meditate on your righteousness all the day long. Alleluia, alleluia, alleluia.[75]

We have seen the true Light

Through Holy Communion, the Christian receives into himself the true Light. His soul is united to Christ, the Sun of righteousness. His intellect is 'wholly intermingled with God and illumined through and through by the divine light'.[76] For the person who has partaken of Him, Christ becomes:

Light and peace and joy, life, food and drink,
clothing and cloak, a tabernacle and divine dwelling…
a sun that truly never sets, a star that ever shines,
a lamp shining forth within the house of the soul.[77]

We have received into our souls not simply 'some ray of light, but the very orb' of the sun. By grace we have become suns attending upon the one unique Sun. For Christ, 'having embraced all things with His illumining power, gives to those who are worthy perpetual light, and makes them new suns'.[78]

---

[75] This hymn was first sung at this point during the patriarchate of Sergius of Constantinople, in the year 624 (Paschal Chronicle, Olympiad 351, PG 92.1001). Cf. Ps. 70: 8.

[76] Discourse on Abba Philemon, Philokalia, vol. 2, p. 355.

[77] St Symeon the New Theologian, Hymn 45, 32–39, SC 196, p. 104.

[78] St Nicholas Cabasilas, On the Life in Christ, 4, PG 150.584D; St Gregory Palamas, Refutation of Acindynus, V.6.22, Chrestou 3, p. 302.

Revealing experiences from his own holy life, St Gregory Pala-mas speaks of man's entry into the realm of the true Light: not only has Christ united His own divine hypostasis with human na-ture, but He is constantly 'uniting Himself also with these human hypostases as He mingles Himself with each believer through their Communion of His holy Body. He becomes one body with us, and transforms us into a temple for the Godhead as a whole, since in the Body of Christ *the whole fullness of deity dwells bod-ily* [Col. 2: 9]. How then will He not illumine with the divine ra-diance of His Body — which is within us — the souls of those who commune worthily, as once He illumined the bodies of the disci-ples on Tabor?'[79]

The light of Christ illumines the whole person, leading him to the vision of the mysteries of God: 'Simple and unified, the pres-ence of divine light gathers within itself the souls that participate in it and converts them to itself... It leads their intellect's faculty of sight towards the depths of God, so that they contemplate the great mysteries and become initiates and mystagogues.'[80]

The eucharistic Mystery — the Mystery of the Sun of right-eousness — dawned upon our world from the Light of the Father; it is celebrated by the Light of the world, which is Christ; and it is sanctified through the Light of the Paraclete. Before the coming of Christ, the Prophet David prophesied: *In Your light shall we see light* (Ps. 35: 10). Now we too, after Holy Communion, 'have seen and discovered the Son of God as light, from the light of the Father, by the light of the Holy Spirit. And we proclaim this as a succinct and simple theology of the Holy Trinity... Light and light and light, but one Light, one God.'[81]

When created man is wholly illumined by the divine Light, he is separated from creation and united with God:

---

[79] *In Defence of the holy Hesychasts*, 1.3.38, *Chrestou* 1, p. 449.
[80] St Nikitas Stithatos, *One Hundred Texts on Spiritual Knowledge*, 20, *Philo-kalia*, vol. 4, p. 145.
[81] St Gregory the Theologian, *Homily 31*, 3, PG 36.136C.

Again the Light seems to me to shine forth, again it is clearly
      seen,
again it opens the heavens, again it cuts through the night,
again it puts aside all things, again it is seen on its own,
again it places me outside all visible things...
And as I am in the midst of everything, it places me outside
      everything.[82]

Christ, the Light of the world, dispels the darkness of the present age. He opens the heavens and leads us into the realm of the
new age. There we see the Light which is 'the beauty of the age
which is to come and which endures, the Kingdom of God without beginning or successor'. There, in the Kingdom, *night shall be
no more; they need no light of lamp or sun* (Rev. 22: 5). There *the
light of* [Christ's] *countenance watches.*[83]

* * *

The entire Liturgy, as an image of the Kingdom which is to
come, is illuminated by the light of Christ. The martyr St James of
the Holy Mountain had the purity of vision to see the invisible:
'As the priest began to vest for the Liturgy, the light of the angels
shone in front of him, like the light of dawn. When he began the
Service of Preparation, four companies of angels went and stood
at the four corners of the church, and after he finished and covered the precious Gifts with the holy veils, they were covered
with abundant light — for the visible veils signify the intelligible
light which covers the Holy Gifts. When it was time for the Great
Entrance and the priest came out with the Holy Gifts, light went
before him and covered all the faithful, and when the Holy Gifts
were placed on the Altar, that light surrounded them, like the orb
of the moon. In the middle of the luminous ring was the priest with

---

[82] St Symeon the New Theologian, *Hymn 40*, 1–4, 15, *SC* 174, pp. 484–6.

[83] St Gregory Palamas, *In Defence of the holy Hesychasts*, 2.3.54, *Chrestou* 1, pp.
586–7; Divine Liturgy, Anaphora prayer (after the Consecration).

the Holy Gifts, while outside it the angels stood with reverence, not daring to approach. That light does not depart from a pure priest but becomes one with him, and a shining flame comes out of his mouth when he reads the Gospel and the prayers. And when he lifts up his hands, light pours from all his fingers.'

And the saint continues: 'After the Consecration, I saw the Lord as an infant, lying on the Paten surrounded by light... And when the Liturgy ended, I saw the divine Infant... ascending to heaven in glory and honour together with the holy angels.'[84]

Be exalted, O God, above the heavens

Having placed the Holy Gifts on the Altar, the priest censes them three times and recites the psalm verse, *Be exalted, O God, above the heavens, and Your glory over all the earth* (Ps. 56: 6). 'When you hear the words *Be exalted*, do not imagine that the Prophet David is asking God to take additional glory unto Himself, for He has no need of glory... Principally, it indicates the way in which God is praised in heaven, where the holy angels exalt and glorify Him. But [the Prophet] wants God's glory to be exalted over all the earth, as it is in heaven.'[85] Furthermore, when these words are said, it is as if we are saying to Christ: 'Even though You abased Yourself for our sake by the voluntary self-emptying of Your In-carnation, and became *obedient even unto death* [Phil. 2: 8], ascend again now, Lord, to heaven, for after Your ascent, You will also fill the whole earth with Your glory.'[86]

---

[84] Life of the Monk and Martyr Jacob of the Holy Mountain (1 November). Cf. *Megas Synaxaristis*, vol. 11, 5th edn (Athens: Mathaios Lagges, 1979), pp. 43–4, and *Thavmata kai apokalypseis apo tin theia Leitourgia* [*Wonders and revelations from the Divine Liturgy*] (Oropos, Attiki: Paraklitou Monastery, 1997), pp. 79–80.

[85] See St Nikodimus of the Holy Mountain, *Ermeneia eis tous 150 psalmous*, [*Commentary on the 150 Psalms*], vol. 2 (Thessaloniki: Orthodoxos Kypseli, 1981), note to p. 61.

[86] St Athanasius the Great, *On Psalm 56*, PG 27.260C.

Every time the Divine Liturgy is celebrated, Christ comes down from heaven for our salvation. At this moment, He ascends to heaven once again. With the eyes of the soul, the faithful see the Ascension of Christ, and like the disciples at the Ascension, 'praise and bless God with great joy' (cf. Luke 24: 52–3), for the light of His glory and love remains also on earth and illuminates the world.

* * *

With the Communion of the faithful, we reach the end of the eucharistic Mystery. The priest and people conclude with thanksgiving and praise: *Let our mouth be filled with praise, O Lord...* It is as if to say: 'We are not fit even to offer You a hymn worthy of the good things that You have vouchsafed to us, but we ask You to grant us this grace. How? By filling our mouths with praise...'. In what follows, 'The faithful pray that the sanctification which they have received may remain with them, and that with the help of the Lord Himself they may not betray this grace or lose this gift: "*Keep us in Your sanctification...*we who *meditate on Your righteousness all the day long*". *Righteousness* means here God's wisdom and love for mankind as these are manifested through the Holy Mysteries... Meditation on this righteousness is able to preserve the sanctification within us, for it increases our faith in God and kindles our love.'[87]

> The Deacon, standing before the Royal Doors, says: *Stand upright. Having received the divine, holy, pure, immortal, heavenly, life-giving and dread Mysteries of Christ, let us give worthy thanks to the Lord.*

[87] St Nicholas Cabasilas, *Comm. Liturgy*, 41, *PG* 150.456D–457A.

Choir: *Lord, have mercy.*

Deacon: *Help us, save us, have mercy on us, and keep us, O God, by your grace.*

Choir: *Lord, have mercy.*

Deacon: *Having asked that the whole day may be perfect, holy, peaceful and sinless, let us entrust ourselves and one another and our whole life to Christ our God.*

Choir: *To you, O Lord.*

The Priest, in a low voice, says the Prayer of Thanksgiving:

We thank you, Lord, lover of mankind, benefactor of our souls, that you have counted us worthy today too of your heavenly and immortal Mysteries. Make straight our way, establish us all in the fear of you, watch over our life, and make firm our steps, through the prayers and intercessions of the glorious Theotokos and Ever-Virgin Mary, and of all your Saints.

(aloud) *For you are our sanctification, and to you we give glory, to the Father, and to the Son, and to the Holy Spirit, now and for ever, and to the ages of ages.*

Choir: *Amen.*

I have no words, my Saviour

This Prayer of Thanksgiving calls to mind the corresponding giving of thanks by the disciples at the end of the Last Supper: *When they had sung a hymn, they went out to the Mount of Olives* (Matt. 26: 30). St John Chrysostom observes: 'The final prayer of the Liturgy is a symbol of that prayer. The Lord gave thanks before giving the disciples His holy Body and Blood, that we also may

give thanks. And after the offering, He again gave thanks and sang a hymn, so that we might do likewise.'[88]

St John composed the following liturgical Prayer of Thanksgiving after Holy Communion. The saint feels unable to express in words the gratitude due to Christ, the Giver of gifts, and he asks the Lord to preserve the celebrants and the faithful 'in an honourable and a reverent way of life' and worthy of the heavenly Table till the last moment of their lives:

> What praise or what hymn or what thanks can we give You in repayment, our God who loves mankind? For when we were condemned to death and immersed in sins, You bestowed freedom upon us and gave us a share in the immortal and heavenly delight of the holy Body and Blood of Your Christ. Therefore we pray You, keep us and Your servants the deacons free from condemnation. Preserve with us the people here present in an honourable and a reverent way of life; count us worthy until our last breath to partake at this mystical Table unto sanctification of soul and body, that we may be accounted worthy of Your heavenly Kingdom with all who have been well-pleasing to You: by the prayers of the all-holy, pure Theotokos and Ever-Virgin Mary and of all Your saints. For You are holy God and love mankind, and to You we give glory, to the Father and to the Son, and to the Holy Spirit, now and for ever, and to the ages of ages. Amen.[89]

Similarly, in the following hymn, St Symeon the New Theologian, in spite of the heavenly gift of theology which he had received, says that he cannot find words to describe the magnitude of the benefaction of Holy Communion and give thanks for it:

---

[88] *On Matthew*, 82.2, PG 58.740. In St John Chrysostom's time, this prayer of thanksgiving was the final prayer of the Liturgy. See also n. 1, p. 308, below.

[89] This used to be the Prayer behind the Ambo in the Liturgy of St John Chrysostom (Trembelas, *Leitourgiai*, p. 155).

Creator of all, Maker and master,
whom the Seraphim may not approach,
You do not only see and speak to me and feed me,
but You have granted to me even to hold and eat
Your flesh, in all reality,
and to drink Your all-holy Blood...
The mind is at a loss, the tongue enfeebled,
and I find no words, my Saviour,
to proclaim the works of Your goodness
which You have performed for me Your servant...
You have united Yourself with me, Lover of mankind,
in Your measureless compassion...
You have swept out the house that was all begrimed
and come in to dwell there, O Trinity, my God,
and then You made me a throne of Your divine Godhead
and a house of Your unapproachable glory and Your Kingdom.[90]

---

[90] *Hymn 20*, 55–203, *SC* 174, pp. 114–26.

8. DISMISSAL

Priest: *Let us go forth in peace.*[1]
Choir: *In the name of the Lord.*
Deacon: *Let us pray to the Lord.*
Choir: *Lord, have mercy.*

The Priest, standing in front of the icon of Christ, says aloud the Prayer behind the Ambo: *O Lord, Who bless those who bless you, and sanctify those who have put their trust in you: save your people and bless your inheritance; protect the fullness of your Church; sanctify those who love the beauty of your house;[2] glorify them in return by your divine power, and do not forsake us who hope in you. Give peace to your world, to your churches, to the priests, to our rulers, to the army, and to all your people. For every good gift and every perfect gift is coming from above, from you, the Father of lights;[3] and to you we give glory, thanksgiving and worship, to the Father, and to the Son, and to the Holy Spirit, now and for ever, and to the ages of ages.*

Choir: *Amen.*

---

[1] In the early centuries, the Liturgy ended with this exhortation from the celebrant. These words marked the conclusion of the eucharistic assembly and the dismissal of the faithful. The prayer recited by the celebrant following this was added later and is called the Prayer behind the Ambo, because it was originally said in the middle of the church, behind the ambo (pulpit). On the Holy Mountain, the celebrant begins the prayer inside the sanctuary, and as he says the words *bless your inheritance* he comes out and blesses the people, and continues the prayer before the icon of Christ.

[2] Ps. 25: 8.

[3] Jas. 1: 17.

Let us go forth in peace

The Divine Liturgy is a journey whose purpose is man's encounter and union with God. This goal has now been realised: we have reached the end of our journey, we have seen the true Light, we have seen the Lord transfigured on the Mount Tabor of the Liturgy, we have partaken of His holy Body and most pure Blood. And as we venture to utter to our exalted Visitor, *Lord, it is good for us to be here* (Matt. 17: 4), our Mother Church reminds us that the end of the liturgical journey must become the starting-point for our spiritual journey: *Let us go forth in peace.* We have to leave the Mountain of the Transfiguration in order to return to the world and tread the way of martyrdom of our lives. This journey becomes our *martyria*, our witness to Christ — the Way and the Life — who has become our guest.

During the Divine Liturgy, we received Christ within us. Now we are invited to pass Him on to the world, to become witnesses to the life of Christ. 'We should come out of the sacred assembly...as if we had descended from heaven itself', so that when our family, our friends or our enemies see us, they will all understand the benefit we have received from the Church.[4]

After Holy Communion, we go out into the world as Christ-bearers and Spirit-bearers. Thereafter, we strive to preserve the Light we have received ever-burning, and to keep undefiled the gifts of grace which we have received. Then, even without words, our presence will transmit the Grace we have received to the souls of our brethren who were not present at the Liturgy. For the Christ-bearing believer is earth that *brings forth fruit of itself* (Mark 4: 28).

The Divine Liturgy began 'in peace', and in its course the peace of God was given to us many times. Now that the celebrant 'dismisses us from the assembly, he once again petitions [peace] for

---

[4] St John Chrysostom, *On 'If your Enemy is hungry'*, 4, PG 51.179.

us, saying: "Go in peace." And without this peace, it is altogether impossible to say or do anything.'[5]

Peace and love are at once the root and the fruit of our prayer at the Liturgy: 'This peace and love do not simply make our prayer acceptable, but are also engendered by prayer itself and arise out of it like twin divine rays, and grow and become perfected.'[6] The faithful too are now called to offer to the world the fruits of the liturgical assembly, its love and peace.

The fullness of the Church

The Prayer behind the Ambo calls the faithful the *fullness* (*pleroma**), that is, the whole body of Christ's Church. The Church is Christ's ship journeying through this world, and all who belong to her form the complement of the ship. 'The world is like a sea on which the Church, like a ship upon the deep, is buffeted by storms but not lost; for she has Christ, the skilled helmsman, with her. And at her centre [like a mast] is the Cross of Christ, which she carries with her as a token of victory over death... Her tillers are the two Testaments, and the ropes that stretch around her are the love of Christ which binds the Church together... As the wind the Spirit from heaven is present, by whom those who believe are sealed... She has also mariners on the right and on the left, assistants like the holy angels.'[7]

As she crosses the stormy sea of life, the ship of the Church is bound for the harbour of the Kingdom of God: 'The Church as a whole is like a great ship, transporting people from different places through foul weather, people who want to dwell in the same city, the city of the good Kingdom. In this representation,

---

[5] St John Chrysostom, *Against the Jews*, 3.6, PG 48.870. The words 'Go in peace' have today been replaced with *Let us go forth in peace*.

[6] Sts Kallistos and Ignatius Xanthopoulos, *On those who have chosen to live in Hesychia*, 8, *Philokalia* [Greek edition], vol. 4, p. 202

[7] St Hippolytus of Rome, *On Christ and Anti-Christ*, 59, PG 10.777B–780A.

the King of the city is God, the helmsman of the ship can be compared to Christ, the first mate to the bishop...the passengers to the multitude of the faithful, the depths of the sea to the world, the contrary winds to temptations, while persecutions, dangers and afflictions of every kind can be likened to the storms.'[8]

Christ has liberated us from sin and death, regenerated us through Baptism and made us the complement of His Church. He is 'the true Ecclesiastes, who gathers into one complete whole the scattered [sheep], and summons to one assembly those who have been led astray in various ways by the multifarious deceptions' of the world. He makes us members of His blessed people, that we may become 'all one Church, and one people, and one bride, under the one Ecclesiast and Leader and Bridegroom, as we are united and acquire the Communion of a Body'.[9]

Choir: *Blessed be the name of the Lord, from this time forth and for ever more* (three times).

The Priest goes to the holy Prothesis and says, in a low voice: *O Christ, our God, who are the fulfilment of the Law and the Prophets, and have fulfilled all the dispensation of the Father, fill our hearts with joy and gladness, always, now and for ever, and to the ages of ages. Amen.*

---

[8] St Clement of Rome, *Epistle to James*, 14, PG 2.49AB.

[9] St Gregory of Nyssa, *On Ecclesiastes*, 1, PG 44.620B; *On the Song of Songs*, 6, PG 44.905A. Christ is called the 'Ecclesiast' here based on the classical sense of the word, in that He 'summons the assembly' of the Church.

Blessed be the name of the Lord

This final praise of the name of the Lord comes from Psalm 112. This psalm is the first of a series of six psalms that were sung by the Jews at the Passover meal. It is therefore virtually certain that the Lord and His disciples would have sung *Blessed be the name of the Lord* at the conclusion of the Last Supper (cf. Matt. 26: 30).

The faithful, Christ's present-day disciples, also glorify the all-holy name of their heavenly Father before leaving the upper room. For, as St John Chrysostom says, 'through this name death was abolished...the doors of Paradise opened wide, the Holy Spirit descended upon us, slaves became free men, enemies became sons, strangers became heirs, humans became angels. Angels, did I say? God became man, and man god. Heaven received the nature that came from earth. The earth received Him who sits upon the Cherubim together with the angelic host. The dividing wall [between God and humans — cf. Eph. 2: 14] has been destroyed, the barrier has been removed, what was separated is united, darkness has been abolished, light has shone forth.'[10]

For all these innumerable benefactions we cry out to the Lord, *How wonderful is Your name in all the earth* (Ps. 8: 2). Indeed, 'by means of this name uncountable things have been accomplished, and by it we are initiated into the sacred mystagogy. So the Psalmist, reflecting on the many marvellous things that are achieved through the name of the Lord,...says, *Holy and terrible is His name!* [Ps. 110: 9]. And if it is holy, then the mouths that praise it should also be holy, holy and pure.'[11] It is precisely for this reason that after our mouths have been sanctified by Communion in Christ, who is the only Holy One, the fount of sanctification, our Church has appointed us to praise the Lord's all-holy name.

---

[10] *On Psalm 8*, 1, PG 55.107.
[11] St John Chrysostom, *On Psalm 110*, 7, PG 55.289.

Fill our hearts with joy and gladness: 'What manner of joy is meant here? Is it the joy of this world? Perish the thought!... [Those who say this prayer] have in mind that joy which has nothing in common with this present life, they mean the joy of the angels, heavenly joy. And they do not simply ask for it; they ask for it in abundance; for they do not say "give" but "fill", and they do not say "us", but "our hearts", since this joy is above all a joy of the heart.'[12]

Deacon: *Let us pray to the Lord.*
Choir: *Lord, have mercy.*
Priest: *May the blessing of the Lord and his mercy come upon you, by his divine grace and love for mankind, always, now and for ever, and to the ages of ages.*
Choir: *Amen.*
Priest: *Glory to you, Christ, O God, our hope, glory to you.*
Reader: *Glory to the Father, and to the Son, and to the Holy Spirit, now and for ever, and to the ages of ages. Lord, have mercy; Lord, have mercy; Lord, have mercy. Holy Master, give the blessing.*
The Priest then turns towards the people and says:[13] *May Christ our true God, through the prayers of his all-pure and holy Mother, by the power of the precious and life-giving Cross, through the protection of the honoured, Bodiless Powers of heaven, through the intercessions of the honoured, glorious Prophet, Forerunner and Baptist, John, of the holy, glorious and all-*

---

[12] St John Chrysostom, *On Matthew*, 55.5, PG 58.547.
[13] On Sundays: *May Christ our true God, who rose from the dead, through the prayers....*

praised Apostles, of the holy, glorious and triumphant Martyrs, of our venerable and God-bearing Fathers and Mothers who have shone forth in the ascetic life, of our Father among the Saints John Chrysostom, Archbishop of Constantinople, of the holy and right-eous forebears of God, Joachim and Anna, of Saint [name, to whom the church is dedicated], *of Saint* [name] *whose memory we keep today, and of all the Saints, have mercy on us and save us, for he is good and loves mankind.*

Through the prayers of our holy Fathers, Lord Jesus Christ, our God, have mercy upon us.

Choir: *Amen.*

The Priest then distributes the *antidoron,** saying to each recipient: *May the blessing and mercy of the Lord come upon you.* As he gives the *antidoron* to the final recipient he adds: *By his grace and love for mankind, always, now and for ever, and to the ages of ages. Amen.*

The blessing of the Lord and His mercy

The Divine Liturgy has reached its conclusion. The priest, 'having blessed the people by making the sign of the cross over them and having prayed that the blessing of the Lord may come upon them, performs the dismissal. He calls upon our true God, Christ, to have mercy upon us and to save us all, through the intercessions of His most holy Mother and all the saints. At the same time he proclaims and testifies that through the divine economy of Christ our Saviour and the celebration of the divine service, we have been and will be saved. He also testifies that the prayers of the Theotokos contribute to our salvation, since she is the servant of

the greatest Mystery [that of God's Incarnation], as do the prayers of all those who have been sanctified by that Mystery.'[14]

The priest prays 'that God may have mercy on us so that we may be saved, since we have nothing of ourselves that is worthy of salvation, but we rely solely on the love for mankind of Him who is able to save us. That is why at this point he commemorates many intercessors who will help us in this, and above all the All-holy Mother of God, thanks to whom mercy was first brought to us.'[15]

* * *

Finally, the celebrant distributes the *antidoron*. The Greek word means literally that which is given in place of (*anti*) the one and only Gift (*doron*): 'It is given in place of the Gifts...to those who have not partaken of those Gifts.' The *antidoron* 'is distributed as a way of transmitting ineffable blessing to those who partake of it with faith'.[16]

The bread that is distributed as *antidoron* has been sanctified because it has been offered to God. And the faithful 'receive it with all reverence and kiss the right hand of the priest, which only shortly before had touched the all-holy Body of Christ the Saviour, and which, thus sanctified, now passes on that sanctification to those who touch it with faith.'[17]

The *antidoron* is 'a type of the virginal body' of the Mother of God. It is the bread from which the Lamb was cut to become the

---

[14] St Symeon of Thessaloniki, *On the holy Liturgy*, 100, PG 155.304AB.

[15] St Nicholas Cabasilas, *Comm. Liturgy*, 53, PG 150.489D.

[16] St Symeon of Thessaloniki, *Church Building*, 101, PG 155.745D; St Germanus, *Contemplation*, PG 98.452D.

[17] St Nicholas Cabasilas, *Comm. Liturgy*, 53, PG 150.489C. In earlier times, the priest would not go back into the sanctuary after saying the Prayer behind the Ambo, but would distribute the *antidoron* while the hymn *Blessed be the name of the Lord...* was sung, together with Psalm 33. Later, when *May the blessing of the Lord and His mercy...* and the dismissal *May Christ our true God...* were added, distribution of the *antidoron* and the Psalm were moved to before *Through the prayers of our holy Fathers....*

Body of Christ, just as Christ, the Bread of life, was born ineffably from His All-holy Mother. At the Divine Liturgy, 'through participation in the immaculate Body of Christ our God, who was born of her,...sanctification and adoption come to the faithful. But spiritual blessing and other good things are undoubtedly given to the race of Christians by the distribution of the bread of the body of the Theotokos', that is to say, the *antidoron*.'[18]

Those who did not receive the Gift, the *Doron*, receive a spiritual blessing through the *anti-doron*. The blessing and mercy of the Lord extend to the whole complement of the faithful.

---

[18] St Germanus, *Contemplation*, PG 98.452D–453A.

III. THANKSGIVING
AFTER HOLY COMMUNION

Whenever you have had Communion
Of the life-giving and transcendent Gifts,
At once give praise and heartfelt thanks
And from your soul say fervently to God:
Glory to you, O God. Glory to you, O God. Glory to you, O God.

THANKSGIVING AFTER HOLY COMMUNION

After distributing the *antidoron*, the Priest goes to the holy Prothesis and consumes the contents of the holy Chalice. He then reads the following prayers of thanksgiving:

Anonymous

I thank you, Lord my God, because you have not rejected me a sinner, but have counted me worthy to be a communicant of your holy things. I thank you, because you have counted me, the unworthy, worthy to share in your most pure and heavenly Gifts. But, Master, Lover of mankind, who died for our sake and rose again, and gave us these your awe-inspiring and life-giving Mysteries, for the well-being and sanctification of our souls and bodies, grant that these may bring me too the healing of soul and body, the repelling of every adversary, the enlightenment of the eyes of my heart, peace of my spiritual powers, faith unashamed, love without pretence, fullness of wisdom, the keeping of your commandments, increase of your divine grace and the gaining of your Kingdom; that preserved through them by your sanctification, I may always remember your grace, and no longer live for myself but for you, our Master and Benefactor. And so, when I leave this present life in the hope of life eternal, I shall find everlasting repose where the sound of those who feast is unceasing, and the delight

*of those who see the ineffable beauty of your face is un-
bounded. For you are the true desire and the inexpressible joy of those who love you, Christ, our God,
and all creation hymns you to the ages. Amen.*

By Saint Basil the Great

*Master, Christ God, King of the ages, and Creator of
all things, I thank you for all the good things you have
given me, and for Communion in your most pure and
life-giving Mysteries. Therefore I pray you, O Good
One, Lover of mankind: guard me under your protection and in the shadow of your wings; and grant that
until my last breath I may share worthily and with a
pure conscience in your holy things for forgiveness of
sins and everlasting life. For you are the Bread of life,
the source of sanctification, the giver of blessings; and
to you we give glory, with the Father and the Holy
Spirit, now and for ever, and to the ages of ages. Amen.*

By St Symeon the Translator

*You who willingly give me your flesh for food,
Who are a fire consuming the unworthy;
Do not burn me up, my Maker;
But penetrate the structure of my limbs,
All my joints, my inner parts, my heart.
Burn up the thorns of all my offences,
Purify my soul and sanctify my mind.
Strengthen my knees, together with my bones;
Enlighten the five-fold simpleness of my senses;
Nail down the whole of me with fear of you.
Always protect, guard and keep me
From every soul-destroying deed and word.*

Hallow me, purify me, bring me to harmony,
And give me beauty, understanding, light;
Show me to be your dwelling, the Spirit's house alone,
And no more the dwelling-place of sin;
That, by the entrance of Communion,
Every evil-doer, every passion,
May flee from me, your house, as from a fire.
As intercessors I bring you all the Saints,
The companies of the Bodiless Hosts,
Your Forerunner, the wise Apostles,
And with them your most pure and holy Mother;
Accept their prayers, O my compassionate Christ,
And make your worshipper a child of light.
For you alone are the sanctification of our souls,
O Good One, and their brightness,
And fittingly to you, as to our God and Master,
We all give praise and glory every day.

Anonymous

May your holy Body, Lord Jesus Christ, our God, bring me eternal life, and your precious Blood forgiveness of sins. May this Eucharist bring me joy, health and gladness; and at your dread Second Coming make me, a sinner, worthy to stand at the right hand of your glory, at the prayers of your All-pure Mother and of all your Saints. Amen.

Anonymous. To the All-holy Theotokos

All-holy Lady, Theotokos, the light of my darkened soul, my hope, protection, refuge, comfort, joy, I thank you, because you have made me, the unworthy, worthy to become a partaker in the most pure Body and

precious Blood of your Son. But, O you who gave birth to the true Light, enlighten the spiritual eyes of my heart; you who bore the source of immortality, give life to me, who have been slain by sin; you, the compassionate Mother of the merciful God, have mercy on me and give me compunction and contrition in my heart, humility in my ideas, and release from the imprisonment of my thoughts. And count me worthy, until my last breath, to receive without condemnation the sanctification of the most pure Mysteries, for healing of soul and body; and grant me tears of repentance and thanksgiving, to praise and glorify you all the days of my life. For you are blessed and glorified to the ages. Amen.

I give thanks to You, O Lord

Through Holy Communion, the Lord has given the highest thing He can give man — His own self. The faithful have become one body with Christ. 'This Mystery is called "communing" or "partaking", because through it we partake of the divinity of Jesus.'[1]

At the beginning of the Holy Anaphora, the celebrant enumerated the divine gifts and exhorted the faithful to give thanks and glory to the Giver: *Let us give thanks to the Lord*. Now, after this zenith of all good things, the celebrant and people spontaneously feel the need to thank the Lord again. This brief service is a small but essential thank-offering which everyone who has received Communion should offer to the Lord who loves mankind.

The gifts afforded by Holy Communion are innumerable. Man becomes a partaker of eternal life, as Christ Himself affirmed:

---

[1] St John of Damascus, *On the Orthodox Faith*, 4.86, PG 94.1153A.

Whoever eats my flesh and drinks my blood has eternal life (John 6: 54). But the benefactions start in this present life: 'When Christ enters within us…He kindles our reverence for God; He mortifies our passions, not charging to our account the transgressions in which we are embroiled, but instead taking care of us as people who are sick.' 'The soul makes progress because it has received life of the Holy Spirit, it has tasted the Lamb, it has been anointed with His Blood and eaten the true Bread, the living Word.'[2]

When man considers the magnitude of the good things that God has bestowed on his sinful person, 'then his heart breaks, however stony it might be'. And he cries out:

Therefore, with grateful mind and grateful heart,
with the grateful members of my soul and flesh,
I worship and magnify and glorify You, my God,
for You are blessed now and to the ages.[3]

---

[2] St Cyril of Alexandria, *On John*, 4.2, PG 73.585A; *Macarian Homilies*, 47.11, PG 34.804A.

[3] Elder Paisios of the Holy Mountain, in: Hieromonk Isaak, *Vios Gerontos Paisiou* [*Life of the Elder Paisios*], 6th edn (Holy Mountain, 2008), p. 413; St Symeon the New Theologian, Service of Preparation for Holy Communion, prayer 7.

EPILOGUE

My Mysteries are for me and those who are mine

In presenting these interpretative commentaries on the Divine Liturgy, an effort has been made to convey to today's reader, who is struggling to live the Christian life, the Christ-centred liturgical experience of the Church Fathers. The compiler of this patristic anthology feels that he must ask the forgiveness of his brethren in Christ, the readers, because his spiritual weakness has prevented him from transmitting the treasures of the Fathers pure and unalloyed. He prays unworthily at the terrible Altar: 'Do not on account of my sins withhold the grace of Your Holy Spirit from the Gifts here set forth'[1] — the gifts of the holy Fathers to our brethren in Christ. And once again, he gives the ultimate word to the holy Fathers:

In all that 'we have said, we have not been speaking for ourselves but on the basis of the writings of the holy Fathers, and in particular those of the teachers of the faith, who have given us exalted theology on these matters'.[2]

'But the reader of these pages should not think that the explanation of the venerable mysteries of the Divine Liturgy is now complete. He should consider rather that he is like a person who wants to see the wonderful and unseen glories of some city, and meets a guide; and with the help of that guide he manages to see, as if through a window, the luminosity and brightness radiated by that city but not the actual nature of the treasures to be found within it. For the Lord says: *My Mysteries are for me and those*

---

[1] Liturgy of St Basil, prayer before the Lord's Prayer.
[2] St Symeon of Thessaloniki, *Church Building*, 101, PG 155.748A.

who are mine [Isa. 24: 16, Theodotion]. So, since I have not only strayed far from the Lord but separated myself completely also from those who approach Him, how is it possible that could I understand His Mysteries or say anything worthy of them? Yet, whatever we do according to the measure of our capacities is well-pleasing to Christ, provided only that our treatment of the subject does not contradict His doctrines and commandments. If, therefore, some reader finds something of value in these present writings, let him say a prayer to God for me who has laboured over them, for the forgiveness of my sins. And then let him thank God for the divine enlightenment which He is accustomed to grant, *from the everlasting mountains* [Ps. 75: 5], to [the holy Fathers] who have been found worthy to perceive things with their spiritual eyes.

'For to Him is due all glory, honour and worship, to the Father and to the Son and to the Holy Spirit, now and ever and to the ages of ages. Amen.'[3]

---

[3] Theodore of Andida, *Protheoria*, 40, *PG* 140.468BC.

The Catechetical Homily of St John Chrysostom[4]

'If any is devout and loves God, let him enjoy this fair and radiant festival. If any is a grateful servant, let him enter rejoicing into the joy of his Lord [cf. Matt. 25: 23]. If any has wearied himself with fasting, let him now enjoy his recompense.

'If any has worked from the first hour, let him today receive what is his due [cf. Matt. 20: 1-16]. If any has come after the third hour, let him keep the feast in thankfulness. If any has arrived after the sixth hour, let him be in no doubt: it is in no way prejudicial to him. If any has delayed until the ninth hour, let him draw near without misgivings.

'If any has arrived only at the eleventh hour, let him not be afraid on account of his tardiness. For the Master is munificent and receives the last even as the first. He gives rest to him who has come at the eleventh hour as to him who has laboured from the first. He has mercy on the last, and He takes care of the first. To the one He gives, and to the other He gives gratuitously. He accepts the works, and He welcomes the resolve. He honours the deed and commends the intention. Enter therefore, all of you, into the joy of your Lord: enjoy your recompense, both you that were first and you that came later.

'Rich and poor, dance together. You that are sober and you that are heedless, honour the day. You that have fasted and you that have not fasted, be glad today. The Table is full; sate yourselves, all of you. The Calf is ample; let no one go away hungry. May all of you enjoy the banquet of faith; may all of you enjoy the richness of goodness.

'Let no one lament his poverty, for the Kingdom common to all has appeared. Let no one bewail his sins, for forgiveness has dawned

---

[4] This homily is printed here at the end of this commentary on the Divine Liturgy because it constitutes a theological recapitulation of the eucharistic Mystery, and its allegorical reference to the eucharistic Table is manifestly clear. It is read in church immediately before the celebration of the Divine Liturgy on Easter Sunday morning, proclaiming that the Eucharist is the feast of the Resurrection of Christ.

from the tomb. Let no one fear death, for the Saviour's death has set us free. Through being held by death, He quenched death.

'He who descended into Hades has despoiled Hades. He embittered him when Hades tasted His flesh. Foreseeing this, Isaiah cried out: *Hades from below was embittered to meet you* [Isa. 14: 9]. He was embittered, for he was abolished. He was embittered, for he was deceived. He was embittered, for he was put to death. He was embittered, for he was destroyed. He was embittered, for he was taken captive. He received a body, and encountered God. He received earth, and met heaven. He received what he saw, and fell whither he saw not.

'O death, where is your sting? O Hades, where is your victory? [cf. Hos. 13: 14]

'Christ is risen, and you are cast down.

'Christ is risen, and demons have fallen.

'Christ is risen, and angels rejoice.

'Christ is risen, and life reigns.

'Christ is risen, and there is none dead in the tomb. For Christ, raised from the dead, has become the first-fruit of those who have fallen asleep.

'To Him be glory and dominion unto the ages of ages. Amen.'[5]

---

[5] St John Chrysostom, *Catechetical Homily on Easter*, PG 59.721-4; cf. I. F. Hapgood (tr.), *Service Book of the Holy Orthodox-Catholic Apostolic Church*, 4th edn (Brooklyn: Syrian Antiochian Orthodox Archdiocese, 1965), p. 235, and Holy Transfiguration Monastery (tr. & ed.) *A prayer book for Orthodox Christians*, 4th edn (Boston Massachusetts: 2005), pp. 182-4.

GLOSSARY AND INDEXES

GLOSSARY

AER (VEIL) (ἀήρ): A large embroidered cloth with which the celebrant covers the Holy Gifts at the holy Prothesis.* During the
Great Entrance the deacon or the priest wears the *Aer* on his
shoulders; subsequently it is placed over the Holy Gifts on the
Altar, and then during the reciting of the Creed it is held aloft
and shaken over the Gifts. Additionally there are two smaller
veils which are used to cover the Chalice and the Paten.

AGAPE MEAL (ἀγάπης δεῖπνον, literally: meal of love): The common meal shared by the first Christians, during which the
Mystery of the Divine Eucharist took place (cf. Acts 2: 42, 46).

ALLELUIA (ἀλληλούια): A Hebrew word meaning 'Praise be to God'
which has remained untranslated in Christian texts. It entered Christian worship together with the Psalms. See also
pp. 157–8 above.

AMEN (ἀμήν): A Hebrew word meaning 'indeed, verily, truly, so
be it', which has remained untranslated in Christian texts,
hymns and prayers in all languages. See also p. 109, n. 10 above.

ANAMNESIS OF CHRIST (ἀνάμνησις Χριστοῦ): In accordance with
the words of Christ at the Last Supper, *do this in remembrance of me* (Luke 22: 19), the liturgical *anamnesis* (calling to
mind) of Christ is the Mystery of the Divine Liturgy. The faithful who participate in the Sacrament of the Divine Liturgy
mystically live the life, death and resurrection of Christ. The
Divine Eucharist is also the remembrance of God's benefactions for which we offer up hymns of thanksgiving to Christ
the Lord.

ANAPHORA (Ἀναφορά): Another name for the Divine Eucharist referring in particular to the part of the Liturgy which begins
Let us stand aright; let us stand with fear; let us attend, that

we may offer the Holy Anaphora in peace, and ends with the Consecration of the Holy Gifts. The word *anaphora* comes from the Greek verb *anaphero*, meaning to bring or lift up, and the Divine Liturgy is also called the Holy Anaphora because through it we offer up ourselves and the Holy Gifts to God.

ANTIDORON (ἀντίδωρον): Small pieces of bread cut up from the oblation loaves (*prosphora**) used in the Proskomide* (Service of Preparation) which are blessed by the priest after the Holy Gifts have been consecrated by passing them over the Gifts. Originally they were offered to the faithful who did not take Communion, *anti* (in place of) the *doron* (gift) — that is to say, in place of Holy Communion. Today all receive the *antidoron* at the end of the Divine Liturgy including those who have communicated.

ANTIMENSION (ἀντιμήνσιον): A consecrated cloth usually imprinted with an image of the entombment of Christ upon which the Divine Eucharist is celebrated. If the Altar has not been consecrated, the *antimension* must have sewn into it a fragment of a holy relic. It symbolises the sheet in which the modest Joseph wrapped the all-holy Body of the Lord. According to the prevailing view of its etymology, the word comes from the Greek *anti* (in place of) and the Latin *mensa* (table).

ANTIPHON (ἀντίφωνον): Originally this was the name given to the psalms whose verses were sung alternately by two choirs. Later the term antiphon was also applied to the response (the so-called *ephymnio* or refrain*), such as *At the prayers of Your saints, save us, O Lord*, that is made after the chanting of a verse from the psalms.

APOLYTIKION (ἀπολυτίκιον): The Dismissal Hymn, a *troparion** that refers to the feast or saint of the day, principally chanted at the Dismissal at Vespers or Matins.

APOSTICHA (ἀπόστιχα): Verses chanted at the end of Vespers and Matins, preceded by a verse from the psalms that refers to the theme of the feast.

BOWS and PROSTRATIONS (μετάνοιες): At various points and times
during worship the faithful, making first the sign of the
cross, incline their bodies at the waist and bow their heads before Christ or the saints; this is called in Greek a small
metanoia. At other times the faithful, making first the sign of
the cross, fall to their knees inclining their heads to the
ground; this is a full prostration or great *metanoia*. By kneel-
ing the created being humbly pays homage to the magnifi-
cence of the Creator.

CANON (Κανών): An long hymn chanted at Matins, which com-
prises three, four, eight or nine odes* (canticles) and has as its
common theme the festal event of the day. The eight first
odes of the Canon correspond to the eight odes of the Old Testament. The ninth ode is dedicated to the All-holy Mother of
God and is taken from the New Testament.

CATECHISM (κατήχησις): Instruction for those who wish to become members of the Christian Church concerning its truths,
doctrines and faith.

CENSER (THURIBLE) (θυμιατήριον): A liturgical vessel that hangs
from three chains adorned with small bells in which incense
is burned and which is used to cense the church, the sanctuary and the people at various times throughout the ecclesiastical offices and services.

CHALICE, HOLY (ἅγιον Ποτήριον): A richly embellished long-
stemmed drinking cup made of precious metal into which,
during the Proskomide, are poured wine and water. The commingled wine and water when consecrated in the Divine
Liturgy are changed into the holy Blood of Christ.

CHERUBIC HYMN (Χερουβικὸς Ὕμνος): The hymn beginning with
the words 'We who mystically represent the Cherubim . . .'
which is chanted at the Great Entrance, and by extension all
other hymns that are chanted at this moment.

COMMEMORATION (μνημόνευσις): The naming and remembrance
of the faithful, both living and dead, made by the priest dur-

ing the Proskomide as he takes out small particles for them from the oblation bread. See also p. 90.

COMMUNION, HOLY (*Θεία Κοινωνία*): The Communion of the holy Body and Blood of Christ is so called because it endows union of the faithful with Christ.

COMMUNION HYMN (*Κοινωνικόν*): The hymn which is chanted while the clergy and the faithful receive Holy Communion. Canonically, the words of the hymn are from the verse of a psalm that refers to Holy Communion or the feast of the day. The words of the oldest known Communion Hymn are *Taste and see that the Lord is good* (Ps. 33: 9). The Communion Hymn would earlier have been a complete psalm. Psalms so used included Pss. 22, 33, 116, 144.

COMMUNION SPOON (*λαβίδα*): A long-handled spoon of precious metal with which Holy Communion is given to the faithful.

COMPLINE (*ἀπόδειπνον*): The office read by the faithful after the final meal of the day and before sleep.

CONSECRATION (*καθαγιασμός*): The changing of the Holy Gifts into the Body and Blood of Christ which takes place during the Divine Liturgy. The term in English (in Greek *ἐγκαίνια*) is also used for the solemn rite of setting apart Altars, churches and eucharistic vessels exclusively for the service of God.

COSMOS (*κόσμος*): The universe as an ordered whole. The primary meaning of cosmos in Greek is 'ordered' or 'arranged' and it also has the meaning of an 'adornment', an 'ornament'.

DEACON (*διάκονος*): The first degree of the higher rank of clergy. A deacon takes part in all the ecclesiastical offices, serving the bishop and the officiating priest, but he can not himself celebrate any of the Mysteries.

DIPTYCHS (*δίπτυχα*): A catalogue in which is written the names of the living and the dead who are commemorated in the Divine Liturgy. It is kept permanently on the holy Prothesis and is called *diptychs* (meaning two folds) because it most usually consists of two parts, one for the living and one for the dead.

Formerly it was read after the Consecration; thus this section of the Divine Liturgy is called *Diptychs and Prayers.*

DISMISSAL ('Aπόλυσις): The prayer spoken by the priest at the end of every ecclesiastical office. The celebrant asks, on behalf of all the faithful, for the mercy of God together with the intercessions of the Most-holy Theotokos, of the saint of the day, and of all the saints.

DOORS, ROYAL, also known as the HOLY DOORS: see Iconostasis.

DOXASTIKON (δοξαστικόν): The *troparia* (pl.) (usually *idiomela**) preceded by the phrase 'Glory to the Father and to the Son and to the Holy Spirit' which bring the *stichera* to a close.

ECONOMY, DIVINE (θεία Οἰκονομία): The totality of miraculous events worked by God to bring man once more into union with Him (from the noun *oikos,* meaning house, and the verb *nemo,* meaning to administer or put in order) and to make him once more His own, that is, belonging to His household. The main events were the Incarnation of the Word of God, the Crucifixion, the Resurrection, the Ascension, and the Descent of the Holy Spirit. See also p. 15 above.

EILETON (CORPORAL) (εἰλητόν): A silk cloth that is spread on the Altar when the Divine Liturgy is celebrated. Today its use has essentially been replaced by the *antimension.**

EIRMOS (εἰρμός): The first *troparion* (stanza) of each ode (canticle) of the Canon. Each *eirmos* has its own melody according to which the rest of the stanzas of the same ode are chanted.

ENGOMIA (ἐγκώμια): The three series of short hymns chanted during Matins on Holy Saturday, relating to the Lord's entombment. *Engomia* are similarly chanted for the Dormition of the Theotokos.

ENTRANCE, GREAT (μεγάλη Εἴσοδος): The point in the Divine Liturgy when the prepared Holy Gifts are carried by the celebrant(s) from the holy Prothesis through the north door of the sanctuary into the nave of the church, and then through the Holy Doors to the Altar where they will be consecrated. During the Great Entrance the Cherubic Hymn is chanted.

ENTRANCE, LITTLE (μικρὴ Εἴσοδος): The point in the Divine Liturgy when the Gospel Book is carried from the Altar through the north door of the sanctuary into the nave of the church, and then back into the sanctuary through the Holy Doors where it is once more placed on the Altar. The entrance takes place during the chanting of the third antiphon, and is also known as the Entrance with the Gospel Book. Formerly, the Gospel Book was carried from the sacristy into the centre of the church for the Gospel reading.

EPIKLESIS (INVOCATION) (ἐπίκλησις): The prayer in the Divine Liturgy in which the celebrant asks God the Father to send down the Holy Spirit upon the Holy Gifts, and to change them into the holy Body and Blood of Christ.

EPIGONATION (ἐπιγονάτιον): A lozenge-shaped, stiffened piece of material, bearing the image of the Cross or the Resurrection, which hangs from the priest's girdle on the right side. Originally it was a vestment worn only by bishops but in more recent times it has also been permitted for archimandrites and archpriests. Its name derives from the fact that it hangs at (epi) the knee (gonaton).

EPIMANIKIA (CUFFS) (ἐπιμανίκια): Embroidered cuffs that are fastened at the wrist over the sticharion* (tunic) of bishops, priests and deacons for the celebration of the Divine Liturgy and the other Holy Mysteries.

EPITRACHELION (STOLE) (ἐπιτραχήλιον): A narrow embroidered vestment which is worn around the neck and hangs down to the bottom of the sticharion (tunic) and ends in a fringe. It is a symbol of the priesthood of bishops and priests, and must be worn for the celebration of all the Mysteries and offices of the Church. Its name derives from the words epi (at) and trachelos (neck).

EUCHARIST, DIVINE (Θεία Εὐχαριστία): The Divine Liturgy is also known as the Divine Eucharist because it is, par excellence, the Mystery in which we give thanksgiving (eucharistia) to God for the infinitude of His benefactions to us.

EUCHOLOGION (*Εὐχολόγιον*): The liturgical book containing all the services of the Holy Mysteries, the prayers of the priests and the offices of the Church.

EXAPOSTILARION (*ἐξαποστειλάριον*): The *troparion* related to the feast or the saint of the day which is chanted immediately before the Lauds.

FAN (*ριπίδιον*): A fan which was used by the deacon in earlier times to drive away any insects that might be hovering above the Chalice during the Anaphora.

FAST (*νηστεία*): Primarily, the abstinence from food. The Orthodox Church has appointed certain days and periods as fasts and has established the degree of abstinence from food on those days. The purpose of fasting is to make the flesh submissive to the spirit and presupposes in parallel an intensified spiritual struggle.

FRACTION (*κλάσις ἄρτου, μελισμός*): The breaking into fragments of the holy Body of Christ which takes place before Communion. The Breaking of Bread was the name that the first Christians gave to the Divine Eucharist (cf. Acts 2: 42).

HOURS, ROYAL (*μεγάλες Ὧρες*): The four offices of the daily liturgical cycle corresponding to four basic times of the day – the first (daybreak), third (mid-morning), sixth (midday) and ninth (mid-afternoon) – which in accordance with the Byzantine method of calculation are called Hours. The Royal Hours are chanted on the eves of Christmas, Epiphany and Easter; they are longer than the daily Hours as they include *troparia* and readings that refer to the feast.

ICONOSTASIS (*τέμπλον, εἰκονοστάσιον*): The screen of icons separating the sanctuary from the body of the church, and which usually has three doors. The central doorway, which is closed by double gates and a curtain, is known as the Royal or Holy Doors, and is used only by the clergy.

IDIOMELON (*ἰδιόμελον*): A *troparion* with its own (*idion*) melody (*melon*); thus it does not follow any model, unlike the *prosomoion,** for example.

INVOCATION: *see* Epiklesis.

KAIROS (*Καιρός*): The short office celebrated in front of the *iconostasis** (usually before Matins) by the clergy who are to celebrate the Divine Liturgy.

KATHISMA (*κάθισμα*): The Psalms of David have been divided for liturgical use into twenty *kathismata* (pl.). Thus *kathisma* is also the name given to the *troparion* sung after the reading of a *kathisma* of the Psalter at the beginning of the Matins.

KONTAKION (*κοντάκιον*): Formerly the *kontakia* (pl.) were a series of several *troparia* chanted in the same mode and metre that referred to the feast or the saint of the day. Today the term *kontakion* is only applied to the first of these *troparia*, and is read during Matins before the Synaxarion of the day, and in the Divine Liturgy as the last *troparion* after the Little Entrance.*

LAMB ('*Αμνός*): The central square part of the seal stamped on the oblation bread (*prosphora**) which bears the letters ΙΣ ΧΣ – ΝΙ ΚΑ standing for 'Jesus Christ conquers'. It is called the Lamb because it is the piece that is changed at the Divine Liturgy into the holy Body of Christ, who is *the lamb of God who takes away the sin of the world* (John 1: 29).

LANCE, HOLY (*ἁγία λόγχη*): A lance-shaped, double-edged knife which is used to cut out, and then to spear, the Lamb, and also to cut out the other portions of the oblation bread in memory of the Theotokos, the saints and all who are commemorated in the Proskomide.

LAUDS (*Αἶνοι*): The three last psalms of the Psalter (148, 149 and 150), chanted in the final section of the office of Matins. The four or six last verses are prefixed to certain *prosomoia* that refer to the feast of the day.

LIKENESS OF GOD (*ὁμοίωσις Θεοῦ*): Man was created 'in the image and likeness of God' (cf. Gen. 1: 26). By making man according to His likeness, God gave His rational creature the possibility of resembling his Creator to the degree that he has the capacity to do so. To help man attain this perfection, the grace of

the Holy Spirit is given to him at all times by God, but for perfection to be attained the necessary disposition and endeavour on the part of man himself is also needed. The saints, known and unknown, are human beings like us, who struggled valiantly and earnestly, and attained the likeness of God.

LITANY (ἐκτενής): A prayer in the form of petitions which the celebrant addresses to God; after each petition the people or choir respond 'Lord, have mercy' (Kyrie, eleison) or sometimes 'Grant this, O Lord'.

LITURGICAL TIME AND SPACE (λειτουργικὸς χρόνος καὶ χῶρος): During the celebration of the Divine Liturgy the category of time as we understand it in the linear sense is transcended. Yesterday, today and tomorrow become, through grace, as one. In this mystery we live in some as yet unrevealed manner both the past and the future of the divine Economy.* In the same way, space is transformed into liturgical space. Space and time in the Divine Liturgy are sanctified by Him who is beyond 'place and time and name and understanding'. Christ, who is in heaven, is together with us in the Divine Liturgy.

LITURGY OF THE PRESANCTIFIED GIFTS (Λειτουργία τῶν Προηγιασμένων Δώρων): The office celebrated during Great Lent (except on Saturday and Sunday) in order to permit the faithful the possibility of receiving Holy Communion on days which, owing to their mournful character, no Divine Liturgy is celebrated. The Liturgy of the Presanctified Gifts is essentially a service of Holy Communion, as the Holy Gifts are presanctified in a previous Divine Liturgy.

LITY (Λιτή): The word means supplication, and the office of the Lity has the character of a supplication. It is chanted on important feasts and is usually celebrated in the narthex of the church after the Entrance of the priest at Vespers. Formerly it was a procession of both clergy and people out of the church and back again.

MATINS (Ὄρθρος): The daily morning office which is chanted in honour of the saint or the feast of the day. If the Divine Liturgy is to be celebrated, it is preceded by Matins during which the priest carries out the Proskomide. In the Slavic Churches, Matins is celebrated immediately after Vespers on the previous evening.

MYSTAGOGY (μυσταγωγία): In a general sense it means instruction in preparation for initiation into a Mystery, for instance that of Holy Baptism; but it refers pre-eminently to the Divine Liturgy, for it is this that leads us into the mystery of God's love.

MYSTERIES (Μυστήρια): The Holy Mysteries or sacraments in the Orthodox Church are vessels of the mystical participation of mankind in divine grace. In a general sense, the Orthodox Church considers everything which is in and of the Church as sacramental or mystical. The sacraments, like the Church, are both visible and invisible. In every sacrament there is a combination of an outward visible sign with an inward spiritual grace. St John Chrysostom wrote that they are called Mysteries because what we believe is not the same as what we see; instead, we see one thing and believe another. The sacraments are personal — they are the means whereby God's grace is bestowed on each individual Christian. In most of the sacraments, the priest mentions the Christian name of each person as he administers it. Generally, the Church recognises and counts seven (though not only seven) Mysteries: Baptism, Chrismation, Eucharist, Confession, Holy Unction, Marriage, Ordination. The sanctified bread and wine are also called Mysteries, being the holy Body and Blood of Christ.

OCTOECHOS (Ὀκτώηχος, literally: eight tones): The music of the Eastern Orthodox Church is based on an eight tone (or mode) system. *Octoechos* is the main ecclesiastical book in which these tones are given, which is also known as the *Parakletiki*, and contains all the hymns of the weekly liturgical cycle divided into eight sections according to the eight tones.

ODE (CANTICLE) (ᾠδή): A collection of stanzas (*troparia*) derived from the nine canticles of the Old Testament which make up a subdivision of a Canon* and which are sung in the same musical tone.

OMOPHORION (ὠμοφόριον): A long, embroidered, narrow length of brocade decorated with crosses which is worn only by bishops when they celebrate. It is placed round the shoulders and falls to the ground in front, and represents the lost sheep which was sought out by Christ and which He took upon His shoulders and brought back to His Father's house.

ORARION (ὀράριον): A long, thin, embellished stole-like vestment worn by deacons only. It is usually draped over the left shoulder, wrapped round the chest and back, then brought forward over the left shoulder. However, when preparing for Communion the deacon will place the *orarion* around his waist bringing the ends cross-wise up over his shoulders and then down in front over the chest. Its use is first mentioned in the Council of Laodicea (4th century). The prevailing explanation of the etymology of the word is that it comes from the Latin *os, oris*, meaning mouth, as in former times, after the faithful had communicated by drinking from the chalice held by the deacon, they would wipe their mouths on his stole-like vestment. Some derive the term from the Latin *orare*, 'to pray', because the deacon holds the front portion of the *orarion* in his right hand as he pronounces the petitions.

PATEN (ἅγιον Δισκάριον): The small round metal disk with a stemmed base on which is placed the Lamb which is to be consecrated as well as the other particles taken out from the oblation bread in honour of the Theotokos, the saints, and for the help of our brethren who have been commemorated in the Proskomide.

PHELONION (CHASUBLE) (φαιλόνιον): A richly adorned cape-like vestment, without sleeves and largely cut away in the front from the waist down to facilitate movement, which is worn by bishops and priests over the other vestments.

PLEROMA (πλήρωμα): The term refers to a condition of plenitude – a totality, fullness, completion, perfection. The Church is the *pleroma* of Christ (cf. Eph. 1: 23).

PROKEIMENON (προκείμενον): A verse, which canonically should be from the Psalter, that is sung before a reading from Holy Scripture; from the verb *prokeimai*, meaning 'to set forth'. The words of the appointed *prokeimenon* are related to the reading or the feast of the day.

PROSKOMIDE (Προσκομιδή): From the verb *proskomizo* meaning 'to carry' or 'to convey to', Proskomide was originally the name given to the Great Entrance when the Holy Gifts were carried to the Altar. Today it primarily refers to the actual Service of Preparation, which takes place before the Divine Liturgy, during which the priest prepares the eucharistic Gifts of bread and wine for the celebration of the Mystery.

PROSOMOION (προσόμοιον): A *troparion* whose psalmody follows the model of an *idiomelon*.*

PROSPHORA (OBLATION BREAD) (προσφορά): A round, usually hand-kneaded, leavened loaf, stamped before baking with a special seal from which is taken the portion that will become the Body of Christ in the Divine Liturgy. The seal leaves a schematic imprint on the *prosphora* in which the 'Lamb' is depicted in the form of a square with the letters ΙΣ ΧΣ – ΝΙ ΚΑ from the first and last letters in Greek of the name Jesus Christ and the word *nika*, meaning 'conquers'. *Prosphora* comes from the verb *prosphero*, meaning 'to offer', and it can be understood as both that which is offered and the act of offering, that is, the eucharistic Mystery. For this reason the Divine Liturgy is also known as the Eucharistic Prosphora.

PROSTRATIONS: *see* Bows.

PROTHESIS, HOLY (ἁγία Πρόθεσις): The area at the north end of the sanctuary, most often set within a conch, where the priest makes ready the Holy Gifts of the bread and wine before they are carried to the Altar. The word is derived from the verb

pro-tithemi, meaning 'to place before'. The Service of Preparation, the Proskomide, is also known as the Prothesis.

READER (ἀναγνώστης): The lowest rank in the clerical hierarchy.
In earlier times the duty of the reader was to read and inter-
pret passages from the Old Testament and the Epistles, and to
put the church in order. Today his responsibility is limited to
reading aloud, or intoning, the prescribed biblical passages.

READING (ἀνάγνωσμα): A passage from the Old or the New Testament which is read during the church offices or in the Divine
Liturgy. Its provenance is shown by the descriptive terms
'Gospel Reading', the 'Epistle', 'Reading from the Old Testament'.

REFRAIN (ἐφύμνιον): Formerly a phrase repeated by the people in
response to a verse from the Psalms chanted by the choir. Re-
frains that are still chanted today, now by the choir, include
Alleluia (thrice), *At the prayers of Your Saints, save us, O
Lord* and *Through the prayers of the Theotokos, O Saviour,
save us.*

SACRISTY (διακονικόν or σκευοφυλάκιον): The southern part of the
sanctuary where the holy vessels and vestments, and liturgical items in general, are usually kept and maintained under
the deacons' care.

SEAL (σφραγίς): A wooden circular disc, carved with schematic em-
blems of Christ, the Mother of God, and the nine orders, used
to stamp the oblation bread that is used in the Divine Liturgy. The same word is used for the imprint in the bread itself.

SPACE, LITURGICAL: *see* Liturgical Time and Space.

SPONGE (μοῦσα): A small thin circular sponge which is used to
gather together the particles of the oblation bread from the
Paten (or which may have fallen onto the *antimension*) and to
wipe them into the Chalice.

STAR or ASTERISK (ἀστερίσκος): Two arched metal bands joined at
their apex by a rivet so that they may be opened in the shape
of a cross. The opened asterisk is placed over the Paten so that

the veil that covers it should not come into contact with the 'Lamb' and the other portions of the oblation bread placed upon it. It symbolises the star of Bethlehem.

STASIS (στάσις): Long texts written in poetic meter are divided into *stases*. Thus each *kathisma* in the Psalter is divided into three *stases*, as are the *Engomia*.*

STICHARION (στιχάριον): A long narrow vestment with loose sleeves that fastens at the neck and is worn as an under vestment by bishops and priests. Made of fine white material, it symbolises the luminous garment of Baptism. The outer vestment worn by deacons and subdeacons is also called a *sticharion* and usually it is more elaborately decorated, open down the side and held shut with buttons.

STICHERON (στιχηρόν): A *troparion* to which a verse taken from the Psalms is prefixed. It may be either *idiomelon* or *prosomoion*.

SYNAXIS (ASSEMBLY) (σύναξις): The gathering together of many people for a particular purpose. The liturgical *synaxis* is the gathering of the faithful within the church for the celebration of a Mystery or a service. The presence of Christ in the celebration of the Divine Liturgy gives this particular *synaxis* another dimension: all the children of God come together where heaven and earth, and the past, the present, and the future, are concelebrating.

THEANTHROPOS (Θεάνθρωπος): The principal name of Jesus Christ. It derives from the words *Theos* (God) and *anthropos* (man), and means that for our salvation the Son and Logos of God became perfect man while remaining perfect God.

THEOTOKION (θεοτοκίον): A *troparion* in honour of the Theotokos.

THEOTOKOS (Θεοτόκος): The principal name of the All-holy Mother of Christ. Since Christ is God and man, His Mother who gave birth to Him is called the Birth-giver of God (from *tokos*, meaning 'birth', and *Theos*, meaning 'God'). See also p. 248 above.

THRICE-HOLY HYMN: *see* Trisagion hymn.

THRONE ON HIGH (*ἄνω Καθέδρα*): A liturgical term for the Episcopal Throne which traditionally was situated in the apse behind (that is, to the east of) the Altar and which symbolises the throne of God. After the *iconostasis* was introduced the Episcopal Throne was moved into the main body of the church and today it stands on the right side of the nave.

TIME, LITURGICAL: *see* Liturgical Time and Space

TRISAGION HYMN (*Τρισάγιος Ὕμνος*): The hymn *Holy God, Holy Mighty, Holy Immortal, have mercy on us*, which is repeated three or more times. It is a combination of the angelic hymn heard by the Prophet Isaiah when he was called to the prophethood (cf. Isa. 6: 3), and the verse from the Psalms, *My soul thirsted for God, the mighty, the living* (Ps. 41: 3).

TRIUMPHAL HYMN (*ἐπινίκιος Ὕμνος*): The combination of the angelic thrice-holy hymn heard by the Prophet Isaiah when he was called to the prophethood and of the hymn with which the people greeted the *Theanthropos** as He entered the holy city of Jerusalem: *Holy, holy, holy, Lord of Sabaoth, heaven and earth are full of Your glory. Hosanna in the highest. Blessed is He who comes in the name of the Lord. Hosanna in the highest.* (See p. 229 above.)

TROPARION (*τροπάριον*): A short hymn of one stanza, varying in length, chanted at different times in the offices of the Church, and most often referring to the feast of the day.

VEIL: *see* Aer.

VESPERS (*ἑσπερινός*): The first service of the daily cycle of liturgical worship in the Orthodox Church which, as the liturgical day begins at sunset, is traditionally served in the early evening.

VESSELS, HOLY (*ἱερὰ σκεύη*): The vessels and utensils which are used for the celebration of the Mysteries and other services. Those necessary for the celebration of the Divine Liturgy are the Chalice, Paten or disk, asterisk or star, lance, communion spoon and sponge. (See the separate entries for these items.)

WINE, COMMUNION (*νᾱμα*): The wine used for Holy Communion must be made from the grape and be dark red in colour.

ZEON (*ζέον*): The boiling water that is poured into the Chalice after the commingling within it of the Holy Gifts. For Communion, the holy Body and Blood of Christ should, as at His Crucifixion, be warm.

ZONE (GIRDLE) (*ζώνη*): The *zone* is tied around the celebrant's waist to secure the *sticharion* (tunic) and *epitrachelion* (stole) in place. It symbolises the sobriety with which the celebrant should be arrayed.

List of main Patristic Texts
concerning the Divine Liturgy

St Dionysius the Areopagite
   On the Church Hierarchy, Ch. 3, PG 3.424B–445C

St John Chrysostom
   On the Incomprehensible, Discourse 6, PG 48.747–56
   Against the Jews, Discourse 3, PG 48.861–72
   On Repentance, Discourse 9, PG 49.343–50
   On the Nativity of our Saviour Jesus Christ,
      PG 49.351–62
   On the holy Baptism of Jesus Christ, PG 49.363–72
   On the Betrayal of Judas, Homily 1, PG 49.373–82
   On Isaiah, Homily 6, PG 56.135–42
   On Matthew, Homily 82, PG 58.737–46
   On John, Homilies 46 and 47, PG 59.257–70
   On 1 Corinthians, Homilies 24, 27 and 28,
      PG 61.197–206 and 223–40
   On Ephesians, Homily 3, PG 62.23–30
   On 1 Timothy, Homily 5, PG 62.525–30
   On Hebrews, Homily 17, PG 63.127–34

St Maximus the Confessor
   Mystagogy, PG 91.657–717

St Germanus of Constantinople
   Church History and Mystical Contemplation,
      PG 98.384–453

Theodore of Andida
   On the Symbols and Mysteries in the Divine Liturgy,
      PG 140.417–68

St Nicholas Cabasilas

> *Commentary on the Divine Liturgy*, PG 150.368–492

St Symeon of Thessaloniki

> *On the holy Liturgy*, PG 155.253–304
> *Commentary on the holy Church Building, the holy Vestments and the divine Mystagogy*, PG 155.697–750

INDEX OF SCRIPTURAL REFERENCES

INDEX OF SUBJECTS AND NAMES

prayer for, 123
throne of, 154, 169, 343
vesting of, as representation Incarnation, 122
vestments, 56, 122

blessing:
at Dismissal, 314
Christ, blessing of the Father, 98
gift of Holy Trinity, 219
myrrh symbol of priestly, 52
mystical, 78
of God to man and world, 24, 97–8, 125–6, 128, 227, 242
of peace, 208
to God from man, 98–9
transmitted by the distribution of *antidoron*, 315–6

Blood of Christ:
adoption by God and, 264
faithful become one in, 23
from His side, 25, 75, 78–9, 230, 278
God's mercy given through, 263
Last Supper and, 68, 235–6
love and, 293
nourishes and is mingled with us, 296–7
Resurrection and, 289
salvation of our souls, 132, 218, 296
union of with holy Body, 277
wine and, 68–9, 238

Body of Christ, 286–7
antidoron and, 315–16
bread and, 67–70
breaking of, 275–6
Christ's 'clothing', 95
Church and, 25–6, 69–70, 88, 259, 277
Divine Eucharist and, 23, 25–6, 69, 78
elevation of, 272
faithful become one body with, 23, 26, 69–70, 88, 211, 296–8, 301
Last Supper and, 5, 25, 68, 71, 236
love and, 293
Resurrection and, 289

Theotokos and, 249
union of with holy Blood, 277
unity of, 224

body:
as a musical instrument, 139
cooperation of in worshipping God, 39
glorification of God in, 38–9
Holy Trinity and, 20
nave of 'mystical Church', 120
preparation of for participation in the Eucharist, 38
purity of, 182–3, 274
soul and, 139, 161
source of spiritual power, 161
standing position as sign of reverence, 165, 215
temple of Holy Spirit, 38, 120

boldness:
before God, 136–7, 263, 264–5
obtained through baptism, 142–3
of Theotokos as mother, 282–3

bow(s), 38, 331
bowing of the head, 268
Bread of life, xvii–xviii, 68, 100, 188, 203, 259, 269
brought forth by Theotokos, xvii, 248–9

bread:
distributed as *antidoron*, 315–6
like a veil of divinity, 270
symbol of unity of the Church, 69–70
the offering of, 67–70
See also prosphora

Breaking of Bread (Fraction), 275–7, 335

Candle(s):
in Great Entrance, 193
Light of Christ symbolised by, 161
reveal intelligible light, 162
symbol of Forerunner at Little Entrance, 150